Switching to a Mac®

PORTABLE GENIUS

Switching to a Mac®

PORTABLE GENIUS

by Paul McFedries

Wiley Publishing, Inc.

Switching to a Mac® Portable Genius

Published by
Wiley Publishing, Inc.
10475 Crosspoint Blvd.
Indianapolis, IN 46256
www.wiley.com

Copyright © 2009 by Wiley Publishing, Inc., Indianapolis, Indiana

Published simultaneously in Canada

ISBN: 978-0-470-43677-6

Manufactured in the United States of America

10 9 8 7 6 5 4 3 2 1

For general information on our other products and services or to obtain technical support, please contact our Customer Care Department within the U.S. at (877) 762-2974, outside the U.S. at (317) 572-3993 or fax (317) 572-4002.

Wiley also publishes its books in a variety of electronic formats. Some content that appears in print may not be available in electronic books.

Library of Congress Control Number: 2009920907

WILEY

About the Author

Paul McFedries is a Mac expert and full-time technical writer. Paul has been authoring computer books since 1991 and he has more than 60 books to his credit. Paul's books have sold more than three million copies worldwide. These books include the Wiley titles *Teach Yourself VISUALLY Macs, Macs Portable Genius*, and *iPhone 3G Portable Genius*. Paul is also the proprietor of Word Spy (www.wordspy.com) a Web site that tracks new words and phrases as they enter the language. Paul invites you to drop by his personal Web site at www.mcfedries.com.

Credits

Senior Acquisitions Editor
Jody Lefevere

Project Editor
Sarah Cisco

Technical Editor
Paul Sihvonen-Binder

Copy Editor
Scott Tullis

Editorial Manager
Robyn B. Siesky

Vice President & Group Executive Publisher
Richard Swadley

Vice President & Publisher
Barry Pruett

Business Manager
Amy Knies

Senior Marketing Manager
Sandy Smith

Project Coordinator
Patrick Redmond

Graphics and Production Specialists
Ana Carrillo
Jennifer Henry
Andrea Hornberger

Quality Control Technician
Melissa Cossell

Proofreading
Melissa D. Buddendeck
Jessica Kramer

Indexing
Christine Spina Karpeles

For Karen and Gypsy.

Acknowledgments

The only thing more fun than switching from Windows to Mac is writing about switching from Windows to Mac! So, yes, I had a great time writing this book, but that task was made all the more pleasant by the great people I got to work with. They include Senior Acquisitions Editor Jody Lefevere, who was kind enough to ask me to write the book; Project Editor Sarah Cisco, who made this an immeasurably better book by offering lots of good advice and asking the right questions at the right time; Copy Editor Scott Tullis, whose eagle-eye for all things ungrammatical made me look like a better writer than I am; and Technical Editor Paul Sihvonen-Binder, who offered excellent suggestions throughout the manuscript. Many thanks to all of you for outstanding work on this project.

Contents

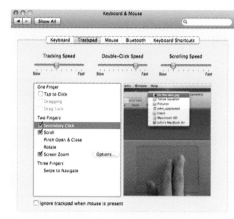

chapter 3

How Do I Perform Everyday Mac Tasks?

chapter 4

How Do I Transfer E-mail, Contacts, and Calendars to My Mac?

chapter 5

How Do I Move My Other Windows
Data to My Mac?   124

chapter 6

How Do I Work with Files,
Folders, and Programs?   146

chapter 7

How Do I Connect and Work with
Devices?   184

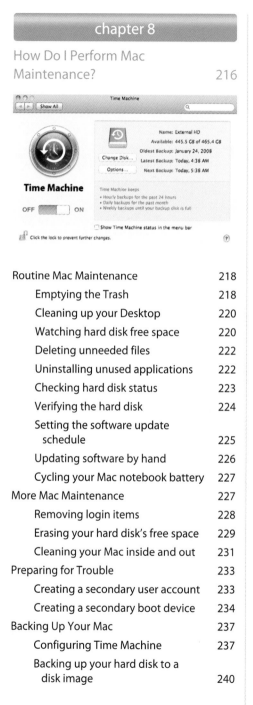

appendix a

Mac Online Resources   330

introduction

The stats tell us that people are switching from Windows to the Mac in record numbers, but those stats don't tell us why. Perhaps it's because Windows users would like to actually enjoy using a computer for a change. Perhaps it's because Macs just work: you take them out of the box, plug them in, and within minutes you're doing your thing. Perhaps it's because Macs just look so darn good that Windows folks can't help but admire their stylishness and innovative design. Or, perhaps, it's those funny and strangely irresistible commercials.

Whatever your reason for switching to the Mac, the bottom line is that you've made the move and now your new Mac life is about to begin. It's true that any computer is going to have problems, but your Mac is likely to have far fewer problems than any other type of system, particularly any Windows system.

The Mac uses a graphical, mouse-centric interface like Windows, but only some of your Windows know-how will transfer to the Mac. While the Mac can handle most types of data, you will face the task of getting your data onto your Mac in a form you can use. There's no doubt the Mac is dead simple to use out-of-the-box, but some of its most useful and powerful features are hidden away in obscure parts of the operating system. Sure, the Mac's robust design makes it a reliable machine day after day, but even the best built machine can have problems.

What you need is a version of the Genius Bar that you can access at your finger tips. What new Mac users like you really need is a "portable" genius that enables you to be more productive and solve problems wherever you and your Mac happen to be.

Welcome, therefore, to Switching to a Mac Portable Genius. This book is like a mini Genius Bar all wrapped up in an easy to use, easy to access, and eminently portable format. In this book you learn how to get comfortable in your new Mac home by learning the ins and outs of the interface, what programs to use, how to perform the most important everyday tasks, and how to get your precious data onto your Mac. You also learn how to work around Mac challenges, prevent Mac problems from occurring, and fix many common problems yourself.

This book is for ex-Windows users who already know their way around a computer, and just want to transfer and apply that know-how to the Mac. It's a book for people who want to get productive, efficient, and creative with their new Mac without have to wade through long and ponderous tutorials. It's a book I had a blast writing, and I think it's a book you'll enjoy reading.

What Are the Differences Between Mac and Windows?

f you were going to move to a new country, you'd probably spend a bit of time learning as much as you could about the culture of your new home. In particular, you'd want to learn how the new place is different from your old country. For things like currency and customs, dress and driving, food and finance, it's important to know how things are different. It's the same when you make the move from a Windows PC to a Mac. Yes, they're both computers, but the similarities pretty much end there. Everything from windows and menus to using the mouse and the keyboard is different on a Mac, and this chapter takes you through the most important of these differences.

Understanding Interface Differences

An old TV ad for a camera told us that "Image is everything." That's probably true for a camera, but not (I hope) for the rest of life. When you're switching from Windows to the Mac, it's probably true that "Interface is everything." That's because, as with any computer, you must use the Mac interface to get things done, but the Mac interface is quite a bit different than the Windows interface you're used to, so mastering the interface should be your first chore.

The next few sections help you do that by showing you how the new Mac interface differs from the old Windows interface that you're leaving behind. (I'll also point out where they are similar, so you know the parts of the Mac terrain where the learning curve isn't so steep.)

The Dock

When you start your Mac, one of the first things you probably notice once the desktop shows up is the colorful ribbon of icons that appears along the bottom of the screen, as shown in figure 1.1.

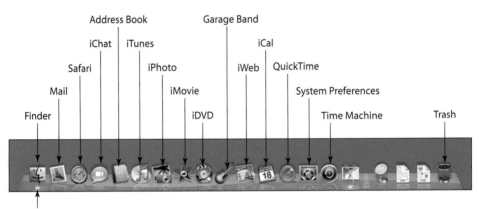

Blue dot indicates the program is running

1.1 The collection of icons along the bottom of the Mac desktop is the Dock.

This strip is the *Dock* and you might think it's the Mac OS X equivalent of the taskbar in Windows. Actually, although it does have its taskbar-like moments, the Dock is quite a bit different than the taskbar. The main difference is that you can search high and low but you won't find anything like the Windows Start button on the Dock. In fact, the Mac doesn't have an equivalent to the Start menu at all (although see my discussion of the Apple menu in the next section). Instead, the Dock itself is a kind of amalgam of the Windows Quick Launch toolbar and taskbar:

- Each Dock icon represents an application, and you click an icon to launch that application. This is just like the Windows Quick Launch toolbar.

- When you launch one of the Dock applications, Mac OS X indicates that the program is running by adding a blue dot under the icon (see the Finder icon on the far left in figure 1.1). If you launch a non-Dock application, Mac OS X adds an icon for that application to the Dock (and displays the blue dot under the icon). For example, figure 1.2 shows the Calculator application running, and you can see that Mac OS X has added an icon for Calculator to the Dock. This is very similar to the Windows taskbar, which displays a button for each running application.

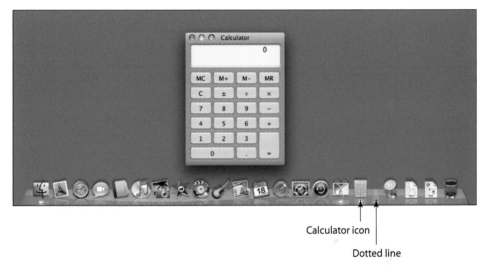

Calculator icon
Dotted line

1.2 When you launch a non-Dock application, Mac OS X temporarily adds an icon for that program to the Dock.

Unlike the Quick Launch toolbar or the taskbar, the Dock differentiates between applications and folders. Examine the Dock closely and you see a dotted line. Everything to the left of the dotted line is an application; everything to the right of the dotted line is a folder, a stack of items, an open file, or an open window.

The menu bar

One of the main (and, for the Mac newcomer, most confusing) differences between Mac and Windows is the strip that sits across the top of the screen. This is the *menu bar* and its weirdest characteristic is that it *never* goes away! You can't turn it off; you can't move it; you can't hide it; and you can't cover it with an application window. (There are some exceptions to this, because a few applications can run in *full-screen mode*, which means they take up the entire screen, including the menu bar.)

The menu bar is divided into three sections:

- **Apple menu.** Click the Apple icon on the left side of the menu bar to see the Apple menu shown in figure 1.3. This menu is home to a few key commands, such as Software Update and System Preferences. Because this menu also includes Sleep, Restart, Shut Down, and Log Out commands, it's the closest thing you'll find to the Windows Start menu in Mac OS X.

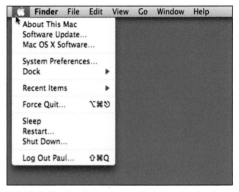

1.3 Click the Apple icon to pull down the Apple menu.

- **Menu extras.** These icons appear on the right side of the menu bar, and the number of icons you see depends on the configuration of your Mac. (As you see throughout this book, there are many icons you can display here.) You use these icons to see the status of certain Mac features (such as your wireless network connection) and to configure other features. For example, you can use the volume icon to adjust the Mac's sound volume, as shown in figure 1.4.

1.4 Use the menu extras on the right to monitor and configure certain Mac features, such as the sound volume shown here.

- **Application menu.** Between the Apple icon and the menu extras lies the application menu area (see figure 1.5), and this is the source of much Mac confusion. That's because this area changes each time you switch to a different application. For example, when you first start your Mac, you see seven menu names: Finder, File, Edit, View, Go, Windows, and Help. These are the menus associated with the Finder application, which (as I discuss in more detail a bit later) is always running. However, if you launch System Preferences (click the System Preferences icon in the Dock, or click the Apple icon and then click System Preferences), those menus go away and are replaced by a new collection: System Preferences, Edit, View, Windows, and Help, as seen in figure 1.5. In general, whenever you switch to a different application, that program's menus appear in this area.

Genius

With each new set of application menus, note that the leftmost menu always uses the name of the application (such as Finder or System Preferences), and that name appears in bold type. This makes it easy to be certain which application's menus you're using, particularly when you have a bunch of applications on the go.

Application menu

1.5 When you switch to a different application, the menu bar reconfigures itself to display the application's menus.

Window features

One thing that Mac OS X and Windows have in common is that they both display programs and content within windows. That's the good news. The bad news is the layout of a typical Mac OS X window is quite a bit different than a typical Windows specimen, and (as you see in the next couple of sections) how you size and move those windows is also different.

To help you get your bearings, figure 1.6 shows an example Mac OS X window, and points out a few key features.

Close

Minimize

Zoom   Title bar   Toolbar   Scroll bar

Status bar   Scroll arrows

                                                        Resize control

1.6 A typical Mac OS X window

Here's a summary of some of the window features pointed out in figure 1.6 and how they make Mac OS X windows different from (or in some cases the same as) their Windows cousins:

- **Close.** Click this button to close the window. This works just like the Close button in Windows.

- **Minimize.** Click this button to minimize the window to an icon that will appear on the right side of the Dock.

> You can also minimize the current window by pressing ⌘+M.
>
> **Genius**

8

- **Zoom.** Click this button to expand the window so that it's large enough to display all of its content, or it's large enough to fill the screen vertically (although without covering the menu bar or Dock). This is sort of like the Windows Maximize command, except that Zoom rarely fills the entire screen. Click Zoom again to restore the window to its original size (so this acts like the Windows Restore button).

- **Scroll arrows.** These work the same way as they do in Windows, but the difference is that both arrows appear at the bottom of the vertical scroll bar. (If you're working with a horizontal scroll bar, the scroll arrows both appear on the right side of the scroll bar.)

Moving windows

In Mac OS X you can use the same technique for moving a window as you can in Windows: Use your mouse to click and drag the title bar. However, Mac OS X goes Windows two better by also enabling you to use the following techniques to move a window:

- Click and drag any empty section of the toolbar.
- Click and drag the status bar (expect for the resize control).

Resizing windows

Changing the size of a window in Mac OS X is quite a bit different than in Windows, and (in my opinion) quite a bit less efficient. In Windows, you resize a window by clicking and dragging any edge of the window, and you resize two sides at once by dragging the corner where they meet.

Things are much simpler in Mac OS X, but there are some things to get used to. For instance, to resize a window in Mac OS X, you click and drag the resize control in the bottom-right corner of the window (pointed out in figure 1.6). Yup, that's all there is to it. That's great if you want to resize the window to the bottom or to the right, but if you want to resize the window to the top or left, you're out of luck. To work around this, first move the window up or to the left to the position you want, and then resize the window down or to the right to get the size you need.

 If you don't see the resize control, it means the window size is set and you can't change it.

Note

Understanding Hardware Differences

One of the major differences between a Mac and a Windows PC is that only one company makes Macs (Apple, of course), while all kinds of companies make Windows PCs. This is the main reason why Macs are so much more reliable than Windows PCs, but it also means that you'll notice quite a few hardware differences when you switch to the Mac. The three main areas where Mac and Windows diverge on the hardware front are the keyboard, mouse, and CD/DVD drives and discs, and the next three sections detail those differences.

Keyboard differences

If you expected the Mac keyboard to be identical to the Windows keyboard, you probably got quite a shock when you set up your Mac. Yes, the QWERTY keys are all there and are (thankfully!) arranged in the same pattern, and many of the other usual keyboard suspects are in place, including Esc, Tab, Caps Lock, Shift, the function keys, Home, End, Page Up, Page Down, and, on the larger Mac keyboards, a standard numeric keypad.

However, after that things get funky pretty quickly. What's up with the Command and Option keys? Is Control the same as Control? What about the Return key? Here's a rundown of these and other unusual Mac keys that should answer these and any other questions you might have:

- **Command (⌘).** This is the Mac's main modifier key. A *modifier key* is a key that you press in conjunction with one or more other keys to launch some action. In Windows, for example, you're probably familiar with pressing Control+S to save a document, and in this case Control is the modifier key. On the Mac, almost all keyboard shortcuts involve the ⌘ key. Its closest Windows equivalent would be the Control key.

- **Option.** This is another modifier key, and it's most often used in combination with ⌘. For example, in most Mac applications that have a toolbar, you can press Option+⌘+T to toggle the toolbar on and off.

- **Control.** This is another modifier key, although it's used only rarely in keyboard short- cuts. For example, you can restart your Mac by pressing Control+⌘+⏏. Note that on some smaller notebook keyboards, the Control key is displayed as Control. The most common use for this key is to hold down Control and click an object (such as a file) to display the object's shortcut menu.

- **Return.** This is the Mac equivalent of the Enter key, so you use it for the same kinds of things. On Mac keyboards with a separate numeric keypad, you usually see an Enter key, which almost always does the same thing as Return.

● **Delete.** This is the Mac equivalent of the Backspace key, which means that it deletes the character to the left of the insertion point cursor. Don't confuse this with the Delete key on a Windows keyboard, which deletes the character to the right.

● **Delete (⊠).** This is the Mac equivalent of the Windows Delete key, which means that it deletes the character to the right of the insertion point cursor (this is called a forward delete). To help differentiate the two Delete keys, note that forward delete appears only on a separate numeric keypad and always includes the ⟨⊠⟩ symbol.

Genius

On keyboards without a numeric keypad, you can still perform a forward delete by holding down the Fn key and pressing Delete.

● **Fn.** You use this key to change the behavior of certain other keys that are configured to perform double-duty. For example, on most modern Mac keyboards there's a key that has an icon of a speaker (with no sound waves) in the middle, and F10 in smaller type in the corner. The speaker icon with no sound waves tells you this is the Mute key, and the F10 text tells you this is also a function key. When you press the key on its own, you toggle the volume off and on; however, if you hold down Fn and then press the key, you initiate the F10 function key.

● **Navigation keys.** All Mac keyboards come with Up, Down, Left, and Right Arrow keys, which are the same as their Windows equivalents. All larger Mac keyboards also have separate Page Up, Page Down, Home, and End keys which are, again, no different than their Windows cousins. However, on smaller Mac keyboards, you don't see these last four keys. Instead, you need to hold down Fn and press Up Arrow (for Page Up), Down Arrow (for Page Down), Left Arrow (for Home), or Right Arrow (for End).

● **Eject (⏏).** Press this key (or, on some Macs, hold down the key for a second or two) to eject the currently inserted CD or DVD.

● **Function keys.** These are the top row of keys, and they usually show both an icon and standard function key text. The latter starts at F1 and can run as high as F19, although most Mac keyboards don't go beyond F12. Table 1.1 presents a summary of the special features associated with F1 through F12 on most modern Mac keyboards.

Caution

The function key associations for the special features listed in Table 1.1 are standard on most current Mac keyboards, but Apple seems to change them regularly. So not only might your old Mac keyboard not be set up this way, it's quite possible that future keyboard designs might change this layout yet again.

Table 1.1 Special Features Associated with Standard Function Keys

Key	What the Icon Represents
F1	Reduce screen brightness
F2	Increase screen brightness
F3	Launch Exposé
F4	Launch Dashboard
F5	Reduce keyboard brightness
F6	Increase keyboard brightness
F7	Skip to beginning of current media track or to previous media track
F8	Play/Pause current media
F9	Skip to next media track
F10	Toggle volume mute
F11	Reduce volume
F12	Increase volume

Genius

You might prefer to use F1 through F12 as standard function keys. That is, pressing the F1 key initiates F1 (usually the Help system) and to reduce screen brightness you must press Fn+F1. To set this up, click System Preferences in the Dock, click the Keyboard & Mouse icon, and then click the Keyboard tab. Select the Use all F1, F2, etc. keys as standard functions keys check box.

Having to learn the functions of all these new (or different) keys is a tough job, to be sure. Apple helps by displaying keyboard shortcuts beside many commands. For example, you can see in figure 1.7 that Finder's different views (Icons, List, Columns, and Cover Flow; see Chapter 6 for the details) use the shortcuts ⌘+1 through ⌘+4. However, check out the keyboard shortcut for the Hide Toolbar command. What does that first symbol represent?

1.7 Most Mac menus list the keyboard shortcuts associated with the commands.

Similarly, pull down the Apple menu and examine the shortcuts associated with the Force Quit and Log Out commands (see figure 1.8).

You can examine your Mac keyboard with a magnifying glass but you won't find those symbols anywhere, but I can help by showing you what they mean. Table 1.2 lists the most common menu symbols and which key each one represents.

| Finder | File | Edit | View | Go | Window | Help |

About This Mac
Software Update...
Mac OS X Software...

System Preferences...
Dock ▶

Recent Items ▶

Force Quit... ⌥⌘⏏

Sleep
Restart...
Shut Down...

Log Out Paul... ⇧⌘Q

1.8 What do the key symbols associated with the Force Quit and Log Out commands mean?

Table 1.2 Key Symbols Used in Mac OS X Menus

Menu Symbol	Corresponding Key
⌘	Command
⌥	Option
⌃	Control
⇧	Shift
⇥	Tab
↩	Return
⌤	Enter
⌫	Delete
esc	Escape
⇞	Page Up
⇟	Page Down
↖	Home
↘	End

A great way to learn these symbols is to keep the Keyboard Viewer on-screen while you work.

Follow these steps to display Keyboard Viewer:

1. **Click System Preferences in the Dock.** The System Preferences window appears.

2. **Click the International icon.** The International preferences appear.

13

3. **Click the Input Menu tab and select the Keyboard Viewer check box.**

4. **Select the Show input menu in menu bar check box.** This check box should be checked by default.

5. **Click Close to quit System Preferences.**

6. **Click the input menu icon in the menu bar.** The input menu icon is a flag, and the flag you see depends on which keyboard your Mac is set up to use. If you're in the U.S., you most likely use the U.S. keyboard layout, so the input menu icon is an American flag.

7. **Click Show Keyboard Viewer.** The Keyboard Viewer appears, as shown in figure 1.9 (although the layout of the Keyboard Viewer will vary depending on your Mac).

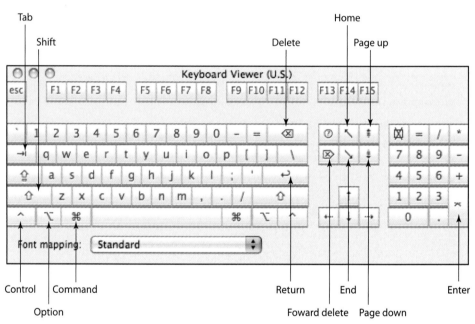

1.9 Use the Keyboard Viewer to help learn your Mac keyboard.

Mouse differences

The Mac keyboard throws a few curveballs your way when you first encounter it, but the Mac mouse is more straightforward. Almost all the basic mouse maneuvers — moving the pointer, clicking, double-clicking, clicking-and-dragging, and scrolling — work identically on the Mac as they do in Windows.

However, *almost* is the operative word, and I think you know what I'm talking about. If you're using the mouse that came with your Mac, or if you've picked up Apple's Mighty Mouse, then you may have noticed by now that it doesn't do the right-click thing. Instead, if you tap the right side of the mouse, it acts like a garden-variety left click. You won't get a shortcut menu pop-up like you do in Windows.

However, Mac OS X *does* come with shortcut menus, lots of them. (Apple often calls them *contextual menus* because the commands that appear depend on what you right-click.) So how do you get at them?

If you have a standard two-button mouse connected to your Mac, you display the Mac shortcut menus the same way you display them in Windows: right-click something. So if you're using an Apple Mighty Mouse, you're out of luck, right? Nope. You can display an object's shortcut menu by holding down the Control key and clicking the object.

Configuring right-clicking on a Mighty Mouse

If you prefer right-clicking to Control-clicking, the good news is that Mac's flexibility lets you do this. If you have an Apple Mighty Mouse, say goodbye forever to Control-clicking by following these steps:

1. **Click System Preferences in the Dock.** The System Preferences window appears.

2. **Click the Keyboard & Mouse icon.** The Keyboard & Mouse preferences appear.

3. **Click the Mouse tab.**

4. **Locate the list that points to the front right side of the mouse, and then select Secondary Button in that list, as shown in figure 1.10.**

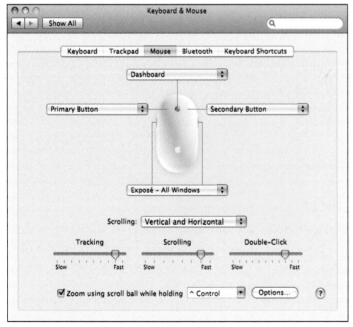

1.10 To enable right-clicks on your Mighty Mouse, choose Secondary Button in the list that points to the front right side of the mouse.

5. Choose System Preferences ⇨ Quit System PreferencesConfiguring right-clicking on a trackpad.

If you have a notebook Mac, you've probably noticed that the button below the trackpad doesn't right-click either, which means you need to hold down Control and click any part of the button to bring up a shortcut menu. Unfortunately, the trackpad button does *not* have a secret right-click personality like the Mighty Mouse. Not to worry, though, because you *can* configure the trackpad to display shortcut menus without needing to press the Control key. Follow these steps:

1. **Click System Preferences in the Dock.** The System Preferences window appears.

2. **Click the Keyboard & Mouse icon.** The Keyboard & Mouse preferences appear.

3. **Click the Trackpad tab.**

4. **Select the Secondary Click check box, as shown in figure 1.11.** On some Mac note-books, you need to select the For secondary clicks; place two fingers on the trackpad and then click the button check box, instead.

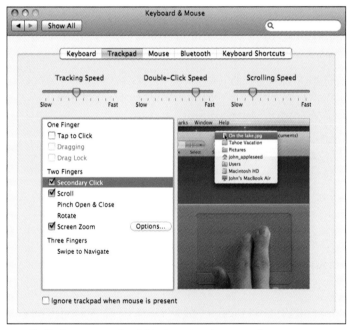

1.11 To display your notebook Mac's trackpad to open shortcut menus without requiring the Control key, select the Secondary Click check box.

5. **Choose System Preferences ⇨ Quit System Preferences.**

Genius You'll need to experiment with the three-finger "right-click" to find out the most comfortable way to do it. My preferred method is to put my middle finger and index finger on the trackpad and tap the button with my thumb.

What you've done here is configured your Mac notebook to display a shortcut menu by placing the mouse pointer over an object, resting two fingers on the trackpad, and then using a third finger to tap the button. It seems awkward at first, but you get used to it quite quickly.

Useful Mighty Mouse techniques

If you're using an Apple Mighty Mouse, you should know that this deceptively simple-looking device comes with a few hidden techniques that are often surprisingly useful. Here they are:

- **Tap the scroll ball.** You normally use the teensy scroll ball in the middle of the Mighty Mouse to scroll a window or document up, down, left, or right (by turning the ball toward the front, back, left, or right of the mouse). However, if you tap the scroll ball, your Mac displays the Dashboard (which you learn about in Chapter 6). Tap the scroll ball again to close the Dashboard.

- **Hold down Control and turn the scroll ball.** You use this technique to zoom the Mac window. Hold down Control and turn the scroll ball forward to zoom in; hold down Control and turn the scroll ball backward to zoom out.

- **Press the two side buttons.** The Mighty Mouse comes with a button on each of its flanks. If you press those two buttons simultaneously, your Mac displays Exposé (which, again, is part of Chapter 6). Press the two buttons again to close Exposé.

You can customize each of these techniques by following these steps:

1. **Click System Preferences in the Dock.** The System Preferences window appears.

2. **Click the Keyboard & Mouse icon.** The Keyboard & Mouse preferences appear.

3. **Click the Mouse tab.**

4. **Use the list that points to the scroll ball to select the action that your Mac performs when you tap the scroll ball.**

5. **Use the list that points to the two side buttons to select the action that your Mac performs when you press those buttons at the same time.**

6. **You can turn off scroll ball zooming by deselecting the Zoom using scroll ball while holding check box.** If you leave this feature selected, you can use the list to choose the key you hold down to zoom: Control, Option, or Command.

7. **Choose System Preferences ⇨ Quit System Preferences.**

Useful trackpad techniques

If you've got yourself a MacBook, MacBook Pro, or MacBook Air, you can always connect an external mouse, but you might prefer just to use the trackpad for your mousing around. That's certainly convenient when you're out and about, but it helps to know how to use the hidden features of the trackpad. You saw earlier that you can unlock the trackpad's ability to display shortcut menus, but it has a few other tricks up its digital sleeve. Here's a summary:

- **Two-finger scrolling.** If you need to scroll a window or document, don't bother dragging the scroll bar. Instead, drag two fingers along the trackpad: drag them left and right to scroll horizontally; drag them up and down to scroll vertically. (Or, if you prefer, place two fingers on the trackpad and then drag just one finger to scroll.)

- **Dragging.** To drag an object with the trackpad, press and hold the trackpad button and then drag a finger along the trackpad.

- **Control+scroll.** You use this technique to zoom the Mac window. Hold down Control and drag two fingers toward the top of the trackpad to zoom in; hold down Control and drag two fingers toward the bottom of the trackpad to zoom out.

- **Trackpad clicking.** Many ex-Windows users are confused because on a Mac you can't click something by tapping the trackpad. Instead, you have to click the button. However, Mac provides a solution. Open System Preferences, click Keyboard & Mouse, and then click the Trackpad tab. Select the Clicking check box. (On multitouch Macs, this check box is named Tap to Click.) You can now tap the trackpad to click stuff. Sweet!

Note
On some Macs, the Trackpad tab includes a check box named For secondary clicks. Place two fingers on the trackpad and then click the button. When you select the Clicking feature, the name of that check box changes to Tap trackpad using two fingers for secondary clicks. In other words, selecting the Clicking feature gives you a bonus: You can display any shortcut menu by double-tapping the trackpad.

Note
The next two items also use the Keyboard & Mouse preferences, so you might want to leave that window open for now.

● **One-finger dragging.** The two-finger drag methods that I showed you earlier work, but it would be easier if you could just use one finger to do it. No problem! In the Keyboard & Mouse preferences, click the Trackpad tab, select the Clicking (or Tap to Click) check box, and then select the Dragging check box. You can now drag windows and other objects without having to hold down the trackpad button. To do this, move the mouse pointer over the object and double-tap the trackpad, but leave your finger on the trackpad. (If you take your finger off, your Mac assumes you're double-clicking.) Drag your finger along the trackpad to drag the object along with it.

● **Drag Lock.** If you've got a long way to drag something, even the simple one-finger drag might not work very well. To work around this, you can use the Drag Lock feature. To turn this on, open the Keyboard & Mouse preferences, click the Trackpad tab, select the Clicking (or Tap to Click) check box, select the Dragging check box, and then select the Drag Lock check box. To use Drag Lock, position the mouse pointer over the object and double-tap the trackpad, but leave your finger on the trackpad. Drag your finger along the trackpad to drag the object along with it. After you've dragged the object, you can remove your finger, and then resume dragging at any time because your Mac is "locked" in drag mode. To exit drag mode, tap the trackpad.

Useful multitouch trackpad techniques

If you've got a Mac notebook with a multitouch trackpad (such as the MacBook Air or a 2008 or later MacBook Pro model), you get even more techniques to play around with:

● **Pinch and spread.** You use these techniques to zoom in on or out of an object such as a photo or a Web page. To pinch means to move two fingers closer together on the track-pad, and you use it to zoom in; to spread means to move two fingers apart on the track-pad, and you use it to zoom out.

● **Rotate.** You use this technique to rotate an object such as a photo clockwise or counter-clockwise. Place two fingers on the trackpad, about an inch apart. Drag the fingers clock-wise on the trackpad to rotate the object clockwise; drag the fingers counterclockwise on the trackpad to rotate the object counterclockwise.

● **Three-finger navigation.** You use this technique to move from one object to the next in applications that can display multiple objects. For example, if you have multiple photos open in the Preview application (see Chapter 6), swipe three fingers quickly across the trackpad to the right to navigate to the next item; swipe three fingers to the left to navi-gate to the previous item.

Hard disk and CD/DVD differences

The way your Mac treats hard disks and optical discs (CDs and DVDs) is radically different than the Windows way. With Windows, as you know, every disk drive on your system gets assigned a drive letter (A, C, D, and so on) and when you open the Computer window (or My Computer in Windows XP), you see icons for each of those drives, even if it's a DVD drive with no disc.

Your Mac does disks differently:

- **No drive letters.** Your Mac doesn't do drive letters. To prove this for yourself, click Finder in the Dock and then choose Go ⇨ Computer (or press Shift+⌘+C). As you can see in figure 1.12, the Computer window shows your Mac's drives with just an icon and a name.

1.12 Your Mac doesn't assign drive letters to its disk drives.

- **No disc or connection? No icon.** Your Mac shows you a drive only if it has a disc in it or if it's connected to the Mac. As soon as you insert a CD or DVD or attach an external hard disk, your Mac adds an icon to the desktop, as shown in figure 1.13. Eject the disc or disconnect the drive, and the icon goes away.

Your Mac deals with six different disk types, and there are icons for each type in figure 1.12, shown earlier. Here's what each icon represents:

1.13 When you connect a disk or insert a CD or DVD, your Mac adds an icon to the desktop.

⚬ **Network.** This icon represents the network to which your Mac is connected.

⚬ **Macintosh HD.** This icon represents your Mac's hard disk.

⚬ **External HD.** This icon represents an external hard disk attached to your Mac via USB or FireWire.

⚬ **Mac OS X Install Disc 1.** This icon represents a CD or DVD disc inserted in your Mac's optical drive. (In general, whenever you have a CD or DVD inserted, your Mac shows the name of that disc.)

⚬ **Downloads.** This icon represents a shared folder from a network server to which your Mac is connected. (Don't confuse this with the Downloads folder that's part of your user profile.) Note that in the Computer window's Sidebar (the pane on the left side of the window), connected servers appear in the Shared section, not the Devices section (see figure 1.12).

⚬ **Paul's iPod.** This icon represents a connected iPod or iPhone.

Genius

You can control what disk icons appear on your desktop. Click Finder in the Dock, and then choose Finder ➪ Preferences. Click the General tab, and then select the check box for each type of disk you want to display on the desktop: Hard disks; External disks; CD, DVDs, and iPods; and Connected servers.

You can't disconnect the Macintosh HD (or any internal hard disk) or the Network, but you can eject the other disk types. The best way to do this depends on what part of Mac OS X you've got on-screen:

⚬ **If you're working in Finder.** Click the eject icon that appears to the right of the disk's icon in the Sidebar.

⚬ **If you can see the desktop.** Click the disk icon and drag it to the Trash icon in the Dock. As you can see in figure 1.14, the Trash icon turns into an Eject icon. Drop the disk on the Eject icon to eject or disconnect the disk.

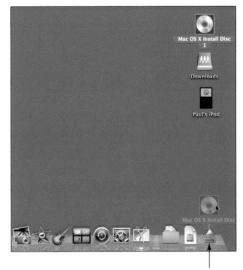

Trash icon becomes Eject

1.14 Click and drag a disk icon and drop it on the Trash (Eject) icon.

21

Understanding System Differences

As you might expect, there are some very basic (and very important) differences between how the Mac and Windows systems operate. Your Mac's operating system is called Mac OS X (pronounced oh-ess-ten), and it's based on another operating system called UNIX (yoo-niks). Windows and UNIX are as different as the proverbial chalk and cheese, but Mac OS X papers over many of those differences by implementing an interface that includes many Windows-like elements, including windows, dialog boxes, icons, and mouse-friendly elements such as buttons and menus. However, as you see in the next few sections, Mac OS X still does lots of things quite differently compared to Windows.

Finder versus Windows Explorer

The Finder program is more or less the Mac equivalent to Windows Explorer. That is, as with Windows Explorer (see figure 1.15), you use Finder to view and work with (rename, move, copy, delete, and so on) your files, folders, and disk drives (see figure 1.16). However, Windows Explorer is a program just like any other that you can open, use, and then close. Finder plays a much more fundamental role on your Mac. That is, it loads automatically when you first start your Mac, remains running throughout your session, and only closes when you shut down your Mac.

1.15 In Windows, you use Windows Explorer to work with files, folders, and disks.

| Finder | File | Edit | View | Go | Window | Help |

```
000                          ⇧ paul
◄ ►        ⬚⬚ ≡ ▥ ▰▰    ◉   ⚙ ▾              Q

▼ DEVICES
   ▤ Macintosh HD        📁          📁          👤
   ▣ iDisk
   ◎ Remote Disc      Desktop     Documents    Downloads
 ▶ SHARED
 ▼ PLACES
   ▨ Desktop          🏛          🎞          🎵
   🏠 paul
   ⚶ Applications      Library      Movies       Music
   📄 Documents
 ▶ SEARCH FOR
                      📷          ◈          ⊗
                      Pictures     Public       Sites

                9 items, 45.29 GB available
```

1.16 The Mac equivalent of Windows Explorer is Finder.

Because Finder is always running, you can always switch to it from another application. You can do this in various ways, but the following three are the easiest:

- Click the Finder icon on the left side of the Dock.
- Hold down ⌘, repeatedly tap the Tab key until the Finder icon is highlighted, and then release ⌘.
- Click an empty section of the desktop.

Genius Clicking the desktop switches to Finder, but it doesn't display the open Finder windows. Instead, the menu bar switches to the Finder menus, which is handy if all you want to do is run a Finder command and not interact with an open Finder window.

For much more about Finder, see Chapter 6.

System Preferences versus Control Panel

In Windows, you use Control Panel (see figure 1.17) to configure all kinds of different aspects of your system, from security to sound, colors to keyboards, programs to printers.

If you found yourself regularly accessing Control Panel's icons, then you'll want to get to know the Mac equivalent, which is System Preferences (see figure 1.18).

1.17 In Windows, you use Control Panel to configure various aspects of your system.

1.18 The Mac equivalent of Control Panel is System Preferences.

You can load this application in various ways, but the following two methods are the most common:

- Click the System Preferences icon in the Dock.
- Pull down the Apple menu and choose the System Preferences command.

24

As shown in figure 1.18, System Preferences is, much like its Control Panel counterpart, a collection of icons arranged in various categories, such as Personal and Hardware. You learn about System Preferences in detail in Chapter 3, but for now I want to stress perhaps the most important difference between System Preferences and Control Panel:

- **In Control Panel, you apply a changed setting by clicking a dialog box button such as OK or Apply.**

- **In System Preferences, most changed settings are applied automatically *as soon as you make the change*.** For example, if a setting is controlled by a check box, as soon as you select (or deselect) that check box, System Preferences applies the change to the system. In other words, many of the System Preferences sections don't come with a Cancel button that enables you to bail out of your changes before applying them. This means you need to exercise a bit more caution when manipulating preferences on your Mac.

Terminal versus Command Prompt

Many Windows users will go their entire Windows career without requiring the services of the command line, which in Windows is handled by the Command Prompt application. However, some users make use of the command line regularly, if not frequently. If you're in the latter camp, then you'll be happy to know that your Mac comes with a command-line application. It's called Terminal, and you launch it by opening Finder's Applications folder (click Applications in the Sidebar or press Shift+⌘+A), opening the Utilities folder, and then double-clicking the Terminal icon. Figure 1.19 shows the Terminal window that appears.

1.19 Terminal is the Mac's command-line application.

The main difference to notice right away is that Terminal is an application just like any other. That is, it comes with a window and its own menu bar, and there are lots of preferences and settings you can configure to customize the look and feel of Terminal. (Command Prompt, by contrast, has no menu system, just a measly few commands on the system menu, so it's not a "true" application.) Terminal also includes some unusual features such as running multiple sessions in a single window (choose Shell ⇨ New Tab ⇨ Basic) and using standard commands to copy text from the Terminal window (Edit ⇨ Copy or ⌘+C) or paste text to the Terminal window (Edit ⇨ Paste or ⌘+V).

Sleep mode differences

One of the great debates in computing circles is whether it's better to turn off your computer when you're not using it (which saves power), or leave your computer on all the time (which is more convenient). I won't rehash all the arguments' pros and cons here because in the Mac world this debate is almost nonexistent. That's because your Mac solves the on-or-off dilemma with an elegant solution called *sleep mode*. When your Mac goes into sleep mode, it goes into a low-power state that uses only marginally more electricity than if it were powered off altogether. However, the Mac also preserves all your running applications, windows, and documents, so when you bring your Mac out of sleep mode, your stuff is right where you left it.

Okay, I hear you say, Windows has a sleep mode, too, so what's the big whoop? Simple: Your Mac does sleep mode correctly. In Windows XP, sleep mode is called *standby mode*, and it basically does the same thing as sleep mode. The crucial difference is that the average Windows box often takes quite a long time to return from sleep mode, while your Mac is back up and running within a few seconds of jiggling the mouse or pressing a key. Windows Vista's sleep mode is a bit faster, but your Mac is still better.

This makes sleep mode usable enough that you can put your Mac to sleep anytime you won't be using it, even for a few minutes. The fastest way to put your Mac to sleep is to press Option+⌘+⏏, but you can also pull down the Apple menu and choose Sleep. To wake up your Mac, jiggle the mouse to press a key.

Note, too, that your Mac puts itself to sleep automatically if you don't use the computer for a while, usually after 10 minutes. To configure the amount of idle time before sleep mode kicks in, follow these steps:

1. **Click System Preferences in the Dock.** The System Preferences window appears.
2. **Click the Energy Saver icon.** The Energy Saver preferences appear, as shown in figure 1.20. (These are the preferences for a notebook Mac; if you don't see the sliders, click Show Details.)

1.20 Use the Energy Saver preferences to set the amount of idle time required before your Mac puts itself to sleep.

3. **If you have a notebook Mac, use the Setting for pop-up menu to choose either Power Adapter or Battery.**

4. **If you have a notebook Mac, use the Optimization pop-up menu to choose a preset power configuration.** Choose Better Energy Savings (your Mac sleeps after a short amount of idle time), Normal, or Better Performance (your Mac sleeps after a longer period of idle time).

5. **Use the Put the computer to sleep when it is inactive for slider to set the number of minutes or hours of idle time before your Mac sleeps automatically.**

Understanding User Account Differences

As with Windows, you deal with your Mac through the lens of a user account, usually the account you set up when you started your Mac for the first time. You learn how to create a new account and customize your existing account in Chapter 3. For now, let's close this chapter with a quick look at a couple of ways that your Mac user account differs from your Windows user account.

Locating your user data

On your Mac, as with Windows, your user account includes a folder where you can store your documents, photos, music, and other personal data. This was called your *user folder* in Windows, and
you accessed it by choosing an icon from the Start menu. On the Mac, this folder is called the *home
folder*, and you access it via Finder. In keeping with the importance of the home folder, your Mac
offers several ways to open it:

- **In Finder's Sidebar, click your user name in the Places section.**

- **In any Finder window, press Shift+⌘+H.**

- **From the Macintosh HD folder in Finder, open Users and then the folder that has
  your user name (see figure 1.21).**

1.21 Your home folder contains subfolders for various document types.

Here's a quick look at the nine folders that are standard in any Mac user account:

- **Desktop.** This folder contains the icons you see on your Mac's desktop. That is, if you add
  or remove an icon in the Desktop folder, you add or remove the same icon in the desktop. (This is a vice-versa thing, too: add or remove an icon on the desktop and the same
  icon is added or removed in the Desktop folder.)

- **Documents.** Use this folder to store data files that don't fit in any of the other folders.

- **Downloads.** Use this folder to store the files that you download from the Internet.

- **Library.** Your Mac uses this folder to store your settings.

- **Movies.** Use this folder to store videos, animations, and movies.

- **Music.** Use this folder to store music and other audio files. If you use iTunes to manage your music, the audio files are stored in the iTunes Music subfolder.

- **Pictures.** Use this folder to store photos, drawings, and other pictures.

- **Public.** Use this folder to store files that you want to share with other people on your network.

- **Sites.** Use this folder to store Web sites you create using the iWeb application.

Understanding your role as an administrator

The user account you created when you first set up your Mac is a special account in that it acts as the administrator account for the Mac. Certain operations — such as installing system updates, reconfiguring your disks, or modifying user accounts — are so important that your Mac doesn't let just anyone perform them. Instead, it prompts you for a password before it allows you to continue with these operations. More accurately, it prompts you for both a user name and a password, but your Mac won't be content with just any old login data. Instead, although your Mac doesn't always say so, what it really wants is an *administrative* login. That is, it wants the user name and password of that first Mac administrator account.

As you see in Chapter 3, it's possible to set up new administrator accounts.

Which Mac Applications Do I Use?

When you visit a new country, you probably spend at least some time with a map to familiarize yourself with the layout, locations, and landscape of the new place. If you're moving from a Windows PC to a Mac, you're entering a world that may prove to be just as alien and strange as a new country, so you need the Mac equivalent of a map to get your bearings. This chapter serves as your Mac map by pointing out some Mac applications that are available for various categories, such as Web browsers, graphics, and word processors.

General Mac Applications

Your Mac comes with tons of applications, most of which are miles better than the almost-universally crummy software you get with Windows. However, in every software category there are third-party applications that you can install if you're not crazy about the default Mac application. This section introduces you to some Mac applications in a half-dozen general categories: Web browsers, e-mail clients, calendars, address books, and FTP.

Mac Web browsers

You'll no doubt do just as much Web surfing on your Mac as you did in Windows, and you know that the quality of your surfing experience is directly related to the quality of the Web browser you use. Fortunately, the major Web browsers available for the Mac are all top-of-the-line, so the hardest job may be deciding which one to use.

Safari

Safari is the Mac's default Web browser and has been since the June 2003 release of Safari 1.0. The vast majority of Mac users stick with Safari not just because it's the laziest thing to do, but because Safari is quite simply one of the world's best browsers. It renders pages lickety-split, supports Web standards extremely well, is super-secure, offers tabbed browsing (see figure 2.1), and more.

2.1 Safari is the default Web browser on your Mac.

Note

The one area where Mac lags significantly behind Windows is the sheer number of applications available. Windows users outnumber Mac users by about ten-to-one, so software developers almost always cobble together a Windows version of their product, and only a few bother doing a Mac version. Bear that in mind when you're looking for software for your Mac.

Note

See Chapter 5 to learn how to import your Internet Explorer favorites or Firefox bookmarks into Safari.

Firefox

Mac users who want to move away from Safari almost always move to the Firefox browser. That's not surprising because Firefox is a great browser that's loaded with innovative features, including tabs, a pop-up blocker, an anti-phishing feature, one-click bookmarks, and tons of available add-on programs. To download Firefox, head for the following site: www.mozilla.com/en-US/firefox. Figure 2.2 shows the look and feel of the Firefox browser.

2.2 Many Mac users are trying out the Firefox Web browser.

Internet Explorer

The only thing you really need to know about the Mac version of Internet Explorer is that there isn't one. Or, technically, there isn't a *current* one. Oh, sure, Internet Explorer used to be the default browser on new Macs back in the day, but that all stopped when Apple released Safari. Microsoft actually kept Internet Explorer for the Mac available until early 2006, but the program itself hadn't seen any changes since about 2003.

So, yes, you won't find a Mac version of Internet Explorer on the Microsoft site, but there are Web sites that still offer it as a download. (Google "Internet Explorer Mac" and you'll see.) Not that I in any way encourage this, however. The version of Internet Explorer you'll get will be years old and, therefore, hopelessly out of date.

Other Web browsers

For the sake of completeness, here's a list of a few other Mac Web browsers that you might want to take for a test surf:

- **Camino.** http://caminobrowser.org/
- **Flock.** www.flock.com
- **iCab.** www.icab.de
- **OmniWeb.** www.omnigroup.com
- **Opera.** www.opera.com

Note As this book went to press, Google hadn't yet released a Mac version of its Chrome browser. However, there might be a Mac Chrome version by the time you read this, so check out www.google.com/chrome.

Making Safari appear to be another browser

The main reason people switch from Safari to another browser is because a particular Web site doesn't work well (or at all) with Safari. For example, some banking sites may insist that you use another browser, and some primitive or poorly coded Web sites may not show up properly because they don't recognize Safari. There's not much you can do directly to combat this browser discrimination, but you can fight back indirectly at least. You do that by taking advantage of the fact that the site is probably deciding which browsers are legitimate by using code to examine a string called the *user agent* that all browsers provide as a kind of identification. It's possible to configure Safari to provide a *different* user agent string (such as Internet Explorer), thus fooling the site into letting you in.

To perform this trick, you must first configure Safari to display its normally hidden Develop menu. Here's how you do that:

1. **Choose Safari ⇨ Preferences**. The Safari preferences appear.

2. **Click the Advanced tab.**

3. **Select the Show Develop menu in menu bar check box.**

4. **Close the Safari preferences.**

Now check out the Safari menu bar: You see a new Develop menu, which contains lots of commands of great interest to programmers. For your purposes, you need to choose Develop ⇨ User Agent to see a list of user agent strings, as shown in figure 2.3. Choose the string you want to use and then try accessing the site. If you still don't get in, keep trying different user agents.

2.3 With the Develop menu in place, the User Agent command presents a list of user agent strings you can use to fool a site into letting Safari in.

Mac e-mail applications

The e-mail onslaught that you face every day isn't going to stop just because you've moved over to the Mac. (On the contrary, all those letters of congratulations will only add to the blizzard.) Fortunately, there are several excellent e-mail applications for the Mac, as you see in the next few sections.

Mac OS X Mail

If you used either Vista's Windows Mail, or XP's Outlook Express, then you know those programs were solid e-mail clients that did pretty much everything you'd ever need an e-mail program to do. I'm happy to report that the default e-mail program on your Mac — Mac OS X Mail, or just Mail — is in the same league and, in fact, is perhaps a few notches better. For example, it comes with a feature that I think should be standard equipment in all e-mail clients: a Bounce command (it's on the Message menu), which replies to a sender with a message that makes it look as though your account is no longer active. It's devious and fun and a great way to get rid of e-mail pests.

As you can see in figure 2.4, Mail offers an elegant, straightforward layout that makes the program easy to navigate and simple to use.

2.4 Mail is your Mac's default e-mail application.

Note See Chapter 4 to learn how to import your Outlook, Outlook Express, or Windows Mail messages into Mac OS X Mail.

Eudora

Eudora is a famous e-mail program that seems like it has been around since before the Internet was even a gleam in the Defense Department's eye. I kid, of course, but Eudora's longevity is a testament to its reputation as one of the best e-mail programs around. Eudora fans claim that it performs all the basic e-mail tasks with speed and elegance, and that its spam filter is as good as anything else out there. There is, of course, a Mac version (see figure 2.5), which you can download from www.eudora.com.

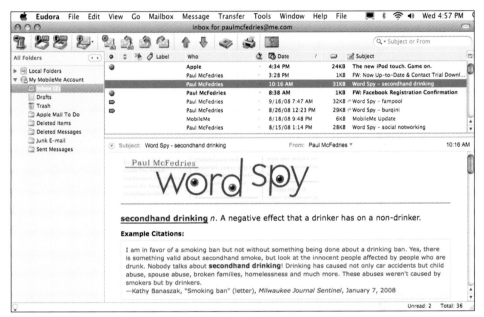

2.5 Eudora for the Mac presents a decidedly homely face to the world.

Entourage Mail

Entourage is the e-mail program that comes with the Mac version of Microsoft Office. The current version is Office 2008, but some older Macs come with test-drive versions of Office 2004. Entourage has lots of powerful tools, but its key feature is that it also combines an address book and calendar (as well as notes and tasks), and these are tightly integrated. For example, you can set up a link between an e-mail message and a calendar event (for example, if the message is setting up a lunch date or a meeting). The interface isn't as nice as Mail's (see figure 2.6). To be fair, this is Entourage 2004, and the interface used by Entourage 2008 is a noticeable improvement. Nevertheless, Entourage is a powerful program. You can download it from www.microsoft.com/mac.

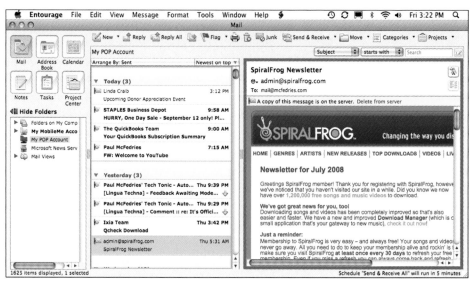

2.6 The Mac version of Microsoft Office uses Entourage for its e-mail chores.

Other e-mail applications

Here are a few other Mac e-mail clients that you might want to check out:

- **GyazMail.** www.gyazsquare.com
- **Mailsmith.** www.barebones.com
- **Odysseus.** http://infinitydatasystems.com/
- **PowerMail.** www.ctmdev.com
- **Thunderbird.** www.mozilla.com

Mac calendar applications

When you meet someone and ask "How are you?" the most common reply these days is a short one: "Busy!" We're all as busy as can be these days, and that places-to-go-people-to-see feeling is everywhere. All the more reason to keep your affairs in order, and that includes your appointments. To do that, you need a calendar program, which acts as a kind of electronic personal assistant, leaving your brain free to concentrate on more important things. Although there aren't tons of Mac calendar applications, the ones that are available are generally pretty good.

iCal

Your Mac comes with a program called iCal that you can use to manage your schedule (see figure 2.7). iCal enables you to create items, called *events*, which represent both your appointments and your all-day activities. For each event, you can specify start and end times (or designate the item as an all-day event), specify a location, and add the names of the attendees. You can also configure an event to repeat at a regular interval, and iCal will even remind you when an appointment is coming up. You can also create multiple calendars (you get a Home and Work calendar by default) and synchronize your calendar with your MobileMe account, if you have one. You can also use iCal to create to-do items, which are tasks to be completed. All in all, iCal is a competent (if not particularly flashy) calendar application.

2.7 The iCal calendar application comes free with your Mac.

Entourage Calendar

Entourage is part of the Mac version of Microsoft Office (Office 2008, but some older Macs come with test-drive versions of Office 2004). Entourage's Calendar feature (see figure 2.8) isn't as easy to use as iCal's, but it performs all the standard calendar techniques without much fuss. The big advantage is that the Calendar feature is integrated with the other Entourage features such as Mail and Address Book, so you can do some powerful things. See www.microsoft.com/mac.

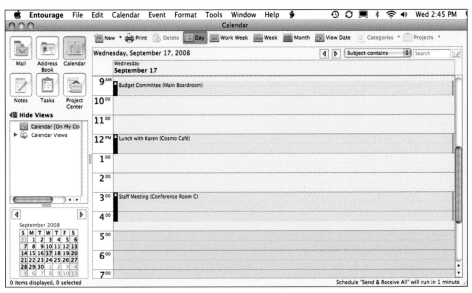

2.8 In Microsoft Office for the Mac, the Entourage application comes with a Calendar component.

Now Up-to-Date

Now Software's Up-to-Date is a calendar application that offers all the standard appointment-tracking features, and presents them in an easy-to-use interface (see figure 2.9). Up-to-Date's key feature is that it makes it easy to share calendars among multiple people. You can share your calendar with other Mac users, Windows users, Web users, and with mobile devices such as cell phones and personal digital assistants. See www.nowsoftware.com.

Other calendar applications

Here are a few other Mac calendar programs that you might want to consider:

- **BdCalendar.** www.baddogapps.com
- **Palm Desktop.** www.palm.com
- **Preminder.** www.hairyhighlandcow.net
- **Sunbird.** www.mozilla.com

2.9 Now Software's Up-to-Date application enables you to share a calendar with multiple users.

Mac address book applications

One of the paradoxes of modern life is that as your contact information becomes more important, you store less and less of that information in the easiest database system of them all — your memory. That is, instead of memorizing phone numbers like you used to, you now store your contact info electronically. When you think about it, this isn't exactly surprising because it's not just a landline number that you have to remember for each person; it might also be a cell number, an instant messaging handle, an e-mail address, a Web site address, as well as a physical address. That's a lot to remember, so it makes sense to go the electronic route and use an address book application.

Address Book

For most Mac users, the "electronic route" means the Address Book application (see figure 2.10), which comes with Mac OS X. Address Book seems basic enough, but it's actually loaded with useful features that can help you organize and get the most out of the contact management side of your life. For example, you can create *smart groups*, which are groups of contacts that Address Book manages automatically based on criteria that you specify (such as a company name).

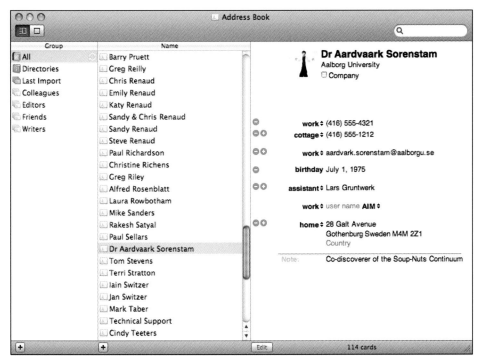

2.10 The Address Book application is part of Mac OS X.

Entourage Address Book

Entourage comes with the Mac version of Microsoft Office (Office 2008, but some older Macs have test-drive versions of Office 2004). Entourage's Address Book feature (see figure 2.11) is a bit clumsier to use than Mac OS X Address Book, but it certainly does the job. The Entourage Address Book is integrated with the other Entourage features such as Mail and Calendar, so all your stuff resides in a single application. See www.microsoft.com/mac.

Now Contact

Now Software's Contact is an address book application that offers all the standard contact management features, and presents them in an easy-to-use interface (see figure 2.12). Contact's main feature is its ability to share address books among multiple people. You can share your contacts with other Mac users, Windows users, Web users, and with mobile devices such as cell phones and personal digital assistants. See www.nowsoftware.com.

2.11 In Microsoft Office for the Mac, the Entourage application comes with an Address Book feature.

2.12 Now Software's Contact application enables you to share an address book with multiple users.

Other address book applications

Here are a few more Mac address book applications to check out:

- **BdContacts.** www.baddogapps.com

- **Contactizer.** www.objective-decision.com

- **Palm Desktop.** www.palm.com

- **Ripplex.** www.ripplex.com

- **Thunderbird.** www.mozilla.com

Mac FTP applications

When you need to download a file from the Internet to your Mac, most often that file is accessible via your Web browser, which enables you to save the file directly to your Mac hard disk. However, many files are also available on special servers that use a technology called File Transfer Protocol (FTP). Although Finder can perform limited FTP duties (choose Go ⇨ Connect to Server and then type the FTP address), your Mac doesn't come with a true FTP application, so you need to download and install one.

Genius

The file you download via FTP may be compressed to save space or to combine multiple files into a single file for easier downloading. If that file is a standard compressed archive that uses the .zip file extension, double-click the file to open it. However, you may occasionally come across a file that uses the .sit extension. This is a StuffIt Compressed Archive File, and to decompress it you need to install the StuffIt utility, available from www.stuffit.com.

Fetch

Fetch is one of the oldest Mac FTP applications, and it's probably the most popular. It fell behind the competition a few years ago when it had a tired interface and only basic functionality, but recent upgrades have pushed Fetch back into the top ranks of Mac FTP programs (see figure 2.13). See www.fetchsoftworks.com.

CyberDuck

CyberDuck is a free Mac FTP client (see figure 2.14). It doesn't have anywhere near as many features as Fetch, Interarchy, or Transmit, but it's also probably the easiest of the Mac FTP clients to use. See http://cyberduck.ch/.

2.13 Fetch is one of the oldest and still one of the most popular Mac FTP applications.

2.14 CyberDuck's clean interface makes it simple to use, and you can't beat the price (free!).

Interarchy

Nolobe's Interarchy application is one of the most popular Mac FTP clients, which isn't surprising considering the raft of powerful features it offers. However, Interarchy's most obvious feature is that it looks and works exactly like your Mac's Finder application (see figure 2.15), so there's almost no learning curve. See www.nolobe.com.

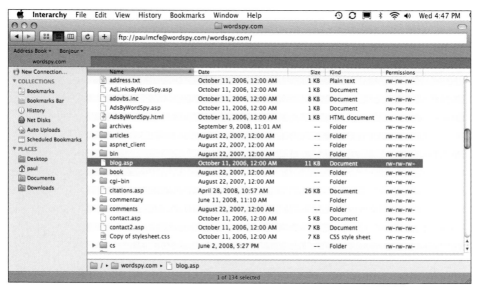

2.15 The Interarchy FTP application is distinguished by its uncanny resemblance to the Mac's Finder program.

Transmit

Panic's Transmit program is an FTP client with a unique two-pane design that shows your local files and folders on the left and the FTP server's files and folders on the right (see figure 2.16). This makes Transmit super-easy to use, and it's loaded with impressive features, such as being able to preview and even edit files before you download them! See www.panic.com.

Other FTP applications

Here are more Mac FTP programs to investigate:

- **Flow.** www.extendmac.com
- **ForkLift.** www.binarynights.com
- **NetFinder.** www.ortabe.com

- **RBrowser.** www.rbrowser.com

- **Yummy FTP.** www.yummysoftware.com

2.16 Panic's Transmit application is a first-rate and easy-to-use FTP application.

Mac Media Applications

Macs are famous for media prowess, and rightly so. Combine a beautiful screen, high-resolution graphics, and uncanny ease of use, and your Mac becomes a media powerhouse right out of the box. But it's not just hardware that makes your Mac graphically great. Whether you're working with music, movies, or photos, you need the appropriate application, and the Mac world is overrun with outstanding media programs. Even better, your Mac comes with quite a few top-notch media applications, and add Apple's iLife suite into the mix, and your Mac's media cupboard is suddenly overflowing.

Mac media players

As a refugee from Windows Nation, you're most likely used to playing your media files in Windows' default application, Windows Media Player, or possibly Windows Media Center. There is no recent version of Windows Media Player for the Mac (and no Mac version of Windows Media Center at all), but not to worry: There are lots of excellent Mac media players.

Note You're probably more concerned about getting all your precious media files from your Windows PC to your Mac. See Chapter 5 to learn how.

iTunes

Your Mac's main media player is the iTunes application (see figure 2.17). Using iTunes, you can cre-ate a library of music and use that library to play songs, albums, and collections of songs called *playlists*; tune in to an Internet radio station; subscribe to podcasts; and listen to audiobooks. You can also use iTunes to listen to music CDs, manage music on an iPod or iPhone, and purchase music from the online iTunes store. On the visual front, you can use iTunes to play movies, video files, and TV shows.

2.17 iTunes is your Mac's main media player.

Note Not only can you listen to music on your Mac, but you can *make* music, too! If you have iLife installed on your Mac, you can use the GarageBand application to record and compose music. See also the Adobe application Audition (www.adobe.com).

QuickTime Player

Your Mac also comes with the QuickTime Player, a stripped-down media player that enables you to view video and audio files in a wide variety of formats. When you open a media file, QuickTime Player loads the media into a simple interface (see figure 2.18) that enables you to control the playback. If you're looking for something more substantial, you can upgrade to QuickTime Pro, which enables you to convert files to different formats, edit media, record audio and video, export media to your iPod or iPhone, and lots more (see www.apple.com/quicktime).

2.18 If you just want to play audio and video files, QuickTime Player does the job.

Genius QuickTime Player supports dozens of audio and video file formats, but two that it *doesn't* support are Windows Media Audio (WMA) and Windows Media Video (WMV). If you want to play Windows Media files on your Mac, take a look at Flip4Mac (www.flip4mac.com), which sells plug-ins that enable QuickTime Player to handle the WMA and WMV formats.

Front Row

What do you do if you want to listen to or watch media on your Mac, but you're not sitting down in front of your Mac? Look no further than the Front Row application, which offers an Apple TV–like interface (see figure 2.19). What's special about Front Row is that although you can maneuver its menus using your Mac keyboard, the device of choice is actually the Apple Remote that came with your Mac (or your iPod). You use the Apple Remote button to navigate to the media you want, launch the media, and control the playback, all without leaving the comfort of your chair or couch.

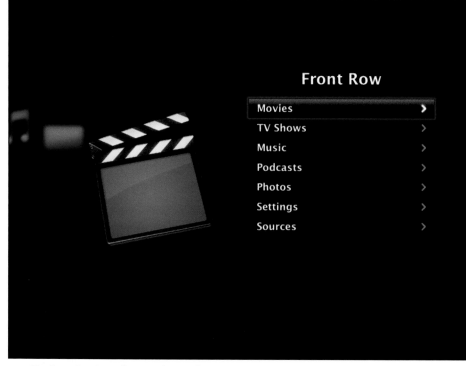

2.19 Use Front Row's Apple TV–style interface to control your Mac media using your Apple Remote.

Other Mac media players

Here are some third-party media players that you might want to try out on your Mac:

- **Adobe Media Player.** www.adobe.com
- **Audion.** www.panic.com
- **Chroma Player.** www.chromaplayer.com
- **RealPlayer.** www.real.com
- **VLC Media Player.** www.videolan.org
- **Windows Media Player for Mac OS X.** www.microsoft.com/mac

Mac graphics applications

The Mac has been *the* computer graphics platform since the first Mac was introduced way back in 1984. This fact is reflected not only in the nice graphics applications that come bundled with your Mac, but more strongly in the incredible number of fantastic graphics programs that are available from third-party developers.

Image Capture

You use your Mac's Image Capture application (see figure 2.20) to connect to a device such as a digital camera or digital camcorder and download the device's photos or videos to your Mac.

Preview

When you want to take a closer look at a photo or other image, your Mac gives you several ways to go about this, as you see in

2.20 You can use the Image Capture application to download media to your Mac from a digital camera or digital camcorder.

Chapter 3. Probably the most common method is to load the file into the Preview application because this is the default application for images (that is, double-click an image and it loads in Preview). Preview shows a full version of the image and enables you to zoom in and out, pan, and select portions of the image. You can also display multiple images in Preview and scroll through them, as shown in figure 2.21. Preview also includes basic image-editing commands that let you flip, rotate, resize, recolor, and annotate a photo.

2.21 Preview is your Mac's default application for viewing photos and other images.

iPhoto

If you have iLife installed on your Mac, you can use the iPhoto application to import photos from your digital camera and organize those photos into albums. iPhoto also comes with some decent photo-editing tools (see figure 2.22) that enable you to rotate, crop, and straighten images, adjust a photo's colors, remove red eye, and apply special effects. You can also sync photos with your MobileMe account, e-mail photos, order prints and other photo gifts, and lots more.

2.22 The iLife suite includes iPhoto, a powerful application for organizing and editing photos.

Photo Booth

Need a quick photo for your Mac's user account picture or your iChat buddy picture? Don't bother pulling out the digital camera. Instead, if your Mac has a built-in iSight camera (as most modern Macs do), you can take a quick snapshot using the Photo Booth application (see figure 2.23). Click the camera icon, smile into the iSight camera, and seconds later your mug shows up in the Photo Booth window. You can then apply the photo to your account, e-mail it, or open it in iPhoto.

2.23 Use Photo Booth to take candid shots using your Mac's built-in iSight camera.

Adobe graphics applications

Adobe (www.adobe.com) currently produces the best graphics software for the Mac, and the company offers lots of different applications with varying levels of sophistication and price, so you should be able to find something that suits your needs and budget. The main Adobe graphics programs to check out are Photoshop, Photoshop Elements (see figure 2.24), Photoshop Lightroom, Illustrator, InDesign, and After Effects.

2.24 Photoshop Elements is a powerful but inexpensive photo-editing program.

Other Mac graphics applications

Here are a few other Mac graphics programs to consider:

- **Aperture.** www.apple.com/aperture
- **GIMP.** www.gimp.org
- **GraphicConverter.** www.lemkesoft.com
- **ImageWell.** www.xtralean.com
- **InstantGallery.** www.thinkmac.co.uk
- **LightZone.** www.lightcrafts.com
- **Painter X.** www.corel.com

Mac video editors

Whether you want to fix up your home movies, put together a video for a corporate presentation, or create a DVD slideshow of your photos, your Mac is up to the task.

iMovie

Apple's iLife suite comes with iMovie, a powerful and easy-to-use video-editing application (see figure 2.25). You can import camcorder video, apply scene transitions, add titles, credits, and a soundtrack, and even export your movie to a DVD.

2.25 iLife's iMovie application is an excellent video editor.

iDVD

iLife also comes with iDVD (see figure 2.26), a program that enables you to set up and burn your own DVD discs (assuming your Mac has a DVD burner attached). You can add movies and create photo slideshows. iDVD offers lots of fun themes, and you can even set up menus and submenus just like the pros.

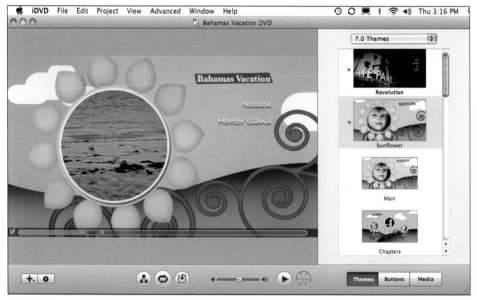

2.26 iLife's iDVD application lets you create and burn your own DVDs.

Final Cut

Apple's top-of-the-line video editor is Final Cut Studio, which offers every possible bell and whistle you can think of for managing, editing, and publishing digital video. Of course, with a price tag of $1,299, it should! If your needs (and pocketbook) are more modest, consider Final Cut Express (see figure 2.27), a scaled-down version of Final Cut Studio that, for the much more comfortable price of $199, still offers amazingly powerful features. See www.apple.com/finalcutexpress.

2.27 Apple's Final Cut Express is a powerful and reasonably affordable video editor.

Adobe Premiere

Adobe Premiere was once the most popular and the most full-featured of the Mac video editors. However, Adobe stopped making Premiere for a while, and that allowed Final Cut to become the king of the Mac video-editing hill. Premiere is back once again, and it remains an excellent product. The high-end version is Premiere Pro (see figure 2.28) which, as the name suggests, is aimed at professional video editors. The price is high-end, too: $799! If your needs aren't so grandiose, you'll want to stick with Premiere Elements, which will set you back $139, but still offers plenty of powerful features.

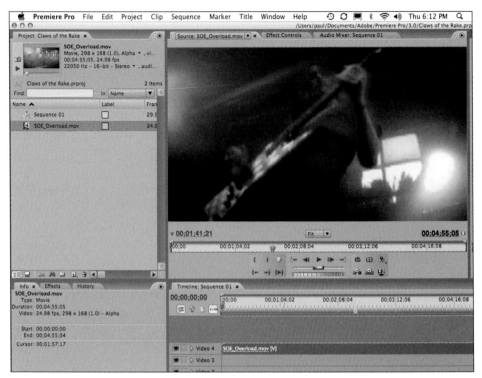

2.28 Mac video-editing applications don't get any more full-featured than Adobe Premiere Pro.

Other Mac video editors

Here are some other Mac video-editing programs to look into:

- **QuickTime Pro.** www.apple.com/quicktime
- **Popcorn.** www.roxio.com
- **FastCut.** www.timesforfun.de
- **MediaEdit.** www.miensoftware.com
- **SimpleMovieX.** www.aeroquartet.com

Mac Productivity Applications

Using your Mac for Web surfing, playing media, and editing photos is all very well, but eventually you'll need to invest in some productivity applications. That is, you need some programs that will help you with your work processing, spreadsheets, presentations, and databases. I used the word "investing" a bit earlier because for the most part your Mac doesn't come with any productivity applications. (The only exception is the TextEdit application, which you can use as a bare-bones word processor in a pinch.) This means that you must install your own applications, and most of the available ones aren't free (although, as you'll see, there are a few exceptions).

Mac office suites

If you need multiple productivity applications, you'll save some bucks by getting an office suite, which combines two or more applications, usually a word processor and spreadsheet, but often programs for presentations and databases as well.

iWork

Apple's iWork suite comes with three programs: Pages, a word processor (see figure 2.29); Numbers, a spreadsheet program; and Keynote, a presentation program. The suite costs $79, but a free trial is also available. Learn more at www.apple.com/iwork.

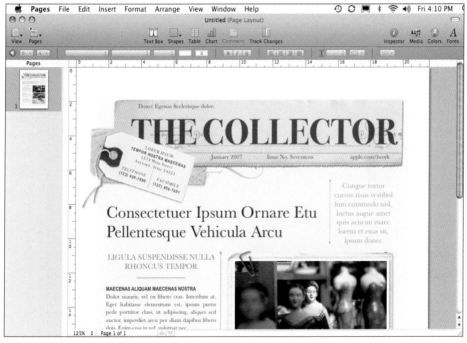

2.29 The Pages word processor comes with Apple's iWork office suite.

Microsoft Office 2008 for the Mac

Like its Office 2004 predecessor, Office 2008 for the Mac comes with four main programs: Word for word processing; Excel for spreadsheets; PowerPoint for presentations; and Entourage for e-mail, contacts, appointments, and tasks. The Home and Student Edition contains just these four applications, and it retails for $149.95; the standard edition also includes support for Microsoft Exchange Server and some built-in workflows for Mac's Automator utility, which you use to automate tasks; the Special Media Edition includes all the features of the regular edition, and also includes Microsoft Expression Media, a program for organizing media files. Find out more at www.microsoft.com/mac.

OpenOffice

The OpenOffice suite includes a word processor, spreadsheet program, presentation application, drawing application, and a database management program. That's a lot of software, so you might think you have to fork over the big bucks for it. Not so, because OpenOffice is complete free! See www.openoffice.org.

Papyrus Office

The Papyrus Office suite includes a word processor, spreadsheet program, desktop publishing application, and a database management program. The suite will run you $99, but you can get a trial version to take for a test drive. See www.rom-logicware.com.

ThinkFree Office

The ThinkFree Office suite is a Microsoft Office for Windows clone that comes with three applications: Write, a word processor; Calc, a spreadsheet program (see figure 2.30); and Show, a presentation program. You can purchase the suite for just $49, but ThinkFree also offers a free trial version. See www.thinkfree.com.

Note

If you're feeling adventurous, you might want to check out NeoOffice, which is an open-source office suite with a great price: Free! It includes programs for word-processing, spreadsheets, and presentations, but it's a work in progress, so expect crashes!

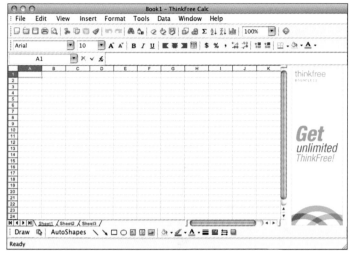

2.30 ThinkFree Office is designed to be a Microsoft Office clone, without also cloning the Microsoft Office price.

Genius

If you just want to view Excel spreadsheets, then consider a nifty little program called icXL, which enables you to open and view any Excel file, even ones that use the new Excel 2007 file format. See www.panergy-software.com.

Mac word processors

Most Mac fans use either Microsoft Word (part of the Office 2008 for the Mac suite) or Pages (part of Apple's iWork suite). If all you need is a word processor, and TextEdit just isn't good enough, check out these stand-alone word processors:

- **AbiWord.** www.abisource.com
- **Mariner Write.** www.marinersoftware.com
- **Mellel.** www.redlers.com
- **Nisus Writer.** www.nisus.com

Mac spreadsheets

If you need to crunch numbers on your Mac, your best bets are either Microsoft Excel (from the Office 2008 for the Mac suite) or Numbers (from Apple's iWork suite). If you don't want to spring for an entire suite, here are some stand-alone spreadsheet applications:

- **Mariner Calc.** www.marinersoftware.com
- **Mesa.** www.plsys.co.uk
- **Tables.** www.x-tables.eu

Mac database applications

Mac database-management programs aren't impossible to find, but they're not exactly thick on the ground, either. None of the major office suites includes a database manager, and of the minor suites only OpenOffice and Papyrus Office do the database thing. If you have data that you need to manage on your Mac, here are a few programs to check out:

- **Bento.** www.filemaker.com/products/bento
- **FileMaker Pro.** www.filemaker.com
- **FrontBase.** www.frontbase.com
- **iData.** www.idata3.com
- **iList Data.** www.lakewoodstudios.com
- **Panorama.** www.provue.com

How Do I Perform Everyday Mac Tasks?

This is the look-before-you-leap chapter. Or maybe it's the walk-before-you-run chapter. Either way, it's the chapter where you get to know your way around your new Mac by learning the techniques associated with tons of day-to-day chores, from customizing your Mac to launching applications to setting up user accounts to playing music and other media. By the time you're done, you and your Mac will be fast friends, and you'll be ready to tackle the more advanced tasks that populate the rest of the book.

Configuring Your Mac

Lots of folks keep their Windows PCs in their out-of-the-box state, but most Mac users are individu-alists and wouldn't dream of such cookie-cutter conformity. True, you and your Mac are just get-ting to know each other, so it may seem a tad premature to be thinking about configuring and customizing your Mac. I hear what you're saying, but in fact your Mac makes configuration chores so ridiculously easy that you can't help but think that you're *supposed* to customize it. Read on to find out how it's done.

Understanding preferences

In Windows, you use the Control Panel to configure your system: hardware settings, desktop back-ground, user accounts, security, and more. Not only that, but many Windows programs come with a command that enables you to play around with the program's configuration, although finding that command often requires a bit of detective work on your part. (Is it on the Tools menu? The Edit menu? The File menu?) So on the one hand it's good that Windows and Windows programs have so many configuration options, but on the other hand it's frustrating that there's no consistent way to find those options.

Well, I'm happy to report that your days of configuration frustration are over because Mac OS X and Mac applications are just as configurable as their Windows counterparts, but on your Mac those configuration options are always easy to find, as you see in the next two sections.

For now, you should know that configuration options and settings are known in the Mac universe as *preferences*. That's a good name for them because it speaks to the heart of the matter: that you customize and configure your Mac and its applications because you *prefer* to set up your system in that way. It really is as simple as that, and you'll soon see that locating and working with Mac pref-erences is faster and easier than configuring Windows.

Caution

You should know right off the bat that when you change Mac preferences there is more potential for making a mistake than when you set Windows options. In Windows, configuration options and settings always appear in a dialog box, and you generally click OK to apply your changes, or you click Cancel if you change your mind or make a mistake. Not so in the Mac scheme of things. In most cases, as soon as you modify a preference, that new setting goes into effect immediately, and the only way to cancel the change is to revert the preference to its previous setting. Bear that in mind as you work with preferences on your Mac.

Displaying the system preferences

The Mac OS X system preferences help you configure and customize various aspects of your Mac, including the colors, desktop background, security, power settings, user accounts, and software updates. A default Mac setup comes with more than two dozen system preference categories, and third-party programs sometimes add new categories to the preferences.

To view the system preferences, your Mac gives you two choices:

◉ Click the System Preferences icon in the Dock (see figure 3.1).

◉ Click the Apple icon in the upper-left corner and then choose System Preferences.

3.1 To view the System Preferences, click the System Preferences icon in the Dock.

Either way, the System Preferences window appears, as shown in figure 3.2.

3.2 You use the System Preferences window to customize and configure your Mac to your liking.

For the most part, you set system preferences by using the following general procedure:

1. **In the System Preferences window, click the icon that represents the preferences you want to work with.** Your Mac displays the preferences.

2. **Make your changes to the preferences**. As in Windows, the Mac preferences appear as controls such as text boxes, check boxes, option buttons, pop-up menus, and lists.

3. **If you want to change preferences in a different category, click Show All to return to the main System Preferences window, and then repeat Steps 1 and 2.**

4. **When you're done, click the Close button or choose System Preferences ⇨ Quit System Preferences.**

For example, if you click the Appearance icon in the System Preferences window, you see the Appearance preferences, shown in figure 3.3. As you can see, this new window is a collection of lists, option buttons, and check boxes that enable you to configure various aspects of Mac OS X.

```
○ ○ ○                        Appearance
◄ ►   Show All                                    [Q          ]

        Appearance: [ ▨ Blue        ▼ ]
                    For the overall look of buttons, menus and windows

     Highlight Color: [   ▨ Blue        ▼ ]
                      For selected text

  Place scroll arrows: ⦿ Together
                       ○ At top and bottom

 Click in the scroll bar to: ⦿ Jump to the next page
                             ○ Jump to here
                             ☐ Use smooth scrolling
                             ☑ Minimize when double-clicking a window title bar

 Number of Recent Items: [ 10   ▼ ]  Applications
                          [ 10   ▼ ]  Documents
                          [ 10   ▼ ]  Servers

   Font smoothing style: [ Automatic – best for main display  ▼ ]
Turn off text smoothing for font sizes [ 4  ▼ ] and smaller.        ⑦
```

3.3 In the System Preferences window, click Appearance to see the Appearance preferences.

Note

Many Windows users find it hard to get used to Mac scroll bars because both scroll arrows appear together. (On a vertical scroll bar, the two arrows appear together at the bottom of the scroll bar.) If you prefer separate scroll arrows, select the Place scroll arrows: At top and bottom option in the Appearance preferences.

Displaying program preferences

The system preferences let you configure your Mac as a whole, but almost all Mac applications are customizable as well, and they come with their own set of preferences. I mentioned earlier that locating options and settings in Windows programs is a frustrating guessing game, but there's no guessing when it comes to finding the preferences for Mac applications. That's because on the

menu bar for every Mac application, you see the name of the program next to the Apple menu. To view the application's preferences, click the program name in the menu bar and then click Preferences.

For example, click any empty section of the desktop to display the Finder menu bar, click Finder as shown in figure 3.4, and then click Preferences.

3.4 To display a program's preferences, pull down the menu named after the program (such as Finder shown here) and then click Preferences.

Genius

In all Mac applications that have preferences (and that's the vast majority of Mac programs) you can also open the program preferences by pressing ⌘+,.

Figure 3.5 shows the Finder Preferences window that appears. This is a typical program preferences window in that it displays several icons across the top: General, Labels, Sidebar, and Advanced. These icons represent the different categories of preferences that the application provides. Click an icon to see the preferences associated with that category. These icons and their preferences are usually called either *tabs* (the term I use in this book) or *panels*.

Here's the general procedure to follow when you work with program preferences:

3.5 The Finder Preferences window is divided into four tabs: General, Labels, Sidebar, and Advanced.

1. **Pull down the menu named after the program and then click Preferences.** The application displays its preferences.

2. **Click the tab that contains the preferences you want to modify.**

3. **Make your changes to the preferences**. As with the system preferences, application preferences appear as controls such as text boxes, check boxes, option buttons, pop-up menus, and lists.

4. **Repeat Steps 2 and 3 to set other application preferences.**

5. **When you're done, click the Close button.**

Unlocking preferences

When you open System Preferences and click an icon, you may find that some or all of the controls in the resulting preferences window are disabled. You might think your Mac has gone haywire, but this actually isn't a glitch or a bug. Instead, it's a security feature designed to prevent unauthorized users from making changes to sensitive system settings. (It's also designed to prevent you from making certain changes without at least having to think about them first.) For example, figure 3.6 shows what the Parental Controls preferences look like when a user without authorization displays the window.

3.6 Your Mac sometimes locks preferences to avoid unauthorized changes.

70

To display or enable the controls, follow these steps:

1. **Click the lock icon in the bottom-left corner of the window.** Your Mac prompts you for the name and password of an authorized user.

2. **Type the name of an administrator account in the Name text box and the account password in the Password text box.**

3. **Click OK.** Your Mac displays or enables the preferences and the closed lock icon changes to an open lock.

Note

When you're done with the preferences, you can click the open lock icon to reset the security for the preferences. However, your Mac resets the lock automatically once you close the preferences, so you don't need to bother with this.

Changing the desktop background

The default desktop background in Mac OS X Leopard is a spectacular image of the aurora borealis. If that's not your cup of tea, or if you'd prefer to gaze at a different background for a while, your Mac comes with dozens of images, patterns, and colors you can use, or you can use one of your own photos.

Follow these steps to change the desktop background:

1. **Click the System Preferences icon in the Dock (or choose Apple ⇨ System Preferences).** The System Preferences window appears.

2. **Click Desktop & Screen Saver.** The Desktop & Screen Saver preferences appear.

Genius

A quicker way to get to the Desktop & Screen Saver preferences window is to right-click (or Control+click) the desktop and then click Change Desktop Background.

3. **Click the Desktop tab and use the list on the left to select an image category.**

   - **Use an Apple preloaded desktop image.** Click one of the following icons: Apple Images, Nature, Plants, Black & White, Abstract, or Solid Colors.

   - **Use your own photo.** Click the Pictures Folder icon or, if you've created some iPhoto albums, click an icon in the iPhoto Albums section.

Figure 3.7 shows the Plants category selected.

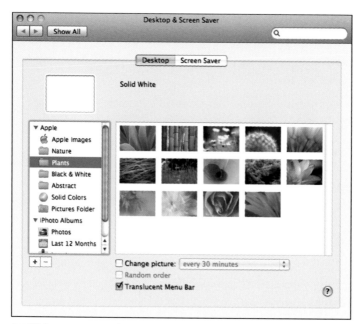

3.7 Click a category such as Plants to see the available images in that category.

4. **Click the image you want to use.** Your Mac changes the desktop background.

5. **Click the Close button or choose System Preferences ⇨ Quit System Preferences.**

Genius

If you want some desktop variety, select the Change picture check box, and then use the pop-up menu to select how often you want your Mac to change the desktop. To really shake things up, also select the Random order check box.

Changing the display resolution

The display resolution (the number of horizontal and vertical pixels used to display the screen output) is generally a bit higher on the Mac than it is in Windows. For example, the MacBook Air boasts a top resolution of 1280 x 800, and the 15-inch MacBook Pro can go up to 1440 x 900, both of which are excellent for smaller screens. The 17-inch MacBook Pro and the 20-inch iMac offer maximum resolutions of 1680 x 1050.

To change the display resolution on your Mac, follow these steps:

1. **Click the System Preferences icon in the Dock (or choose Apple ⇨ System Preferences).** The System Preferences window appears.

2. **Click Displays.** The display preferences appear.

3. **Click the Display tab.**

4. **Use the Resolutions list to select the resolution you prefer, as shown in figure 3.8.**

5. **Click the Close button or choose System Preferences ⇨ Quit System Preferences.**

3.8 Use the Resolutions list to set your preferred display resolution.

Genius

If you find yourself switching display resolutions relatively often, here's a tip that will save you a few steps. Open the display preferences and select the Show displays in menu bar check box. This adds a monitor icon to the right side menu bar. From now on, you can choose a different display resolution by clicking that icon and then clicking the resolution you want to use.

Setting the sleep options

Although you might find that you enjoy your Mac so much that you'd *like* to use it all the time, it's likely your social obligations will prevent that (plus there's the whole sleeping thing). So when it comes to leaving your Mac, you probably don't want it running normally while you're not around, because that's just a waste of energy (and, so, money). Instead, you want to put your Mac into sleep mode so that it uses only a minimal amount of power.

The good news is that Apple knows this, too, so it configured your Mac and its displays to go into sleep mode after 10 minutes of inactivity. Now, I don't know about you, but I quite often sit and stare for 10 minutes at a time, so it bugs me when my Mac goes to sleep on me when I'm still using it (in a fashion). So I always configure my Macs with a more generous sleep timeout value: usually an hour for the Mac itself, and 30 minutes for the display.

If you want to change the default sleep settings on your Mac, follow these steps:

1. **Click the System Preferences icon in the Dock (or choose Apple ⇨ System Preferences).** The System Preferences window appears.

2. **Click Energy Saver.** The Energy Saver preferences appear.

3. **If you're using a notebook Mac, click the Settings for pop-up menu and then click either Power Adapter or Battery.**

4. **If you see the Show Details button, click that button to expand the dialog box, as shown in figure 3.9.**

3.9 Use this expanded version of the Energy Saver preferences to set your Mac's sleep options.

5. **Click the Sleep tab.**

6. **Use the following controls to adjust the sleep settings:**

   - **Put the computer to sleep when it is inactive for.** Use this slider to set the number of minutes or hours of inactivity that must occur before Mac OS X puts your Mac to sleep.

   - **Put the display(s) to sleep when the computer is inactive for.** Use this slider to set the number of minutes or hours of inactivity that must occur before Mac OS X puts your display to sleep.

   - **Put the hard disk(s) to sleep when possible.** By default, this check box is selected, and it means that your Mac puts its hard disk to sleep whenever it detects that the hard disk has not been used for 10 minutes. If you deselect this check box, your Mac still puts the hard disk to sleep, but only after 3 hours of inactivity.

7. **Click the Close button or choose System Preferences ⇨ Quit System Preferences.**

Performing Day-to-Day Tasks

In this book I assume that you were fairly comfortable working with Windows, so you're already familiar with the basics of working with programs, files, e-mail, the Web, and so on. Fortunately, almost all of your hard-won Windows knowledge will transfer seamlessly over to your new Mac, so you won't find yourself back at the bottom of the learning curve. In this section, I take you through a few day-to-day Mac chores and show you how they're done the Mac way, and how that way differs from the Windows way that you're used to.

Launching a program

Just like your Windows PC, your Mac doesn't do much of anything on its own. In fact, just like Windows, after you start your Mac, it patiently waits for action until you're ready to take charge and get a program or three up and running.

The biggest difference between Windows and the Mac as far as program launching goes is the Dock at the bottom of the Mac screen, which offers one-click access to up to 17 applications in the default setup (see figure 3.10). (Smaller Mac screens actually display fewer Dock icons.) Here's a summary of the typical Dock icons you will find on your Mac.

- **Finder.** You use Finder to work with the files on your computer.

- **Dashboard.** You use Dashboard to access several cool and handy mini applications called *widgets*.

- **Mail**. You use Mail to send and receive e-mail messages.

- **Safari**. You use Safari to browse the Internet.

- **iChat**. You use iChat to converse with other people in real time by sending each other text messages.

- **Address Book.** You use the Address Book to store people's names, addresses, phone numbers, and other contact information.

- **iTunes**. You use iTunes to play music files and audio CDs and to add music to your iPod.

- **iPhoto**. You use iPhoto to import and edit digital photos and other images.

- **iMovie**. You use iMovie to import and edit digital video movies.

- **iDVD**. You use iDVD to burn images or video to a DVD disc.

- **GarageBand**. You use GarageBand to create songs, podcasts, and other audio files.

- **iWeb**. You use iWeb to create Web pages.

- **iCal**. You use iCal to record upcoming appointments, birthdays, meetings, and other events.

- **QuickTime Player**. You use QuickTime Player to play audio and video files, music CDs, and other media.

- **System Preferences**. You use System Preferences to customize your Mac.

- **Time Machine.** You use Time Machine to access backups of your files.

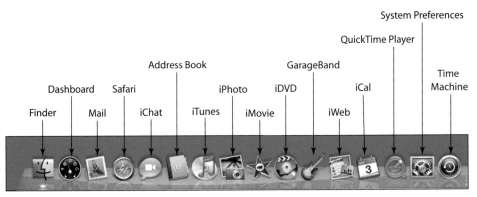

3.10 The Dock offers one-click access to some often-used applications.

Genius

If there are Dock applications that you never use, not to worry because the Dock is readily customizable. To remove an icon from the Dock, right-click (or Control+click) the icon and then click Remove from Dock (or simply click and drag the icon off the dock). (Note that this works for every icon except Finder, which is a permanent part of the Dock.) If you have an application that you use regularly, add its icon to the Dock for quick access. Start the application, right-click (or Control+click) the program's Dock icon and then click Keep in Dock. (You can also drag the application's icon from Finder and drop it in the Dock.)

Otherwise, your Mac gives you two other main ways of starting applications:

- **Finder.** In Finder, choose Go ⇨ Applications or press Shift+⌘+A. Double-click the folder that contains the application (if any), and then double-click the application.

- **Spotlight.** Click the Spotlight icon (the magnifying glass on the far right of the menu bar), type the name of the application, and then click the application in the search results.

Finding a file

If you're coming to the Mac from Windows XP, then you probably know that searching for a file in XP is hair-pullingly, teeth-gnashingly frustrating because XP and its silly Search Companion make you jump through all kinds of hoops, and even after all that you rarely find what you're looking for. Windows Vista is quite a bit better with its Start menu search box and the search boxes that appear in every folder window, but the results are still a bit hit-and-miss.

So you'll no doubt be thrilled to know that searching for files is one of the Mac's strong points. Without any configuration on your part, without tweaking settings or setting tweaks, without any fuss or muss, the Mac's search feature — it's called Spotlight — simply works.

Even better, Spotlight simply could not be easier to use:

1. **Click the Spotlight icon, which is the magnifying glass that you see on the far right side of the menu bar.** The Spotlight search box appears.

You can also display the Spotlight menu by pressing ⌘+Spacebar.

2. **Type a word or phrase that represents the file you're looking for.**
   Spotlight displays a list of every file that matches your search text, organized by category: applications, preferences, documents, folders, Mail messages, images, media, and so on. See figure 3.11 for an example.

3. **If you don't see the file you want, click Show All to see the complete results.**

4. **Click the file you want in the search results.**

Sending an e-mail message

When you first launch Mac OS X Mail, the program prompts you to add an account. After you specify your account details, you're ready to start shipping out messages to all your friends telling them how much you love your Mac.

	🖵 🕘 ⟳ ⚹ 📶 ◀)) Fri 3:51 PM 🔍
Spotlight	mobileme ⊗
	Show All
Top Hit	MobileMe
Definition	An Internet service from Ap...
System Preferences	MobileMe
Documents	INBOX
	Eudora Log
	413050 TOC.8–14.doc
Folders	My MobileMe Account
	apple_mobileme_guidedtour...
Messages	iPhone 3G
	Re: iPhone 3G
	Re: iPhone 3G
	Re: iPhone 3G
Images	photo.jpg — 1075
	photo.jpg — 407
	mobileMeAlbum.png
PDF Documents	9780470381083_DF.pdf
Webpages	MobileMe
	MobileMe Account – Paul Mc...
	MobileMe Login
Movies	apple_mobileme_guidedtour...
	Spotlight Preferences...

3.11 Type your search text in the Spotlight box and you get a list of matching files, organized by category.

Sending an e-mail message is pretty much universal no matter which program you use, but Mail does have a quirk or two that you should be aware of. To get started, click the New Message icon in Mail's toolbar. Figure 3.12 shows an example of a composed e-mail in the New Message window that appears.

If there are file types that you never want to see in the Spotlight results, you can configure Spotlight not to show them. Open the System Preferences, click Spotlight, and then click the Search Results tab. Deselect the check box beside each category you want to remove.

3.12 Use this window to compose and send your e-mail message.

Here are a few notes to bear in mind:

◉ **To send the message to one of your contacts, click Address to open the Addresses list, click the contact, and then click To:, Cc:, or Bcc:.** Mail doesn't give you any indication that it has added the contact, but trust me, it did.

◉ **Perhaps the most glaring oddity in the message window is the lack of a formatting toolbar.** Instead, you need to click Fonts to see the available fonts, styles, and sizes, and you need to click Colors to see the various color palettes. Any other formatting you need is done via the Format menu.

◉ **If you're used to adding a priority to your messages, you can hunt through the menus all day long and you won't find the command you need.** Instead, you need to click the unnamed pop-up menu that appears to the right of the From: field (or the Subject: field if you have just one account), and then click Priority Field.

Surfing to a Web site

Surfing the Web is all about navigating from one site to another to find what you need, check out intriguing links, and explore the vastness of the Web. To get the most out of your online excursions, it helps to know a few navigation techniques beyond just clicking links and entering URLs into Safari's address bar.

Opening a site in a new tab

For efficient Web browsing, it's tough to beat Safari's slick tabs feature, which lets you use a single Safari window to display a bunch of Web pages by opening each page in its own tab. You create a new tab by choosing File ⇨ New Tab or by pressing ⌘+T. However, Safari offers a number of other useful techniques for opening sites in their own tab.

For example, when you click a link, Safari opens the new page in the same tab. However, if you ⌘+click the link (that is, you hold down ⌘ when clicking), Safari opens the page in a new tab. (If you have a two-button mouse, you can also right-click the link and then click Open in New Tab.)

By default, Safari opens the new page in the background, which is great if you want to keep reading the current page. What if you want to start reading the new page right away, instead? To avoid the extra click required to display the new tab, select the link with Shift+⌘+click.

You may find that most of the time you prefer to switch to the new tab right away. Instead of always using the slightly awkward Shift+⌘+click method each time, you can configure Safari to always switch to new tabs that you open. Follow these steps:

1. **Choose Safari ⇨ Preferences to display the Preferences dialog box.** You can also Press ⌘+, .

2. **Click the Tabs pane.**

3. **Select the Select tabs and windows as they are created option.**

Safari also lets you open a site in a new tab from the address bar. Type the URL of the new site and then use either of these techniques:

- Press ⌘+Return to open the new site in a background tab.
- Press Shift+⌘+Return to open the new site in a foreground tab.

Genius

One common scenario is when you want to keep only a single tab open and close all the rest. That's not hard to accomplish when you have only two or three tabs going, but if you're sitting there with a half dozen or a dozen tabs in front of you, you might think you're better off shutting down and restarting Safari. Not so! Instead, select the tab you want to keep open, and then Option+click that tab's Close This Tab icon. Safari leaves the current tab open, and shuts down all the others.

Opening a Site in a New Window

You can use similar techniques to open a site in a new window instead of a new tab:

Press	To
Option+⌘+click	Open a link or bookmark in a background window
Shift+Option+⌘+click	Open a link or bookmark in a foreground window
Option+⌘+Return	Open the address bar URL in a background window
Shift+Option+⌘+Return	Open the address bar URL in a foreground window

Finally, if you have a site saved as a bookmark, you can open it in a new tab from the Bookmarks Bar or the Bookmarks menu:

- ⌘+click the bookmark to open the site in a background tab.
- Shift+⌘+click the bookmark to open the site in a foreground tab.

Using Back and Next to navigate your history

As you navigate from one page to the next in a Safari session, you can retrace your steps by clicking Safari's Back button (or by pressing ⌘+[) and, having done that, you can traverse your history forward by clicking the Next button (or by pressing ⌘+]). This is fine if you just want to go back (or forward) a few sites, but if you need to go back a long way, constantly clicking the Back or Next button can get old in a hurry.

To solve that problem, you need to know that the Back and Next buttons also come with hidden history lists. For example, the Back button stores a list of all the sites in the current session that you've been to prior to the current site. To get at those lists, click and hold down the mouse button over the Back or Next button. As shown in figure 3.13, Safari pops up the corresponding history list, and you then click the page you want to jump to.

3.13 The Back and Next buttons have hidden history lists.

Using the title bar to navigate a site

When a link takes you to a site, you don't always end up on the home page. Instead, you may "deep link" to a page that's buried several layers down in the site's folder hierarchy. That's fine, but if the page you end up on is interesting or entertaining, it's natural to wonder if the site has similar pages. If the site's navigation links don't help, a good strategy is to display the contents of whatever folder contains the current page. You could delete the filename portion of the URL in the address bar, but Safari gives you an easier way: ⌘+click the site title in Safari's title bar. (If you have a two-button mouse, you can also right-click the site title.) Safari displays a list that includes the current page, its parent folder, the folder above that, and so on all the way up to the site's root folder. Figure 3.14 shows a simple example. From there, you click the folder you want to investigate.

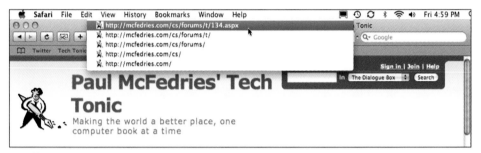

3.14 ⌘+click the site title to see the folder hierarchy associated with the current page.

Bookmarking a site

The unfathomable size of the Web means that if you stumble upon a site today, finding that site again a month from now (when the site no longer appears in Safari's history) is just about impossible. That's why if you like a site or find it useful, you should save it in your browser.

If you've been an Internet Explorer user for the past while, then you're used to referring to these saved sites as *favorites*. Safari, however, calls them *bookmarks*. Here's how you work with them:

- To add a bookmark, surf to the site, choose Bookmarks ⇨ Add Bookmark (or press ⌘+D), choose a location (such as the convenient Bookmarks Bar, which appears just below the Address Bar), and then click Add.

- To navigate to the bookmark, either click it if it appears on the Bookmarks Bar (or one of its menus), or pull down the Bookmarks menu and click the bookmark.

- To work with your bookmarks, choose Bookmarks ⇨ Show All Bookmarks. (You can also press Option+⌘+B or click the Show All Bookmarks icon on the left side of the Bookmarks Bar.)

Adding a contact

Although there are other contact management applications available for the Mac (see Chapter 2), most Mac users are happy enough with the Address Book application. Here's how you use it to add a new contact:

1. **In Address Book, choose File ⇨ New Card, or press ⌘+N.** Address Book displays a blank card.

Genius There's actually another method you can use to get a new contact started. The Address Book window is divided into three panes: Group on the left, Name in the middle, and the right pane, which shows the details of the selected card. At the bottom of the Name pane, you see a plus (+) icon. Click that icon to start a new card. Note that this is a very common technique that's used in many different Mac applications to create something new.

2. **Fill in the fields as needed.**

3. **To add a field now shown, choose Card ⇨ Add Field, and then click the field you want.**

4. **Some fields offer multiple categories, such as Home and Work, so you need to click the category to pop up the menu, as shown in figure 3.15, and then click the category you want to use.**

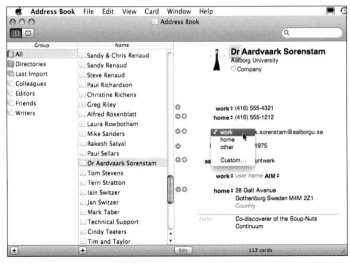

3.15 Click a category field to choose which category you want to assign to the associated contact data.

5. **When you're done, click Edit.**

Scheduling an appointment

Your Mac's iCal application is a solid scheduling program that should serve you well no matter what you were used to on your Windows PC. Here are the basic steps to follow to set up a new appointment in iCal:

1. **Click either Day or Week.**

2. **Navigate to the date on which you want to schedule the appointment.**

3. **Use your mouse to click and drag over the appointment time.** That is, click and hold down the mouse at the exact start time, drag down until you reach the end of the appointment, and then release the mouse.

4. **Type a title for the appointment and then press Return.**

5. **Double-click the appointment.** iCal displays the appointment details, as shown in figure 3.16.

3.16 Double-click an appointment to see the details.

Note Confusingly, the first time you double-click a new appointment, you see the details. After that, however, every time you double-click an appointment you must then also click Edit to see the details.

84

6. **Fill in the details as needed.** For each appointment you can specify a location, set up an all-day appointment, repeat the appointment at a regular interval, add an alarm, add notes, and more.

7. **Click Done.**

Shutting down your Mac

When you're done with your Mac chores for the day, you can either let it go into sleep mode, as described earlier in this chapter, or you can shut down the Mac altogether. You have a couple of choices:

● **Choose Apple ⇨ Shut Down and then click Shut Down when your Mac asks you to confirm.** You can also just leave things be and your Mac will shut itself down after 60 seconds.

● **Press Control+Eject to display the dialog box shown in figure 3.17, and then click Shut Down.**

3.17 Pressing Control+Eject displays this dialog box.

Working with User Accounts

When you start your Mac for the first time, a program takes you through a series of setup chores to get your Mac ready for action. One of those chores involves setting up your Mac's main user account, which acts both as a normal user account for storing documents and preferences, and as an administrative account for updating and configuring the system, as I described in Chapter 1.

If you didn't bother much with your Windows user account, then it's likely you'll have even less to do with your Mac account because in Mac OS X the user account doesn't play much of a role in most day-to-day tasks (at least not overtly; as always, there's tons of stuff going on behind the scenes).

However, it still pays to know a few of the standard user account chores such as logging into your account automatically, changing your user name and password, and setting up and working with multiple user accounts.

Logging into your account automatically

If you're the only person who uses your Mac and you use the Mac at home, then it might seem silly to have to log in to your user account every time you start your Mac. And, you're right, it is silly in most cases. You can save the hassle of dealing with the login screen, as well as make the whole startup process run faster, by configuring your Mac to log into your account automatically. Here's how it's done:

1. **Click the System Preferences icon in the Dock (or choose Apple ⇨ System Preferences).** The System Preferences window appears.

2. **Click Accounts.** The Accounts preferences appear.

3. **If the Accounts preferences are locked, click the lock icon, type your password, and click OK.** System Preferences unlocks the Accounts preferences.

4. **Click Login Options.**

5. **In the Automatic Login pop-up menu, click your user account.**

6. **Click the Close button or choose System Preferences ⇨ Quit System Preferences.**

Caution   If you have any sensitive data on your Mac, think long and hard about whether an automatic login is a good idea. The automatic login is convenient for you, but it's also very convenient for any snoop who happens to fire up your Mac when you're not around. If you have any data on your Mac that you wouldn't want a stranger to see, avoid the automatic login.

Assigning a password to your user account

When you configured your main user account during the Mac setup routine, assigning a password to that account was optional. If security isn't even a tiny bit relevant in your case, you can probably get away with being password-free. However, remember that your main Mac account is also an administrative account on your Mac, which means that it can do anything to your Mac, including updating software and configuring all system preferences. That's a lot of power, and for most people that power should be protected with a good password.

So if you didn't assign a password to your account initially, or if you'd like to assign a more robust password to your account, follow these steps to change your user account password:

1. **Click the System Preferences icon in the Dock (or choose Apple ⇨ System Preferences).** The System Preferences window appears.

2. **Click Accounts.** The Accounts preferences appear.

3. **If the Accounts preferences are locked, click the lock icon, type your password, and click OK.** System Preferences unlocks the Accounts preferences.

4. **In the list of user accounts on the left, click your account.**

5. **Click Change Password.**

6. **If your account has a password, type it in the Old Password text box.**

7. **Type your new password in the New Password text box and in the Verify text box.**

Genius

What do I mean by a strong password? It should be at least eight characters long, and it should include characters from at least three of the following four sets: lower-case letters, uppercase letters, numbers, and symbols.

8. **Use the Password Hint text box to type some text that will help you remember your password if you forget it, as shown in figure 3.18.**

9. **Click Change Password.** System Preferences tells you that the password for your login keychain will be changed to the new password.

10. **Click OK to return to the Accounts preferences.**

11. **Click the Close button or choose System Preferences ➪ Quit System Preferences.**

Old Password:

New Password: •••••••••

Verify: •••••••••

Password Hint: Mother's maiden name and year of
(Recommended) birth

Cancel   Change Password

3.18 It's a good idea to include a vague-but-helpful password hint.

Note

In the Mac scheme of things, a *keychain* is a list of saved passwords.

Changing your user name

In the rush to get your Mac up and computing, you might have rushed through the account setup portion of the show, and now you regret the user name you chose. No worries. Changing your user name is as simple as following these steps:

1. **Click the System Preferences icon in the Dock (or choose Apple ⇨ System Preferences).** The System Preferences window appears.

2. **Click Accounts.** The Accounts preferences appear.

3. **If the Accounts preferences are locked, click the lock icon, type your password, and click OK.** System Preferences unlocks the Accounts preferences.

4. **In the list of user accounts on the left, click your account.**

5. **Use the User Name text box to type the name you prefer to use.**

Note

The name you're changing here isn't the actual name of the user account, but rather your account's display name. The actual account name can't be changed.

6. **Click the Close button or choose System Preferences ⇨ Quit System Preferences.**

Setting up another user account

You probably have family members or colleagues who are clamoring to use your Mac, and who can blame them? Sessions that you supervise are fine, of course, but you probably don't want people messing with your Mac when you're not around because they could accidentally delete important info or modify your settings.

The solution is to let the other person access the Mac using a different user account. You have two ways to go here:

- **Activate the built-in Guest account.** This is a good way to go if you only have to give people occasional access because it's easy to configure and they can't do any damage with the Guest account, which is a highly secure account.

- **Create a new user account.** This is the way to go if you want to allow another person to save files, set up e-mail and chat accounts, and configure his or her own preferences.

Note

Whichever method you choose, you'll probably want the person to be able to log in to his or her account at startup. (Note that the Guest account has no password.) In that case, if you configured your account to log in automatically earlier, then you need to disable this feature. In the unlocked Accounts preferences, click Login Options and then use the Automatic Login pop-up menu to click Disabled.

Activating the Guest account

If the built-in Guest account best serves your needs, follow these steps to activate it:

1. **Click the System Preferences icon in the Dock (or choose Apple ⇨ System Preferences).** The System Preferences window appears.

2. **Click Accounts.** The Accounts preferences appear.

3. **If the Accounts preferences are locked, click the lock icon, type your password, and click OK.** System Preferences unlocks the Accounts preferences.

4. **In the list of user accounts on the left, click Guest Account.**

5. **Select the Allow guests to log into this computer check box.**

6. **Click the Close button or choose System Preferences ⇨ Quit System Preferences.**

Creating a new user account

If a shiny, new user account is what you need, follow these steps to set it up:

1. **Click the System Preferences icon in the Dock (or choose Apple ⇨ System Preferences).** The System Preferences window appears.

2. **Click Accounts.** The Accounts preferences appear.

3. **If the Accounts preferences are locked, click the lock icon, type your password, and click OK.** System Preferences unlocks the Accounts preferences.

4. **Below the list of user accounts, click the plus sign (+).**

5. **Click the New Account pop-up menu and then click one of the following account types:**

   - **Administrator.** This creates a new administrative account. This is just as powerful as your account, so use this type of account only if you explicitly trust the other person.

   - **Standard.** This creates a user account with lower security privileges. For example, the user can't update system software, change many system settings, or unlock system preferences that are locked. This is a good choice for most accounts.

   - **Managed with Parental Controls.** This creates a user account that you can protect with your Mac's built-in Parental Controls feature, which is very similar to the feature of the same name in Windows Vista. This is a good choice if the account is for a young child.

● **Sharing Only.** This creates a user account that you can use to share files and folders with people on your network. Normally others can see your shared files by entering your user name and password. If you don't want to give out that information, use a Sharing Only account instead.

6. **Type the account's display name in the Name text box, and the account's user name in the Short Name text box.**

7. **Type the account's password in the Password and Verify text boxes and a hint in the Password Hint text box.**

8. **Click Create Account.** Your Mac creates the new account and adds it to the list of accounts in the Accounts preferences.

9. **If you still have an automatic login configured, System Preferences prompts you to turn it off, so click Turn Off Automatic Login.**

10. **Click the Close button or choose System Preferences ⇨ Quit System Preferences.**

Switching user accounts

If you activated the Guest account or created one or more new user accounts on your Mac, then you need to know how to switch back and forth between them. Here are the basic steps:

1. **Choose Apple ⇨ Log Out** *User*, **where** *User* **is the name of the currently logged in user.** You can also start the logout by pressing Shift+⌘+Q. Your Mac asks you to confirm the logout.

2. **Click Log Out.** Your Mac logs out the account and displays the login screen.

3. **Click the user account you want to use.** Your Mac prompts you for the account password.

4. **Type the password and click Log in.**

The only problem with this scenario is that your Mac shuts down all your running programs when you log out. If the other person only needs to access their account briefly, it's a real hassle that you have to restart all your programs and open all your documents.

To avoid this, you can configure *fast user switching*, which leaves your programs running when you log out, and reinstates them just as they were when you log back in. Here's how to set this up:

1. **Click the System Preferences icon in the Dock (or choose Apple ⇨ System Preferences).** The System Preferences window appears.

2. **Click Accounts.** The Accounts preferences appear.

3. **If the Accounts preferences are locked, click the lock icon, type your password, and click OK.** System Preferences unlocks the Accounts preferences.

4. **Click Login Options.**

5. **Select the Enable fast user switching check box.**

6. **In the View As pop-up menu, click how you want the accounts to appear in the menu bar.**

7. **Click the Close button or choose System Preferences ⇨ Quit System Preferences.**

You can now switch between accounts by clicking the username in the menu bar, as shown in figure 3.19.

3.19 With fast user switching on the go, click the username in the menu bar to switch user accounts and leave your running programs open.

Working with Media on Your Mac

Your Mac is one mean media machine that's equally adept at managing your music collection, organizing your photos, and editing your digital movies. If your old Windows PC still has your media files captive, you learn how to liberate them onto your Mac in Chapter 5. For now, the rest of this chapter takes you through a few Mac media chores you need to know.

Ripping music from an audio CD

You can use iTunes to rip tracks from an audio CD to your Mac. Why should anyone bother to learn how to do that in this day and age, particularly with the impressive iTunes Store a mere click away? Two reasons. First, if you have a large CD collection gathering dust, it's about time you converted those tracks to digital audio files, and that requires a ripping session (or, more likely, a bunch of ripping sessions). Second, many of us prefer to purchase new CDs only to rip them to our Macs because that way we get full control over the rip process. If you purchase an album from iTunes, the resulting digital audio files use Apple's proprietary Advanced Audio Coding (AAC) file format, which limits your options when it comes to playing those files. Similarly, the bit rate of the purchased music might be as low as 128 kilobits per second (Kbps), which is only so-so. By ripping your own audio CDs, you can create MP3 files, which are supported by all players and programs, and you can ratchet up the bit rate to get the best quality that makes sense given the disk space limitations on your Mac and on your digital audio players.

Setting the file format and bit rate

Before getting to the ripping specifics, take a second to see how you adjust the import file format and bit rate. Here are the steps to follow using iTunes 8 or later:

1. **In iTunes, choose iTunes ⇨ Preferences.** The iTunes program preferences appear.

2. **Click the General tab.**

3. **Click Import Settings.** The Import Settings dialog box appears.

4. **From the Import Using pop-up menu, choose the file format you want to use for the ripped tracks.** For example, to rip the tracks using the MP3 format, choose MP3 Encoder.

5. **From the Setting pop-up menu, choose the bit rate you want to use during your rips.** Note that the available settings depend on the file format you chose in Step 4. If you want to specify your own settings, click Custom (although not all file formats offer this option). Figure 3.20 shows the MP3 Encoder dialog box that appears if you choose Custom for the MP3 Encoder format.

```
                        MP3 Encoder

        Stereo Bit Rate:  [ 320 kbps      ▲▼ ]

                        ☐ Use Variable Bit Rate Encoding (VBR)

                Quality:  [ Medium          ▲▼ ]

       (With VBR enabled, bit rate settings are used for a guaranteed minimum bit rate.)

         Sample Rate:  [ Auto             ▲▼ ]

            Channels:  [ Auto             ▲▼ ]

         Stereo Mode:  [ Joint Stereo     ▲▼ ]

                        ☑ Smart Encoding Adjustments

                        ☑ Filter Frequencies Below 10 Hz

    ( Use Default Settings )          ( Cancel )  (   OK   )
```

3.20 If you choose the Custom setting, you see a dialog box similar to the one shown here for the MP3 format.

6. **If you chose Custom in Step 5, specify your custom settings and then click OK.**

7. **Click OK to return to the iTunes preferences.**

8. **Click OK.**

Note If you're using a version of iTunes prior to version 8, you follow a slightly different procedure. Choose iTunes ⇨ Preferences, click the Advanced tab, and then click Importing. Use the Import Using pop-up menu to choose a file format, and use the Setting pop-up menu to choose the bit rate. Click OK.

Ripping the tracks

By default, when you insert an audio CD into your Mac's optical drive, iTunes loads and asks if you want to import the CD. That's ideal for most situations, but not for the following two:

- **You're ripping tons of CDs.** In this case, you might prefer that your Mac just go ahead and rip away as soon as it detects the disc. To set this up, choose iTunes ⇨ Preferences, click the General tab, and then use the When you insert a CD pop-up menu to choose Import CD and Eject. This fully automates the ripping *and* it tells iTunes to eject the disc as soon as the rip is done.

- **You want complete control over the rip.** Through personal experience I've learned that whereas iTunes is pretty good at retrieving information about each CD, it gets some of that data wrong fairly often. It might be the wrong genre, the wrong album title, or just an inconsistent artist name. So I always prefer to check out and, if necessary, correct the CD data *before* launching the rip. To set this up, choose iTunes ⇨ Preferences, click the General tab, and then use the When you insert a CD pop-up menu to choose Show CD.

In the steps that follow, I show you how to manually edit and import tracks. I assume you're either using the default CD insertion option (Ask to Import CD) or you've chosen the Show CD option:

1. **Insert an audio CD into your Mac's CD or DVD drive.**
2. **If iTunes asks whether you want to import the CD, click No.** The music CD appears in iTunes' Devices category and iTunes shows the contents of the CD.
3. **Examine the CD data to ensure that it's accurate.**
4. **If you need to edit the data, you have three choices:**
   - **To edit a single track:** Right-click (or Control+click) the track, click Get Info, and then click the Info tab.
   - **To edit two or more tracks:** Hold down ⌘ and click each track you want to edit. Right-click (or Control+click) any selected track, click Get Info, and then click Yes when iTunes asks you to confirm.
   - **To edit all the tracks:** Press ⌘+A to select every track. Right-click (or Control+click) any selected track, click Get Info, and then click Yes when iTunes asks you to confirm.

5. **Edit the CD data as needed.** As you can see in figure 3.21, iTunes activates the check box beside any field that you edit.

Multiple Item Information	
Info Video Sorting Options	

Artist
☐ The Be Good Tanyas

Album Artist
☐

Album
☐ Chinatown

Grouping
☐

Composer
☐

Comments
☐

Genre
☑ Folk

Year
☐ 2003

Track Number
☐ of ☐ 14

Disc Number
☐ 1 of ☐ 1

BPM
☐

Artwork
☐

Rating
☑ ★★★★★

Cancel   OK

3.21 When you edit a field, iTunes activates the check box beside it.

6. **Click OK.**

7. **For every track that you don't want to rip, deselect the check box beside the track title.**

8. **Click Import CD.** iTunes imports the tracks.

Playing music

There's nothing rocket-science-y about playing music in iTunes. Basically, you find the song you want to play (using the Library's Music category or an existing playlist) and then either double-click the song or click the Play button. As you can see in figure 3.22, iTunes displays a speaker icon to the right of the current song's track number. Information about the current track appears in the toolbar, which also includes several buttons for playback control: pausing the current song, and skipping forward or backward in the song list.

3.22 To play a song in iTunes, double-click it.

If your hands are on the keyboard, feel free to use the shortcuts listed in Table 3.1 to control the playback.

Table 3.1 iTunes Playback Shortcuts

Shortcut	Description
Return	Start playing the chosen song
Spacebar	Pause/Play the current song
Option+⌘+Right Arrow	Fast-forward the current song
Option+⌘+Left Arrow	Rewind the current song
Right Arrow	Skip to the next song
Left Arrow	Skip to the beginning of the current song; press again to skip to the previous song
Option+Right Arrow	Skip to the next album
Option+Left Arrow	Skip to the previous album
⌘+Up Arrow	Increase the volume
⌘+Down Arrow	Decrease the volume
Option+⌘+Down Arrow	Mute/unmute the volume
⌘+E	Eject an audio CD

95

Most Mac keyboards also come with dedicated keys for controlling media playback, so you can use those as well.

Note

Another way to adjust the overall volume on your Mac is by clicking the volume icon in the menu bar (it's the speaker icon), and then dragging the slider up and down to get the volume level you prefer. If you don't see the volume icon, choose Apple ⇨ System Preferences, click Sound to open the Sound preferences, click the Output tab, and then select the Show volume in menu bar check box.

Importing photos from a camera

Whether you use a dedicated digital camera or a phone with a built-in camera, such as the iPhone, you probably want to get those photos onto your Mac so that you can organize them, edit them, and share them with others.

Your Mac's iPhoto application handles all of these photo chores. Here's how to use it to import photos from your camera:

1. **Connect your camera to your Mac.** iPhoto opens, adds your camera to the Devices list, and displays the photos from your camera's memory card, as shown in figure 3.23.

Note

If you've imported some of your camera's photos in the past, you probably don't want to import them again. That's very sensible of you, and you can prevent that by hiding those photos. Select the Hide photos already imported check box.

2. **Use the Event Name text box to name the event that these photos represent.**
3. **Use the Description text box to type a short description of the event.**
4. **Choose how you want to import the photos:**
   - If you want to import every photo, click Import All.
   - If you want to import only some of the photos, hold down ⌘ and click the ones you want to import. When you've selected the ones you want, click Import Selected.
5. **If you want to leave the photos on your camera, click Keep Originals.** Otherwise, click Delete Originals to clear the photos from your camera.

3.23 When you connect your camera to your Mac, iPhoto shows up to handle the import of the photos.

Preventing iPhone from Synching Photos

Each and every time you connect your iPhone to your computer, you see iPhoto. This is certainly convenient if you actually want to send photos to your computer, but you might find that you do that only once in a blue moon. In that case, having to deal with iPhoto or a dialog box every time could cause even the most mild-mannered among us to start pulling out our hair. If you prefer to keep your hair, you can configure your computer to not pester you about getting photos from your iPhone.

Here's how you set this up:

1. **Choose Finder ⇨ Applications to open the Applications folder.**

2. **Double-click Image Capture.** The Image Capture application opens.

3. **Choose Image Capture ⇨ Preferences.** The Image Capture Preferences window appears.

continued

97

continued

4. **Click the When a camera is connected, open menu and then click No application.**

5. **Choose Image Capture⇨Quit Image Capture.** Image Capture saves the new setting and then shuts down. The next time you connect your iPhone, iPhoto ignores it.

Remember, however, that configuring your Mac to not download photos from your iPhone means that in the future you either need to reverse the setting to get photos, or manually import your photos.

Viewing photos

Once you've got a decent crop of photos on your Mac, you'll no doubt want to view them in all their glory. First, you need to choose the iPhoto object that holds the photos you want to view. You've got several choices:

- If you recently imported the photos, look in the Recent category in iPhoto's sidebar. You'll find the most recently imported photos in the Last Import category. You should also see an item for any recent import events.

- The Events category displays one object for each of your events. In each case, the event icon is a thumbnail of one of the event's images.

- The Photos category displays all your photos, organized by date.

- If you've created any photo albums, click an object in the Albums category.

Note To change the sort order of the photos, choose View⇨Sort Photos and then choose a sort order: By Date, By Keyword, By Title, By Rating, or Manually.

Once you've got the photos you want to view ready, you have two choices for viewing them:

- Double-click the first photo to open it, and then use the Right and Left Arrow keys to navigate the photos.

- Select the first photo and then choose View⇨Full Screen (or press Option+⌘+F) to open the photo in full screen view. Again, you can use the arrow keys to move through the photos, but you can also move your mouse to the bottom of the screen and use the controls that appear. When you're done, press Esc to exit the full screen view.

Creating a Photo Album

iPhoto gives you a few ways to create a new photo album:

- If you know which photos you want in the album, select them, choose File ⇨ New Album from Selection (or press Shift+⌘+N), type a name for the album, and then click Create.

- To create an empty photo album, choose File ⇨ New Album (or press ⌘+N), type a name for the album, and then click Create. You then click and drag the photos you want and drop them on the new album.

- A *smart album* is one that iPhoto maintains automatically based on data such as event names and keywords. Choose File ⇨ New Smart Album (or press Option+⌘+N), type a name for the album, choose your criteria, and then click Create.

Taking a screen shot

You might find that you need to capture the current state of some or all of the Mac screen and save it to a file. For example, you might want to use a dialog box or window as part of a blog post or other Web page material. Similarly, you might want to capture an error message to show to a tech support engineer.

Whatever the reason, your Mac gives you two ways to capture screen shots:

- **Keyboard shortcuts.** Use any of the following three shortcuts to capture some or the entire screen to a file on your desktop:
  - Press Shift+⌘+3 to capture an image of the entire screen.
  - Press Shift+⌘+4 and then drag the mouse to capture an image of the selected area of the screen.
  - Press Shift+⌘+4, press Spacebar, and then click an object to capture an image of that object.

- **Grab.** This is the Mac's built-in screen capture program (and it's the one I used to capture all of the screen shots you see in this book). In Finder, select Go ⇨ Utilities (or press Shift+⌘+U) to open the Utilities folder, and then double-click Grab. The Capture menu gives you four possibilities: Selection (or press Shift+⌘+A) captures the currently selected object; Window (or press Shift+⌘+W) captures the current window; Screen (or press ⌘+Z) captures the entire screen; and Timed Screen (or press Shift+⌘+Z) captures the entire screen after a ten-second countdown.

Import

Import Items

Select the items you want to import.

- Messages
- Accounts
- Rules
- Signatures

Click the right arrow to continue.

◀ 3 ▶

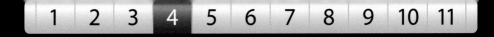

Okay, so *you* have made the switch from Windows to Mac, but unfortunately the same probably can't be said for your data. For example, you might have left behind a large collection of e-mail, contact, and appointment data in Microsoft Outlook. Don't worry, you won't have to enter all that data by hand in your Mac! As long as you still have access to your Windows PC, there are methods you can use to transfer that data to your Mac. This chapter shows you how this is done for e-mail, contacts, and appointments, and in Chapter 5 you learn how to transfer other kinds of data.

Transferring E-mail

If you're a long-time Windows user, then you may have thousands of e-mail messages stored on your Windows PC — messages that you've received and copies of messages that you've sent. That's a precious and valuable store of data, no doubt about it, and it's one that I'm sure you're loath to leave behind. Fortunately, you don't have to! Whether your messages reside in Outlook, Windows Mail, or Outlook Express, you *can* get them from Windows to Mac, as the next few sections show.

Importing messages from Microsoft Outlook

When it comes to getting e-mail messages from Outlook to Apple Mail, there's good news, bad news, and then more great news. The good news is that Outlook offers an exporting feature that writes some or all of your messages to special text files. The bad news is that Apple Mail does *not* offer a feature for importing those special text files. Not to worry, though, because the great news is that you have not one, but *two* ways to transfer your messages.

Transferring messages with O2M

A company called Little Machines (www.littlemachines.com) offers a cute little program called O2M (Outlook-to-Mac) that can read your Outlook e-mail folders and export some or all of your messages to special mbox (mailbox) files. These mbox files are crucial for our purposes because Apple Mail's import feature can work with mbox files, which means you can import your Outlook messages into Mail. Best of all, O2M is a mere $10, and I *know* your Outlook messages are worth more than that! (To sweeten the deal, O2M can also transfer your Outlook contacts and appointments into formats readable by your Mac's Address Book and iCal applications.)

Assuming you've downloaded and installed O2M on your PC and applied your serial number (which you must do to unlock all of O2M's features), follow these steps to create your mbox file:

1. **Shut down Outlook if it's currently running.**

2. **After you start O2M and it has read your Outlook data, click Next.** O2M asks you to select the folder on your PC where it will store the Macintosh format files.

Genius

If you're running O2M under Windows Vista, you'll likely receive an error telling you that O2M can't create temporary files in C:\. This is a security feature in Vista, but it's not a major roadblock as long as you have administrator access to Vista. Shut down O2M, click Start, click All Programs, click the O2M folder, right-click the O2M icon, and then click Run as Administrator. Enter your User Account Control credentials and away you go.

3. **Choose a folder and then click Next.** Ideally, you should select a folder that you can access from your Mac if it's on the same network as your Windows PC. If you're going to be copying the files to a USB Flash drive or other removable drive, then the default My_Outlook_Files folder is fine.

4. **Select the check box beside each of the Outlook mail folders that you want to convert, as shown in figure 4.1, and then click Next.**

4.1 In O2M, select the Outlook mail folders that you want to convert to Macintosh format.

5. **In the Email Date Range dialog box, select one of the following options and then click Next:**

   ● **Convert all of my email, regardless of date.** Select this option if you want to transfer all your Outlook e-mail to your Mac.

   ● **Only convert email that is postmarked.** Select this option if you want to transfer Outlook e-mail that falls only within a specific date range. Use the lists provided to specify a start date and an end date.

6. **In the Skip Large Email Attachments dialog box, select one of the following options and then click Next:**

- **Skip file attachments larger than.** Select this option if you don't want to transfer large e-mail attachments to your Mac. Use the list to select the maximum size you want to transfer.

  - **Don't skip large file attachments — convert everything.** Select this option if you want to transfer all attachments to your Mac, regardless of size.

7. **Use the Skip Windows Email Attachments dialog box to add or remove file types that you don't want to convert, and then click Next.**

8. **I'm going to skip the conversion of contacts here, which is covered later in this chapter, so click Next in the Outlook Contact Lists dialog box.**

9. **I'm going to skip the conversion of appointments here, which is covered later in this chapter, so select No in the Outlook Calendar dialog box and then click Next.**

10. **Click Start.** O2M converts your Outlook messages to mbox files.

11. **Click Exit.**

With your Outlook messages converted, you're ready to get them to your Mac. If your Mac and your Windows PC aren't on the same network, open the folder where O2M stored the mbox files, open the mail folder, copy the files to a USB Flash drive (or something similar), and then connect the drive to your Mac.

Open Apple Mail and follow these steps to import the mbox files:

1. **Choose File ⇨ Import Mailboxes.** The Import dialog box appears.

2. **Select the mbox files option and click Continue.** Mail prompts you to select an mbox file.

3. **Open the drive on your Mac or the network share where your O2M mbox files are stored, click the mbox file you want to import, and then click Choose.** Mail imports the messages.

4. **If you have other mbox files to import, click Go Back and then repeat Steps 2 and 3.**

5. **Click Done.** Your messages appear in a mailbox in Apple Mail named Import that's part of the On My Mac category.

Transferring messages with Thunderbird

If you don't want to fork over the $10 for O2M, there's another method you can use that won't cost you a dime. However, this method is quite a bit more convoluted, so it's only "cheaper" if you don't believe that time is money.

This method uses the free Thunderbird e-mail program, which is available via the Mozilla Foundation at www.mozilla.com/en-US/thunderbird/. The idea is that you use Thunderbird to import your Outlook messages and then export them to a Mac-friendly format.

Download and install Thunderbird on your PC, and then start the program. One of two things will happen:

- **The Import Wizard appears.** Select the Outlook option and then click Next to start the import. Click Finish when it's done.
- **Thunderbird opens.** In this case, choose Tools, Import, select the Mail option, click Next, click Outlook, and click Next to start the import. Click Finish when it's done.

You end up with a folder in Thunderbird called Outlook Mail, which contains your Outlook messages. Now follow these steps to determine the location of the folders and open that location:

1. **In Thunderbird's folder list, right-click Outlook Mail and then click Copy Folder Location.**

2. **Shut down Thunderbird.**

3. **Open the Run dialog box:**
   - **Windows Vista.** Press Windows Logo+R or choose Start ⇨ All Programs ⇨ Accessories ⇨ Run.
   - **Windows XP.** Press Windows Logo+R or choose Start ⇨ Run.

4. **Press Control+V to paste the folder location in the Run dialog box.** The address you see will look something like this (where *User* is your user name and *ProfileID* is a random 8-character value):

   mailbox:/C|/Documents and Settings/*User*/Application Data/Thunderbird/Profiles/*ProfileID*.default/Mail/Local Folders/Outlook Mail

5. **At the end of the address, delete the "Outlook Mail" part.**

6. **At the beginning of the address, change "mailbox:/C|" to "C:".** The address should now look something like this:

   C:/Documents and Settings/*User*/Application Data/Thunderbird/Profiles/*ProfileID*.default/Mail/Local Folders/

7. **Click OK.** Windows opens the Local Folders folder.

8. **Copy the Outlook Mail.sbd folder.**

9. **Paste the folder in a location that you can access using your Mac.** If your Mac is on the same network as your Windows PC, choose a shared network folder; otherwise, paste the folder to a USB Flash drive or other removable drive that you can connect to your Mac.

Open Apple Mail and follow these steps to import the messages:

1. **Choose File ⇨ Import Mailboxes.** The Import dialog box appears.

2. **Select the Thunderbird option and click Continue.** Mail prompts you to select a folder.

3. **Open the drive on your Mac or the network share where your Thunderbird files are stored, click the Outlook Mail.sbd folder, and then click Choose.** Mail displays a list of the folders, as shown in figure 4.2.

4.2 When you choose Thunderbird's Outlook Mail.sbd folder, Mail displays a check box for each mail folder it contains.

4. **Deselect the check box beside any folder you don't want to import, and then click Continue.** Mail imports the messages.

5. **Click Done.** Your messages appear in a mailbox in Apple Mail named Import that's part of the On My Mac category.

Importing messages from Windows Mail

If you've been using Vista's Windows Mail program, you'll want to get your messages into Apple Mail lickety-split. Unfortunately, there's no direct way to go about this because Windows Mail can't export its messages into any format that Apple Mail is on friendly terms with. Fortunately, there's a roundabout way you can go that uses the free Thunderbird e-mail program, which is available via the Mozilla Foundation at www.mozilla.com/en-US/thunderbird/. Using a special add-on, you can use Thunderbird to import your Windows Mail messages and then export them to a format that your Mac can make sense of.

Download and install Thunderbird on your PC, and then start the program. Fire up your Web browser and head for the following site:

http://nic-nac-project.de/~kaosmos/mboximport-en.html

This is the home of the ImportExportTools add-on for Thunderbird, which enhances Thunderbird's importing capabilities to handle Windows Mail messages. Download the add-on and then follow these steps in Thunderbird to install it:

1. **Choose Tools ⇨ Add-ons.** The Add-ons dialog box appears.
2. **Click Install.** The Select an extension to install dialog box appears.
3. **Choose the file you downloaded and then click Open.** Thunderbird asks you to confirm the install.
4. **Click Install Now.** Thunderbird installs the add-on and prompts you to restart the program.
5. **Click Restart Thunderbird.**

Before proceeding, you need to configure Vista to show its hidden folders:

1. **Choose Start ⇨ Control Panel.**
2. **Click Appearance and Personalization.**
3. **Click Folder Options.**
4. **Click the View tab.**
5. **Select the Show hidden files and folders option.**
6. **Click OK.**

107

With the add-on in place and Vista displaying hidden folders, follow these steps to import the Windows Mail messages:

1. **In Thunderbird, choose the folder where you want the messages to be stored on your PC.**

2. **Choose Tools ⇨ Import/Export in mbox/eml format ⇨ Import all eml files from a directory ⇨ just from the directory.** The Browse for Folder dialog box appears.

3. **Open the following folder (where** *User* **is your user name):**

   User\AppData\Local\Microsoft\ Windows Mail\Local Folders

4. **In the list of Windows Mail folders, click the folder you want to import, such as Inbox, as shown in figure 4.3.**

5. **Click OK.** Thunderbird imports the messages.

6. **Repeat Steps 1 to 5 to import Windows Mail messages inside other folders.**

With the import complete, you can now import your Thunderbird mailbox into Apple Mail, as described earlier in the "Transferring messages with Thunderbird" section. Note

Browse For Folder

Select a directory to search the files

- Paul
  - AppData
    - Local
      - AOL
      - AOL OCP
      - Microsoft
        - Assistance
        - Credentials
        - Event Viewer
        - Feeds
        - Internet Explorer
        - Media Player
        - Messenger
        - Portable Devices
        - Windows
        - Windows Defender
        - Windows Live
        - Windows Live Contacts
        - Windows Mail
          - Backup
          - Local Folders
            - Deleted Items
            - Drafts
            - Inbox
            - Junk E-mail
            - Outbox
            - Sent Items

Folder: Inbox

Make New Folder   OK   Cancel

4.3 Choose which Windows Mail folder you want to import.

that in Windows Vista your Thunderbird local folders are located here (where *User* is your user name and *ProfileID* is a random 8-character value):

C:\Users*User*\AppData\Roaming\Thunderbird\Profiles*ProfileID*.default\Mail\Local Folders\

Importing messages from Outlook Express

If your messages are stored in Outlook Express and you still have access to that Windows XP PC, you can get your messages into Apple Mail, but not directly. Instead, you need to first import them into the free Thunderbird e-mail program, which is available via the Mozilla Foundation at www.mozilla.com/en-US/thunderbird/. From there, you use Thunderbird to export your messages to a Mac-friendly format.

Download and install Thunderbird to your PC, and then start the program. One of two things will happen:

- **The Import Wizard appears.** Select the Outlook Express option and then click Next to start the import. Click Finish when it's done.

- **Thunderbird opens.** In this case, choose Tools, Import, select the Mail option, click Next, click Outlook Express, and click Next to start the import. Click Finish when it's done.

You end up with a folder in the Thunderbird e-mail program called Outlook Express Mail, which contains your Outlook Express messages. With the import complete, you can now import your Thunderbird mailbox into Apple Mail, as described earlier in the "Transferring messages with Thunderbird" section. Note that in Windows XP your Thunderbird local folders are located here (where *User* is your user name and *ProfileID* is a random 8-character value):

C:\Documents and Settings*User*\Application Data\Thunderbird\Profiles*ProfileID*.default\Mail\ Local Folders\

Importing messages into Entourage

So far I've assumed that you're using Apple Mail on your Mac, but you might be using Microsoft's Entourage application, which comes with the Office 2008 for Mac and Office 2004 for Mac suites. In that case, you'll no doubt be Jonesing to get your Windows messages into Entourage. Surprisingly, Entourage can't import directly from Outlook (or Windows Mail or Outlook Express). Instead, you have to take a more long and winding road. How you start the journey depends on what Windows application you were using:

- **Microsoft Outlook.** You need to use either O2M or Thunderbird to import your Outlook messages into Apple Mail. (See the section "Importing messages from Microsoft Outlook.") From there, you can import the messages into Entourage, as described next.

● **Windows Mail.** You need to install Thunderbird, install the ImportExportTools add-on tool, import your Windows Mail EML files into Thunderbird, and then import the messages into Apple Mail. (See the section "Importing messages from Windows Mail.") From there, import the messages into Entourage, as described below.

● **Outlook Express.** You need to install Thunderbird, use it to import your Outlook Express message store, and then import the messages into Apple Mail, as described in the section, "Importing messages from Outlook Express." Then import the messages into Entourage, as described below.

In each case, you end up with your messages in Apple Mail, and Entourage *can* import data from Mail. Here are the steps to follow:

1. **In Entourage, choose File ➪ Import.** The Import dialog box appears.

2. **Select an import option and then press Return (or click the right arrow):**

   ● **Entourage 2008.** Select the Information from another application option.

   ● **Entourage 2004.** Select the Information from another program option.

3. **Select the Apple Mail option.** Entourage displays the Import Items dialog box, shown in figure 4.4 (this is the Entourage 2008 version; the 2004 version has a few extra check boxes).

4.4 Use the Import Items dialog box to select the data you want to import from Mail into Entourage.

4. **Deselect the check box beside any items you don't want to import, and then press Return.** Entourage imports the data.

5. **Click Finish.** Your messages appear in a mailbox named Import that's part of the Mail Import category.

Transferring Contacts

Getting your e-mail messages from Windows to Mac is important, but I bet digital dollars to dough-nuts that getting your Windows contacts into your Mac is even more important. That makes sense because although you may have a few current e-mail messages to deal with, and you might refer to old messages from time to time, you probably use your contact data constantly. So you need your contacts ASAP, and the more contacts you have, the more you'll want to automate the pro-cess. The next few sections show you how to do just that.

Importing contacts from Microsoft Outlook

To get your Outlook Contacts folder into your Mac's Address Book application, you can either use the O2M application, or you can export the Contacts folder to a text file. The next two sections show you both methods.

Transferring contacts with O2M

The $10 O2M program offered by Little Machines (www.littlemachines.com) can read your Outlook Contacts folder and export that data to a special vCard file, which you can then import into the Mac's Address Book application.

Assuming you've downloaded and installed O2M on your PC and applied your serial number (which you must do to unlock all of O2M's features), follow these steps to create your vCard file:

1. **Shut down Outlook if it's currently running.**

2. **After you start O2M and it has read your Outlook data, click Next.** O2M asks you to select the folder on your PC where it will store the Macintosh format files.

3. **Choose a folder and then click Next.** Ideally, you should select a folder that you can access from your Mac if it's on the same network as your Windows PC. If you're going to be copying the files to a USB Flash drive or other removable drive, then the default My_Outlook_Files folder is fine.

Genius

If you're running O2M under Windows Vista, you'll likely receive an error telling you that O2M can't create temporary files in C:\. To work around this Vista security fea-ture, shut down O2M, click Start, click All Programs, click the O2M folder, right-click the O2M icon, and then click Run as Administrator. Enter your User Account Control credentials to continue.

4. **Click Next to skip exporting e-mail messages.** O2M asks you to select which contact lists you want to export, as shown in figure 4.5.

```
O2M 2.0 - Little Machines (2002/2003/XP Version)         [_][□][X]

Little Machines                                              [Help]
O2M

Outlook Contact Lists
─────────────────────────────────────────────────────────
If you want to move your contacts to your Macintosh, select the Outlook contact folders
you want converted.

──────────────────────────────────────────────
  Outlook Contact Folders
  └─ ⊠ Contacts
        ├─ □ Colleagues
        ├─ □ Friends
        ├─ □ Editors
        └─ □ Writers



  1 contact list will be converted.

                                      [ < Back ]   [ Next > ]
```

4.5 In O2M, select the Outlook contact lists that you want to convert to the vCard format.

5. **Select the check box beside each contact list you want to export, and then click Next.**

6. **Select the Apple Address Book option and click Next.**

7. **Select the Address Book category where you want the Outlook contacts stored — Work or Home — and then click Next.** O2M asks if you want to export your Outlook Calendar.

8. **I'm going to skip the conversion of appointments here because it is covered later in this chapter, so select No and click Next.**

9. **Click Start.** O2M converts your Outlook contact to the vCard format.

10. **Click Exit.**

With your Outlook contacts converted, you're ready to get them to your Mac. If your Mac and your Windows PC aren't on the same network, open the folder where O2M stored the vCard file, open the contacts folder, copy the Contacts.vcf file to a USB Flash drive (or something similar), and then connect the drive to your Mac.

Open your Mac's Address Book application and follow these steps to import the vCard file:

1. **Choose File ⇨ Import vCards.** The Select vCards to Import dialog box appears.

2. **Open the drive on your Mac or the network share where your O2M vCard file is stored, click the Contacts.vcf file, and then click Open.** Address Book asks you to confirm the import.

3. **Click Import.** Address Book imports the contacts.

Exporting Outlook contacts to a text file

If you don't want to go the O2M route, there's a way to get your Outlook contacts to your Mac directly. First, follow these steps on your PC to export your Outlook data:

1. **In Outlook, choose the Contacts folder.**

2. **Choose File ⇨ Import and Export.** The Import and Export Wizard appears.

3. **Choose Export to a file, and then click Next.**

4. **Choose Comma Separated Values (Windows), and then click Next.**

5. **Make sure the Contacts folder is selected, and then click Next.**

6. **Select a name and location for the file, and then click Next.** For best results, save the file to a network location that you can access with your Mac. If your Mac and your Windows PC aren't on the same network, save the file to a USB flash drive or some other removable drive.

7. **Click Finish.** Outlook exports the contact data to a text file.

Now you can import the contacts into Address Book by following these steps on your Mac:

1. **In Address Book, choose File ⇨ Import ⇨ Text File.** Address Book displays the Select text file to import dialog box.

2. **Choose the text file that you exported earlier from Outlook, and then click Open.** The Text File Import dialog box appears, as shown in figure 4.6.

```
┌─────────────────────────────────────────────────────────┐
│ ○ ○ ○                 Text File Import                    │
│                                                           │
│    Address Book  contacts.CSV                             │
│   Do not import ;  Title                     ▓            │
│          First ;  First Name                 ▓            │
│         Middle ;  Middle Name                ▓            │
│           Last ;  Last Name                               │
│         Suffix ;  Suffix                                  │
│        Company ;  Company                                 │
│     Department ;  Department                              │
│      Job Title ;  Job Title          First Card          │
│ Address (other) ;              Contains Column Headers    │
│         Street ;  Business Street                         │
│         Street ;  Business Street 2   ▴                   │
│           City ;  Business City                           │
│       Province ;  Business State                          │
│    Postal Code ;  Empty                                   │
│        Country ;  Business Country/                       │
│   Do not import ;  Business Street 2                      │
│ Address (other) ;                                         │
│         Street ;  Business Street 3   ▲                   │
│         Street ;  Other Street        ▼                   │
│                                                           │
│ ☑ Ignore first card    ◄  ►         ( Cancel ) ( OK )    │
└─────────────────────────────────────────────────────────┘
```

4.6 Use the Text File Import dialog box to map the Outlook fields to the Address Book fields.

3. **Check to make sure the fields under the Address Book column correspond with the fields in the contacts.CSV column.** If an Address Book field doesn't match with its corresponding contacts.CSV field, click the field in the Address Book column and choose the correct Address Book field from the drop-down list.

4. **Click OK.** Address Book imports the contact data.

Note If nothing happens when you click OK, it likely means that there's one or more corrupted entries in the exported text file. Open the file in a text editor and look for lines that don't begin or end with a quotation mark, or for contact data that appears on two or more lines.

Importing contacts from Windows Contacts

If you're coming to the Mac from Windows Vista and you used Vista's Windows Contacts folder, it's easy to export your contacts and then import them into Mac's Address Book application.

The easiest way to go about this is to export the contents of the Contacts folder to a collection of vCard files. Here are the steps to follow:

1. **On your Windows PC, click Start, click your user icon, and then double-click the Contacts folder.**

2. **Click the Export icon.** The Export Windows Contacts dialog box appears.

3. **Choose vCards and then click Export.** The Browse For Folder dialog box appears.

4. **Select a location for the files.** If possible, save the files to a network location that's available to your Mac. If your Mac and your Windows PC aren't on the same network, save the files to a USB flash drive or some other removable drive.

5. **Click OK.** Windows Contacts exports the contact data to vCard files.

6. **Click OK to return to the Export Windows Contacts dialog box.**

7. **Click Close.**

Now you can import the vCard files into your Mac's Address Book:

1. **On your Mac, open Address Book, and choose File ⇨ Import vCards.** The Select vCards to Import dialog box appears.

2. **Open the drive or network share where your vCard files are stored.**

3. **Click the first .vCard file, hold down Shift, and then click the last vCard file.** This ensures that you select every file.

4. **Click Open.** Address Book asks you to confirm the import.

5. **Click Import.** Address Book imports the contacts.

Importing contacts from Windows Address Book

If you were a Windows XP user, then chances are your contacts are stored in the Windows Address Book. As you see in this section, it doesn't take much effort to export your Windows Address Book data and then import it into your Mac's Address Book application.

First, follow these steps to export your Windows Address Book contacts to a text file:

1. **On your PC, select Start ⇨ All Programs ⇨ Accessories ⇨ Address Book.** The Address Book program appears.

2. **Choose File ⇨ Export ⇨ Other Address Book.** The Address Book Export Tool appears.

3. **Choose Text File (Comma Separated Values) and then click Export.** The CSV Export dialog box appears.

4. **Select a name and location for the file.** Save the file to a network location that you can access with your Mac. If your Mac and your Windows PC aren't on the same network, save the file to a USB flash drive or some other removable drive.

5. **Click Next.** The Address Book Export Tool prompts you to choose the fields you want to export.

6. **Select the check box beside each field you want to include.** For best results, select the First Name and Last Name check boxes, and deselect the Name check box, as shown in figure 4.7.

7. **Click Finish.** Address Book exports the contact data to a text file.

8. **Click OK to return to the Address Book Export Tool.**

9. **Click Close.**

4.7 Use this dialog box to select which Address Book fields you export.

Note The Address Book Export Tool also doesn't select the Personal Web Page and Business Web Page check boxes for export. If you've got Web addresses that you want to preserve, be sure to select these check boxes.

116

Now you can import the contacts into your Mac's Address Book application:

1. **On your Mac, open Address Book, and choose File ➪ Import ➪ Text File.** Address Book displays the Select text file to import dialog box.

2. **Choose the text file that you exported earlier from Outlook, and then click Open.** The Text File Import dialog box appears.

3. **Check to make sure the fields under the Address Book column correspond with the fields in the contacts.CSV column.** If an Address Book field doesn't match with its corresponding contacts.CSV field, click the field in the Address Book column and choose the correct Address Book field from the drop-down list.

4. **Click OK.** Address Book imports the contact data.

Caution

For some reason, your Mac's Address Book doesn't do a good job of importing postal codes. That is, in the Text File Import dialog box, it shows the Postal Code field as Empty, and although it recognizes the Home Postal Code fields from the Windows Address Book, it sets it to Do Not Import. To fix this, click Postal Code and then click Home Postal Code. For the business address, click Postal Code and then click Business Postal Code.

Importing contacts into Entourage

If you're doing the Mac contact thing with Entourage instead of Address Book, you'll be happy to know that it's relatively easy to get your Windows contacts into Entourage. The key here is that Entourage can only import contacts from a comma-separated values (CSV) text file, so your first chore is to export your Windows contacts data to a CSV file:

- **Microsoft Outlook.** Use the same export technique that I described in the "Exporting Outlook contacts to a text file" section.

- **Windows Contacts.** Open the Contacts folder, click the Export icon, choose CSV (Comma Separated Values), and then click Export. Use the Browse For Folder dialog box to choose a location for the files, and then click OK.

- **Windows Address Book.** Use the same export technique that I described in the "Importing contacts from Windows Address Book" section.

With your CSV file ready for action, follow these steps on your Mac to import your contacts into Entourage:

1. **Choose File ⇨ Import.** The Import dialog box appears.

2. **Select an import option and then press Return (or click the right arrow):**

   - **Entourage 2008.** Select the Contacts or messages from a text file option.

   - **Entourage 2004.** Select the Import information from a text file option.

3. **Select the Import contacts from a tab- or comma-delimited text file option, and then press Return.** A Finder dialog box appears.

4. **Choose the CSV file that contains your Windows contacts, and then click Import.** The Import Contacts dialog box appears, as shown in figure 4.8. In the Mapped fields pane, the left column shows the available Entourage fields, and the right column shows which import fields have been mapped to the Entourage fields.

5. **To add a mapping, click and drag the field from the Unmapped fields pane and drop it beside the corresponding Entourage field in the Mapped fields pane.**

6. **Click Import.** Entourage asks if you want to save the field mappings.

7. **Click Save, type a mapping name, and then click OK.** Entourage imports the contacts.

8. **Click Finish.**

4.8 Use the Import Contacts dialog box to map the contact fields before importing.

Transferring Appointments

With your e-mail messages and contacts safely stowed away on your Mac, just one thing remains in the process of transferring your life (well, the *digital* portion of your life) to your new Mac home: your calendar and its various appointments and events. Fortunately, getting your calendar data from your Windows PC to your Mac isn't hard and doesn't take long, so you won't miss a thing.

Whether you use Microsoft Outlook or Windows Mail, the basic process is the same: You export the calendar to a file that uses the Internet Calendaring and Scheduling (ICS) format — more commonly called the iCalendar file format — and you then import that file in your Mac's iCal application.

Exporting appointments from Microsoft Outlook

To export your Outlook Calendar folder into the iCalendar format, you can use either the O2M application or Outlook itself. The next two sections show you both methods.

Exporting appointments with O2M

The O2M (Outlook to Mac) program offered by Little Machines ($10; www.littlemachines.com) can export your Outlook Calendar folder to a special file that you can then import into the Mac's iCal application.

Assuming you've downloaded and installed O2M to your PC and applied your serial number (which you must do to unlock all of O2M's features), follow these steps to create your ICS file:

Genius

If you're running O2M in Windows Vista, you may see an error message that says O2M can't create temporary files in C:\. To bypass this security feature, close O2M, click Start, click All Programs, click the O2M folder, right-click the O2M icon, and then click Run as Administrator. Enter your User Account Control credentials to continue.

1. **Shut down Outlook if it's currently running.**

2. **After you start O2M and it has read your Outlook data, click Next.** O2M asks you to select the folder where it will store the Macintosh format files.

3. **Choose a folder and then click Next.** Ideally, you should select a folder that you can access from your Mac if it's on the same network as your Windows PC. If you're going to be copying the files to a USB Flash drive or other removable drive, then the default My_Outlook_Files folder is fine.

4. **Click Next to skip exporting e-mail messages.** O2M asks you to select which contact lists you want to export.

5. **Click Next to skip exporting contacts.** O2M asks whether you want to export your Outlook Calendar.

6. **Select Yes and click Next.**

7. **Select the Apple iCal option and click Next.** The Calendar Date Range dialog box appears, as shown in figure 4.9.

8. **Select one of the following options and then click Next:**

   - **Convert all appointments, regardless of date.** Select this option if you want to transfer all your Outlook appointments to your Mac.

   - **Only convert calendar appointments that did or will occur.** Select this option if you want to transfer Outlook appointments that fall only within a specific date range. Use the lists provided to specify a start date and an end date.

9. **Select one of the following options and then click Next:**

   - **Only look up email addresses if an invite is addressed to fewer than.** Select this option if your appointments include many meeting invitations that contain a large number of invitees. To greatly speed up the exporting, use the list to select the maximum number of invitees that you want O2M to convert to valid e-mail addresses.

   - **Look up all email addresses in all invitations.** Select this option to force O2M to convert all invitee names to valid e-mail addresses. This is the best way to go if your calendar doesn't include many meeting invitations or if most of your invitations include only a small number of invitees.

10. **Click Start.** O2M converts your Outlook contact to the vCard format.

11. **Click Exit.**

With your Outlook calendar exported, it's time to import the data into your Mac's iCal application. If your Mac and your Windows PC aren't on the same network, open the folder where O2M stored the iCalendar file, open the calendar folder, copy the Calendar.ics file to a USB Flash drive (or something similar), and then connect the drive to your Mac.

O2M 2.0 - Little Machines (2002/2003/XP Version)

Little Machines

O2M

Help

Calendar Date Range

You can convert all of your calendar appointments if you want, or just appointments that fall within a certain date range. Choose one of the options below.

○ Convert all appointments, regardless of date

⊙ Only convert calendar appointments that did or will occur:

	Month	Day	Year
On or After:	Oct ▼	16 ▼	2008 ▼

	Month	Day	Year
On or Before:	Dec ▼	31 ▼	2008 ▼

< Back   Next >

4.9 In O2M, select the range of dates that you want to export.

Exporting appointments with Outlook

You don't need to spend $10 (for O2M) to export your Outlook appointments because Outlook itself gives you a way to do it:

1. **On your PC, open Outlook, and choose the Calendar folder.**

2. **In the Navigation pane, click the Send a Calendar via E-mail link.** The Send a Calendar via E-mail dialog box appears, as shown in figure 4.10.

Send a Calendar via E-mail

Specify the calendar information you want to include.

Calendar: Calendar
Date Range: Today
Sat 1/12/2008

Detail: Availability only
Time will be shown as "Free," "Busy," "Tentative," or "Out of Office"

☐ Show time within my working hours only   Set working hours

Advanced: Show >>

OK   Cancel

4.10 Use the Send a Calendar via E-mail dialog box to export your Outlook calendar.

3. **If you have more than one calendar, use the Calendar drop-down list to choose the one you want to export.**

4. **Use the Date Range drop-down list to choose Whole calendar.**

5. **In the Detail list, choose Full details.**

6. **Click the Show button to expand the dialog box.**

7. **If you have any private items in the calendar, select the Include details of items marked private to export those items.**

8. **In the E-mail Layout list, choose List of events.** The e-mail layout isn't important, but choosing the List of events value is much better than choosing the Daily schedule value because it greatly reduces the amount of time Outlook spends composing the e-mail message.

9. **Click OK.** Outlook asks you to confirm that you want to send the whole calendar.

10. **Click Yes.** Outlook gathers the calendar data, starts a new e-mail message, and attaches an iCalendar file that includes the data.

11. **You have two ways to proceed from here.**

    ○ If your Windows PC and Mac are on the same network, right-click the attached iCalendar file, click Copy, open a shared network folder that you can access with your Mac, and then press Control+V to paste the file into that folder.

    ○ Use the To text box to type your Mac e-mail address, and then click Send. When you receive the iCalendar file on your Mac, open the message, click and drag the attachment icon, and then drop the file on your desktop or in some other folder.

12. **Click Finish.** Outlook exports the contact data to a text file.

Caution If you have a large number of appointments in the past, exporting the whole calendar can take quite a while. To speed things up, use the Date Range drop-down list to choose Specify dates, and then specify the dates you want using the Start and End calendar controls.

With that out of the way, you can now import the calendar into iCal:

1. **On your Mac, open iCal, and choose File ⇨ Import.** iCal displays the Import dialog box.

2. **Select the Import an iCal file option.** An iCal file uses the same format as an iCalendar file.

3. **Click Import.** The iCal: Import dialog box appears.

4. **Navigate to the folder containing the iCalendar file, click the file, and then click Import.** The Add events dialog box appears.

5. **Choose the iCal calendar you want to use to import the Outlook events.** You can also choose New Calendar to import the events into a separate calendar.

6. **Click OK.** iCal imports the calendar data.

Exporting appointments from Windows Calendar

If you're an ex-Vista user and you maintained your schedule using Vista's Windows Calendar program, you'll be happy to hear that you can move your appointments and events to your Mac's iCal application without much fuss and with almost no bother.

Here are the steps to follow to use Windows Calendar to export your appointments to a file that uses the iCalendar format:

1. **In Windows Calendar, choose File ⇨ Export.** The Export dialog box appears.

2. **Select a location for the file.** If possible, save the files to a network location that's available to your Mac. If your Mac and your Windows PC aren't on the same network, save the files to a USB flash drive or some other removable drive.

3. **Click Save.** Windows Calendar exports the appoints to the iCalendar file.

Importing an iCalendar file into iCal

With your iCalendar file exported, you're ready to import it into your Mac's iCal application. Here are the steps to follow:

1. **On your Mac, open iCal, and choose File ⇨ Import.** iCal displays the Import dialog box.

2. **Select the Import an iCal file option.**

3. **Click Import.** The iCal: Import dialog box appears.

4. **Navigate to the folder containing the iCalendar file, click the file, and then click Import.** The Add events dialog box appears.

5. **Choose the iCal calendar you want to use to import the Outlook events.** You can also choose New Calendar to import the events into a separate calendar.

6. **Click OK.** iCal imports the calendar data.

How Do I Move My Other Windows Data to My Mac?

List of files to convert	Format	Size	Containing Folder
01 Leap Of Innocence	.wma	30.001	/Users/karen/Music/iTunes/iTunes Music/Somebody's
02 Wind and The Mountain	.wma	38.951	/Users/karen/Music/iTunes/iTunes Music/Somebody's
03 Stars And Planets	.wma	27.968	/Users/karen/Music/iTunes/iTunes Music/Somebody's
04 Somebody's Miracle	.wma	31.369	/Users/karen/Music/iTunes/iTunes Music/Somebody's
05 Got My Own Thing	.wma	30.819	/Users/karen/Music/iTunes/iTunes Music/Somebody's
06 Count On My Love	.wma	26.357	/Users/karen/Music/iTunes/iTunes Music/Somebody's
07 Lazy Dreamer	.wma	34.489	/Users/karen/Music/iTunes/iTunes Music/Somebody's
08 Everything To Me	.wma	24.440	/Users/karen/Music/iTunes/iTunes Music/Somebody's
09 Closer To You	.wma	23.161	/Users/karen/Music/iTunes/iTunes Music/Somebody's
10 Table For One	.wma	24.389	/Users/karen/Music/iTunes/iTunes Music/Somebody's
11 Why I Lie	.wma	22.381	/Users/karen/Music/iTunes/iTunes Music/Somebody's
12 Lost Tonight	.wma	28.326	/Users/karen/Music/iTunes/iTunes Music/Somebody's
13 Everything (Between Us)	.wma	28.263	/Users/karen/Music/iTunes/iTunes Music/Somebody's
14 Giving It All To You	.wma	27.355	/Users/karen/Music/iTunes/iTunes Music/Somebody's

Switch Sound File Converter

Add File(s) Add Folder Remove Remove All Preferences Play Stop Convert Help

Output to same folder as source files   Output Format .mp3   Encoder Options...

Output Folder /Users/karen/Music   Browse...   Open...   Convert

Express Burn - professional CD Burner www.nch.com.au/burn

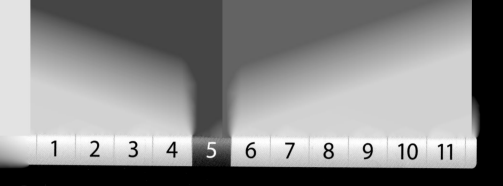

n Chapter 4 you learned how to populate your Mac with some precious data from your Windows PC: your e-mail messages, contacts, and calendar appointments. That's crucial stuff, to be sure, but it's not likely to be the sum total of your Windows data. You probably have word-processing documents, spreadsheets, presentations, databases, music, bookmarks, and who knows what else scattered around your Windows PC's hard drive. Your job now is to get that data onto your Mac so you can work with it, refer to it, or simply sleep better knowing that it's safe. This chapter shows you how it's done.

Moving Data from Windows to Mac

The techniques in Chapter 4 for moving messages, contacts, and appointments from your PC to your Mac all made use of the export and import features of various applications. That makes sense in those cases because each type of data needed to be converted to a format that your Mac understands.

However, you probably have lots of data where no conversion is required on the move from Windows to Mac:

- You might have Windows data that has no corresponding Mac application, so you simply want to store the data on your Mac for safekeeping.

- You might have Windows data that can be opened as-is without conversion on your Mac. For example, if you have Office 2008 for Mac, you can use it to work with any Word, Excel, or PowerPoint file that you created on your Windows PC.

In these and similar "conversionless" moves, you don't need to use applications to export and import the data. Instead, you use the Windows and Mac OS X file systems to transfer the data. As the next few sections show, you have three main ways to go about this: using an external hard disk, using a shared network folder, or using your MobileMe iDisk storage tool.

Copying data using a shared network folder

If you've got quite a bit of data to transfer from your Windows PC to your Mac, then you need to take a second to figure out the fastest and most convenient way to transfer all that info. A network connection is easily the most convenient way to go, assuming your Mac and your PC are on the same network, but is it the fastest? Perhaps. It all depends on whether the connection between your PC and your Mac uses Gigabit Ethernet, which operates at a theoretical transfer rate of 1 Gbps (1000 Mbps), which is faster than any transfer that uses an external hard drive (the method I describe in the next section).

For this to work, you require three things:

- A PC with a Gigabit Ethernet network adapter

- A Mac with a Gigabit Ethernet (also called 1000baseT) network adapter

- A network connection point — a router or switch — that supports Gigabit Ethernet connections

If you don't have all of these, then it means your network connection probably supports only 100 Mbps Ethernet, or it may mean you use a wireless (Wi-Fi) connection. Either way, a fast external hard drive (as described in the next section) is your better choice, so I suggest skipping the rest of this section.

Checking network connection speeds

Not sure about your network connection speed? Here's how to check your Windows PC for a gigabit connection:

- **Windows Vista.** Choose Start ➪ Network and then click Network and Sharing Center. (You can also click the Network icon in the notification area and then click Network and Sharing Center.) Click the View Status link beside your wired connection (which is usually called Local Area Connection). In the Status dialog box that appears, check the Speed value, as shown in figure 5.1. If this value is 1.0 Gbps, then your PC and connection point support Gigabit Ethernet.

- **Windows XP.** Choose Start ➪ All Programs ➪ Accessories ➪ Communications ➪ Network Connections. Double-click the icon for your wired connection (which is usually called Local Area Connection). In the Status dialog box that appears, check the Speed value.

5.1 View the status of your network connection and then check the Speed value.

To check your Mac's network connection speed, follow these steps:

1. **Choose Apple ➪ System Preferences.** The System Preferences window appears.

2. **Click the Network icon.** The Network preferences appear.

3. **Click the Ethernet connection.** On most Macs, this connection is called Built-in Ethernet.

4. **Click Advanced.**

5. **Click the Ethernet tab.**

6. **In the Configure pop-up menu, choose Manually.** This enables the Speed pop-up menu.

7. **Pop up the Speed menu and check the highest value.** If you see the 1000baseT option, as shown in figure 5.2, then your Mac supports Gigabit Ethernet; if you only see a lower value, such as 100baseTX, then your Mac won't do gigabit data transfers.

8. **Click Cancel.**

5.2 If the Speed pop-up menu shows 1000baseT, then your Mac supports Gigabit Ethernet.

Making the transfer

If your network is gigabit-friendly, then you're ready to make the transfer. There are two techniques you can use:

● **Share your Windows data and then use your Mac to access the shared folder.** Once you have the shared Windows folder open, you can then click and drag the data to whatever Mac folder you want to use to store it. This is a good method to use if all or most of your Windows data is in one place. For more details on this type of transfer, see Chapter 10.

● **Share your Mac on the Windows network and then use your Windows PC to access your Mac.** Once you have the shared Mac folder open, you can then click and drag the data from your Windows folders to the Mac. This is a good method to use if your Windows data is scattered in various places. For more details on this type of transfer, see Chapter 10.

Copying data to an external hard disk

If you don't have access to a zippy gigabit network connection, your next best bet is to use an external hard disk. However, it's important that you use a fast hard disk to minimize the amount of time the transfer takes, particularly if you're moving lots of data. You have two choices:

● **USB 2.0.** This is a good general choice because all recent PCs and Macs have at least one USB 2.0 port. Make sure you get USB 2.0, which offers a transfer rate of 480 Mbps, compared to a mere 12 Mbps for USB 1.1.

● **FireWire.** These external drives attach to a FireWire port. (FireWire is an Apple term; in the PC world it's called IEEE 1394.) You can get either FireWire 400 (IEEE 1394a), which offers 400 Mbps data throughput, or FireWire 800 (IEEE 1394b), which offers 800 Mbps data throughput. Most of the latest Macs come with FireWire 800 (the notable exception is the MacBook Air), which is by far the best way to go, but your old PC might not have a FireWire port.

Genius

If your PC doesn't have a FireWire port, one solution would be to purchase a FireWire to USB adapter cable, which connects to the Mac's FireWire port on one end, and to the PC's USB port on the other. Another solution is to purchase a hub that combines both USB and FireWire ports.

Whichever type of external hard disk you use, here's the basic procedure for using it to copy data from your PC to your Mac:

1. **Connect the external hard disk to your PC.** Your Windows PC should install device drivers for the hard disk automatically; if not, insert the disc that came with the drive and install the drivers yourself.

2. **Click Start and then click either Computer (in Vista) or My Computer (in XP).**

3. **Double-click the icon for the external hard disk.** Windows opens the disk.

4. **Click Start and then click either Documents (in Vista) or My Documents (in XP).**

5. **Click and drag the data you want to copy to your Mac, and drop it inside the external hard disk window.**

Genius Instead of clicking and dragging the data, an alternative is to select the data, right-click the selection, click Send To, and then click the external hard disk in the menu that appears.

6. **Repeat Step 5 to copy all the data you want to transfer.**

7. **Close the external hard disk window.**

8. **Disconnect the external hard disk.**

9. **Connect the external hard disk to your Mac.** An icon for the hard disk, named External Hard Disk, appears on your desktop, as shown in figure 5.3.

10. **Double-click the external hard disk icon.** Your Mac opens the hard disk.

5.3 When you connect the external hard disk to your Mac, an icon for the disk appears on your desktop.

11. **Choose File ⇨ New Finder Window.**

12. **Navigate to the Mac folder where you want to store the data from the Windows PC.**

13. **Click and drag some or all of the data from the external hard disk and drop it inside the Mac folder.**

14. **Repeat Steps 12 and 13 to complete the transfer.**

Copying data using your MobileMe iDisk

If you have a MobileMe account (see www.me.com), you get online e-mail, contacts, calendars, and photo sharing. However, each MobileMe account also has access to an iDisk, a bit of online storage real estate that you can use to store files. This is handy because it enables you to store pictures, videos, documents, or whatever else that you think you might want to access from anywhere online. It's also possible to access your iDisk from a Windows PC, so you can use iDisk to transfer your data from Windows to Mac. This is great if your Windows PC and Mac aren't on the same network, and if you don't have a handy external hard disk. Unfortunately, this isn't an ideal way to transfer data:

- Even a broadband Internet connection is a slow way to transfer data.

- You can transfer only one file at a time.

- Your iDisk can hold only so much space (up to a bit less than 20GB).

Genius

By default, MobileMe allocates half your storage space (10GB) to MobileMe Mail and half to iDisk. This isn't the right setting for most people because it's extremely unlikely they'll ever need so much space for e-mail messages. To fix this, access MobileMe, click the Account icon, type your MobileMe password, click Log In, and then click Storage Settings. In the Storage Settings window, choose a smaller value in the Mail list (for example, 500MB). MobileMe automatically allocates the rest of the storage to iDisk. Click Save.

To access your iDisk on your Mac, you have two choices:

- **If you're logged in to your MobileMe account, click the iDisk icon in the toolbar.**

- **Open Finder and click the iDisk icon.** Figure 5.4 shows the iDisk folder that appears.

5.4 The iDisk folder that appears when you access iDisk via Finder.

To access your iDisk from your Windows PC, open a Web browser and enter the address http://idisk.me.com/*username*/, where *username* is your MobileMe member name. When Windows asks you to log on, type your MobileMe member name and password, and then click OK.

iDisk provides you with a collection of folders, some of which you can use to store files. Here's a summary:

- **Backup.** MobileMe uses this folder to store data files created by its Backup feature.

- **Documents.** You can use this folder to store miscellaneous files.

- **Library.** MobileMe uses this folder to store items such as contacts and bookmarks that you've synced with your Mac.

- **Movies.** You can use this folder to store digital video files. If you create Web pages with MobileMe, you can embed these movies in your pages.

- **Music.** You can use this folder to store digital audio files and music playlists.

- **Pictures.** You can use this folder to store digital image files. You can add these images to your MobileMe Web pages.

- **Public.** You can use this folder to share files with other people over the Web. Other people need only enter the address http://idisk.me.com/*username*-Public/, where *username* is your MobileMe member name. No password is required, so others can easily work with these files.

- **Shared.** You see this folder only if you signed up for a MobileMe Family Pack. You use this folder to share files with other accounts in your Family Pack.

- **Sites.** MobileMe uses this folder to store pages you created using the HomePage feature (which was part of the old .Mac service, but is no longer part of MobileMe).

- **Software.** MobileMe uses this folder to store applications and other files that are made available solely to MobileMe members.

● **Web.** You see this folder only after you've used iWeb to publish a Web site to your MobileMe account.

To get files from your Windows PC to iDisk, follow these steps:

1. **In the iDisk window, click the folder you want to use to store the files.**

2. **Click the Upload a File or Files icon.** The Uploads dialog box appears.

3. **Click Choose.** The File Upload dialog box appears.

4. **Choose the file and then click Open.** MobileMe uploads the file.

5. **Repeat Steps 1 through 4 to upload other files.**

6. **Click Done.**

To get files from iDisk to your Mac, you have two choices:

● **Using MobileMe.** In the iDisk window, open the folder you want to use to store the files and then select the files you want to download. Click the Download the Selected Files icon.

● **Using Finder.** Open the iDisk folder that contains the files, and open a Finder window for the folder where you want to copy the files. Click and drag the file or files from the iDisk folder and then drop them inside the second Finder window.

Moving Media from Windows to Mac

To take advantage of your Mac's vaunted media savvy, you need, of course, media. If your music, photos, and videos currently reside on your Windows PC, you need to hire the digital equivalent of a moving van to transport all that good stuff to your Mac neighborhood. The next three sections provide the details.

Moving music using iTunes

Getting music into the iTunes library is generally pretty straightforward, as long as the files are in a format that iTunes recognizes: AAC, Apple Lossless, MP3, MPEG-4, AIFF, or WAV. If your music is in any other format, you need to convert it to one of these formats. (I suggest converting to MP3 because it's the universal music format.) For example, if you've got lots of Windows Media Audio (WMA) tunes on your Windows PC, you'll need to convert them to an iTunes-friendly format (such as MP3, which I discuss in the next section).

Other than that, how you get your music into iTunes depends on whether you've used iTunes yet and where your music files now reside. There are three possible routes to take:

● **If you're a Windows iTunes user and you haven't yet used iTunes on your Mac.** The first time you start iTunes, it scans your Mac to look for music files, and it adds any files it finds to the iTunes library. Therefore, before you start iTunes for the first time, use the techniques from the previous section to move your Windows PC's iTunes Music folder to your Mac's Music ➪ iTunes folder. (If you don't see that folder, create it yourself.) If you use Vista, choose Start ➪ Music to see the iTunes Music folder; in XP, choose Start ➪ My Music.

● **If your music files reside on a network share, external hard disk, or removable disk.** In this case, use iTunes' Add to Library command (see the steps that follow) to locate the music files and add them to the library. iTunes automatically copies the files to the iTunes Music folder on your Mac.

● **If you've already copied the music files to your Mac.** In this case you want to avoid ending up with two copies of your music on your Mac. That can happen because when you use iTunes' Add to Library command (see the steps that follow) to add music, iTunes automatically copies the files to the iTunes Music folder. Note that it copies the files, it doesn't move them, so you end up with two copies of each file. To avoid this, use Finder to move your music files to the Music ➪ iTunes ➪ iTunes Music folder.

Genius

If your music is on your Mac in a folder other than iTunes Music, you may prefer to keep it there. To avoid ending up with duplicates of your music, you can configure iTunes to not create copies in the iTunes Music folder. Choose iTunes ➪ Preferences, click the Advanced tab, click the General subtab, and then deselect the Copy files to iTunes Music folder when adding to library check box. Click OK.

If your music resides on a network share, an external hard disk, removable disk, your MobileMe iDisk, or in the iTunes Music folder on your Mac, use the following steps to add the music to your Mac iTunes library:

1. **In iTunes, choose File ➪ Add to Library, or press ⌘+O.** The Add To Library dialog box appears.

2. **Choose the folder that contains the music files you want to add.**

3. **Click Open.** iTunes copies the files and adds them to the Music section of the library.

Genius

You can also click and drag the folder that contains the music files, and then drop the folder on the iTunes icon in the Dock.

Converting WMA music to MP3

If you use Windows Media Player to rip a bunch of audio CDs on your Windows PC, there's a good chance all that music ended up in the WMA (Windows Media Audio) format that's Media Player's default. Unfortunately, iTunes doesn't deal with the WMA format, so you can't play those files on your Mac. Fortunately, you don't have to waste hours of your life re-ripping your audio CDs to your Mac. Instead, you can use a nifty little program called Switch to convert your WMA files to the MP3 format.

The good news about Switch is that there's a free version, which you can download from www.nch. com.au/switch/. The bad news is that because you'll be converting WMA files, you also need the Flip4Mac plug-in software, which is *not* free: the basic version costs $29. You can purchase Flip4Mac from www.flip4mac.com/. (Technically, there is a free version that you can download, but it converts only half a song, so it's pretty useless.)

Caution

Before slapping down the bucks for Flip4Mac, note that the program will *not* convert any WMA files that are protected by Windows digital rights managements (DRM).

With both Flip4Mac and Switch installed, follow these steps on your PC to convert WMA music to the MP3 format:

1. **In Switch, click Add Folder.** The Locate Folder window appears.

2. **Choose the folder that contains the WMA files, and then click Choose.**

3. **If you want the MP3 files to reside in the same folder as the WMA files, select the Output to same folder as source file check box.** Otherwise, use the Output Folder text box to specify the folder for the MP3 files.

4. **In the Output Format pop-up menu, choose .mp3.**

5. **Click Encoder Options.** The Mp3 Encoder Settings dialog box appears.

6. **Select the Constant Bitrate option, use the Bitrate pop-up menu to choose the bitrate you want, and then click OK.** Figure 5.5 shows the Switch window ready for the conversion.

Note The higher the bitrate you use, the higher the quality of the converted files, but the more hard disk space those files consume.

```
○ ○ ○                    Switch Sound File Converter                              ⊖

  ⬆        📁⁺       ⬇       ⬇        ⚙        ▶      ⬤        ⬇               ?
Add File(s)  Add Folder  Remove  Remove All  Preferences  Play  Stop    Convert          Help

  List of files to convert          Format      Size       Containing Folder
♦  01 Leap Of Innocence             .wma        30.001     /Users/karen/Music/iTunes/iTunes Music/Somebody's
♦  02 Wind and The Mountain         .wma        38.951     /Users/karen/Music/iTunes/iTunes Music/Somebody's
♦  03 Stars And Planets             .wma        27.968     /Users/karen/Music/iTunes/iTunes Music/Somebody's
♦  04 Somebody's Miracle            .wma        31.369     /Users/karen/Music/iTunes/iTunes Music/Somebody's
♦  05 Got My Own Thing              .wma        30.819     /Users/karen/Music/iTunes/iTunes Music/Somebody's
♦  06 Count On My Love              .wma        26.357     /Users/karen/Music/iTunes/iTunes Music/Somebody's
♦  07 Lazy Dreamer                  .wma        34.489     /Users/karen/Music/iTunes/iTunes Music/Somebody's
♦  08 Everything To Me              .wma        24.440     /Users/karen/Music/iTunes/iTunes Music/Somebody's
♦  09 Closer To You                 .wma        23.161     /Users/karen/Music/iTunes/iTunes Music/Somebody's
♦  10 Table For One                 .wma        24.389     /Users/karen/Music/iTunes/iTunes Music/Somebody's
♦  11 Why I Lie                     .wma        22.381     /Users/karen/Music/iTunes/iTunes Music/Somebody's
♦  12 Lost Tonight                  .wma        28.326     /Users/karen/Music/iTunes/iTunes Music/Somebody's
♦  13 Everything (Between Us)       .wma        28.263     /Users/karen/Music/iTunes/iTunes Music/Somebody's
♦  14 Giving It All To You          .wma        27.355     /Users/karen/Music/iTunes/iTunes Music/Somebody's
                                                                                    ◀  ▶

☐ Output to same folder as source files    Output Format  [.mp3        ⬍]  ( Encoder Options... )    ⬇
                                                                                              Convert
Output Folder  [/Users/karen/Music                    ▼]  ( Browse... )  ( Open... )

Express Burn - professional CD Burner www.nch.com.au/burn
```

5.5 The Switch window, ready to convert some WMA files to the MP3 format.

7. **Click Convert.** Switch converts the WMA files to MP3.

Once the files are converted, you need to add them to your iTunes library on your Mac. Use the Add to Library command as described in the previous section.

Moving photos using iPhoto

Moving your Windows photos to your Mac using iPhoto is a bit weird because of the way the iPhoto library works. The iPhoto library is where iPhoto stores your photos, so you'd think it would be a standard-issue folder, something like the iTunes Music folder that I talked about earlier (see "Moving music using iTunes"). And, yes, when you use Finder to open the Pictures folder, you see an item named iPhoto Library, but when you click that item, as shown in figure 5.6, you don't see a folder at all, but a kind of file. Actually, it's a special object called a *package* that includes not only folders and files, but other data as well.

5.6 When you use Finder to click iPhoto Library, you see that it's a special type of file instead of a folder.

Genius

To see what's inside the iPhoto Library package, right-click (or Control+click) iPhoto Library and then click Show Package Contents.

This means that you can't simply copy your photos from your Windows PC to your Mac. Instead, you need to import your photos using the iPhoto application. First, make sure the photos are accessible from your Mac:

- If your Mac and your Windows PC are on the same network, share the folder on your Windows PC that contains the photos.

- If your Mac and Windows PC aren't connected, copy the photos to an external hard disk, USB Flash drive, or some other removable media that you can then insert into your Mac.

Here are the steps to follow:

1. **In iPhoto, choose File ➪ Import to Library, or press Shift+⌘+I.** The Import Photos dialog box appears.

2. **Click the folder that contains the photos you want to import.**

3. **Click Import.** iPhoto imports the photos and then creates a new event for the import.

137

Genius

Another way to import photos into iPhoto is to use Finder to display the folder that contains the photos. Click and drag the folder and then drop it inside the iPhoto window.

Moving videos and movies to your Mac

After having to jump through a few hoops to get your music and photos from your Windows PC to your Mac, you'll be happy to know that there's not a hoop in sight when it comes to getting your videos and digital movie files onto your Mac. On your Mac, your user profile comes with a Movies folder, and that is where you store your video and movie files. That is, you use any of the techniques from the opening section of the chapter. This means you simply move the files from your PC onto your network shared folder, external hard disk (or removable disk), or MobileMe iDisk, and then connect to that source from your Mac. Then you can access the files from your Mac and move them to your Movies folder.

Note

Remember that if any of your digital video files use the Windows Media Video (WMV) format, you need to purchase and install Flip4Mac (www.flip4mac.com) to view those files using your Mac's QuickTime player.

Importing Windows Data

To complete your data's transition from Windows to Mac, the rest of this chapter shows you how to import three different types of data: Internet Explorer favorites, Firefox bookmarks, and RSS feeds.

Importing Internet Explorer favorites

With your switch from Windows to Mac, you might be wondering if you have to give up all your hard-earned Internet Explorer favorites as part of the deal. No way! As long as you still have access to your Windows machine, you can export your favorites from Internet Explorer and import them as bookmarks into Safari.

First, follow these steps to export your Internet Explorer favorites to a file:

1. **On your Windows PC, launch Internet Explorer.**

2. **Start the Import/Export Wizard.**

- In Internet Explorer 7 or 8, click the Add to Favorites icon (or press Alt+Z) and then click Import and Export.

- In all versions of Internet Explorer, choose File ⇨ Import and Export. (To see the menu bar in Internet Explorer 7 or 8, press Alt.)

3. **Click Next.** The Import/Export Selection dialog box appears.

4. **Click Export Favorites, and then click Next.** The Export Favorites Source Folder dialog box appears.

5. **Click the Favorites folder, and then click Next.** The Export Favorites Destination dialog box appears.

6. **Choose a location for the export file.**

   - If your Windows PC and your Mac are on the same network, save the favorites file in a folder that's shared on the network.

   - If your Windows PC and Mac aren't on the same network, insert a USB flash drive into the Windows PC and then save the favorites file to the flash drive.

7. **Click Next.** Internet Explorer exports the favorites to a file.

8. **Click Finish.**

Now you're ready to import your Internet Explorer favorites into Safari by following these steps:

1. **On your Mac, launch Safari, and choose File ⇨ Import Bookmarks.** The Import Bookmarks dialog box appears.

2. **Open the folder that contains the favorites file you exported earlier from Internet Explorer.**

   - If your Windows PC and your Mac are on the same network, open the shared network folder that contains the favorites file.

   - If your Windows PC and Mac aren't on the same network, insert the USB flash drive that contains the favorites file.

3. **Click the favorites file.** In most cases, the file is named bookmark.htm.

4. **Click Import.** Safari adds the Internet Explorer favorites as bookmarks.

Note

If you're using an older Mac that has Internet Explorer for the Mac installed, you may want to import the local favorites. In Safari, choose File ⇨ Import Bookmarks to open the Import Bookmarks dialog box. Choose your user folder, and then choose Library ⇨ Preferences ⇨ Explorer. Click the Favorites.html file, and then click Import.

Importing Firefox bookmarks

If you were a Firefox user on your Windows PC, but have decided to go with Safari on your Mac, you'll want to get your mitts on your precious Firefox bookmarks. Fortunately, this isn't a problem because Firefox can export its bookmarks to a file that you can then import into Safari.

First, here are the steps to follow to export your Firefox bookmarks:

1. **On your Windows PC, launch Firefox.**
2. **Choose Bookmarks ⇨ Organize Bookmarks.** You can also press Control+Shift+B. The Library window appears.
3. **Choose Import and Backup ⇨ Export HTML.** The Export Bookmarks File dialog box appears.
4. **Choose a location for the export file.**
   - If your Windows PC and Mac share a network connection, save the file in a shared network folder that both machines can access.
   - If your Windows PC and Mac aren't on the same network, insert a USB flash drive or other removable media into the Windows PC and then save the bookmarks file to the drive.
5. **Click Save.** Firefox exports the bookmarks to a file.
6. **Choose Organize ⇨ Close.**

Now follow these steps to import your Firefox bookmarks into Safari:

1. **On your Mac, launch Safari, choose File ⇨ Import Bookmarks.** The Import Bookmarks dialog box appears.
2. **Open the folder that contains the exported Firefox bookmarks file.**
3. **Click the bookmarks file.** In most cases, the file is named bookmarks.html.
4. **Click Import.** Safari adds the Firefox bookmarks.

Importing your RSS feeds into Mail

One of Apple Mail's nicest features is its built-in support for RSS (Real Simple Syndication) feeds. (A *feed* is a file that shows the most recent entries from a specific Web site, particularly a blog.) Mail offers an RSS category that lists each of your subscribed feeds, and you can read an entry just by clicking it. In other words, you can do all your e-mail reading and feed reading in a single application.

That's awesome, for sure, but there's a problem: If you have a couple of dozen feeds that you track, how do you tell Mail about those feeds without having to resubscribe to each one individually? Happily, there are actually several ways to go about this. Unhappily, none of these methods is straightforward. (That is, Mail doesn't come with a handy "Import Feeds" command. Bummer.) The next two sections show you two methods that I've used with success.

Importing RSS feeds using NetNewsWire

Newsgator (www.newsgator.com) specializes in RSS feed reading, and it shows: They make excellent products that enable you to read feeds anywhere, anytime. One of their products is a Mac OS X application called NetNewsWire, which is an excellent feed reader that I recommend highly. However, if you're determined to read your feeds in Mail, you can also use NetNewsWire to get your feeds into Mail without much fuss.

Note that the method I'm going to show you is easy, but it doesn't enable you to import multiple subscriptions into Mail at one time. Therefore, use this method if you have a relatively small number of feeds (say, no more than a couple of dozen). For larger feed collections, see the method in the next section.

Assuming you've downloaded and installed NetNewsWire on your Mac, here's the procedure to follow to use that program to get your feeds into Mail:

1. **In whatever Windows program or online service you now use to read RSS feeds, export your feeds to an OPML (Outline Processor Markup Language) file.** How you do this depends on the program or service, so see the help section. Here's what you do if you're using either Internet Explorer or Firefox:

   - **Internet Explorer 7 or 8.** Press Alt to display the menu bar, choose File ⇨ Import and Export, click Next, click Export Feeds, click Next, choose a location accessible from your Mac, click Next, click Finish, and then click OK.

   - **Firefox.** You need to install Sage (http://sage.mozdev.org/), which is a feed reader plug-in for Firefox. In the Sage sidebar (if you don't see it, press Alt+Z), click Options ⇨ OPML Import/Export, select Export OPML, click Next, choose a location accessible from your Mac, click Next, and then click Finish.

2. **In NetNewsWire on your Mac, choose File ⇨ Import Subscriptions.** A Finder dialog box appears.

3. **Choose the OPML file that you created in Step 1, and then click Open.** NetNewsWire imports your RSS feeds. The feeds appear in a folder named Imported Subscriptions *Date*, where *Date* is the date you performed the import, as shown in figure 5.7.

4. **Open Mail.** Position the Mail and NetNewsWire windows so that you can see Mail's sidebar when you switch to NetNewsWire.

5. **Click and drag a feed from NetNewsWire and then drop it inside Mail's sidebar.** Mail adds the feed to the RSS folder.

6. **Repeat Step 5 to add each feed to Mail.**

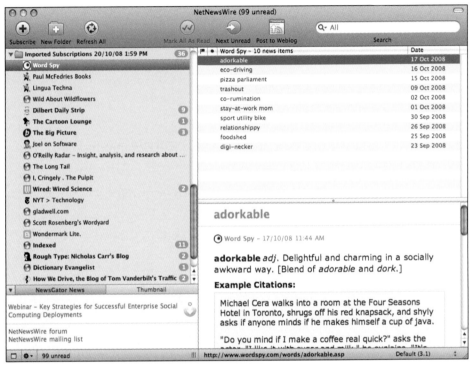

5.7 When you import the OPML file into NetNewsWire, the feeds appear in the Imported Subscriptions folder.

Importing RSS feeds using Firefox and Safari

The NetNewsWire method shown in the previous section is time-consuming because you can click and drag only one feed at a time. If you've got a large collection of feeds that you keep up with, you'll want a faster way to get those feeds into Mail. You got it! There's a method that, strangely, uses Firefox and Safari to get your feeds into Mail.

First, here's the Firefox portion of the show:

1. **On your PC or Mac, launch Firefox and install the Sage feed reader from http://sage. mozdev.org/.**

2. **In whatever Windows program or online service you now use to read RSS feeds, export your feeds to an OPML file on your PC.** How you do this depends on the program or service, so see the help section. If you use Internet Explorer, 7 or 8, press Alt to display the menu bar, choose File ⇨ Import and Export, click Next, click Export Feeds, click Next, choose a location accessible from your Mac, click Next, click Finish, and then click OK.

3. **In the Sage sidebar in Firefox, choose Options ⇨ OPML Import/Export.** If you don't see the Sage sidebar, press Alt+Z.

4. **Select the Import OPML option, and then click Next.**

5. **Select your OPML file from Step 2, and then click Next.** Sage imports the feeds.

6. **Click Finish.**

7. **Choose Bookmarks ⇨ Organize Bookmarks (or press Control+Shift+B).** The Library window appears.

8. **Choose Import and Backup ⇨ Export HTML.** The Export Bookmarks File dialog box appears.

9. **Choose a location for the export file.**

   - If your Windows PC and Mac share a network connection, save the file in a shared network folder that both machines can access.

   - If your Windows PC and Mac aren't on the same network, insert a USB flash drive or other removable media into the Windows PC and then save the bookmarks file to the drive.

10. **Click Save.** Firefox exports the bookmarks to a file.

11. **Choose Organize ⇨ Close.**

Now you need to import the feeds into Safari:

1. **On your Mac, launch Safari and choose File ⇨ Import Bookmarks.** The Import Bookmarks dialog box appears.

Caution

Before continuing, make sure that Safari is the default feed reader on your Mac. Choose Safari ⇨ Preferences, click the RSS tab, and then use the Default RSS reader pop-up menu to choose Safari.

2. **Open the folder that contains the exported Firefox bookmarks file.**

3. **Click the bookmarks file.** In most cases, the file is named bookmarks.html.

4. **Click Import.** Safari adds the Firefox bookmarks.

5. **Choose Bookmarks ⇨ Show All Bookmarks.** In the Bookmarks section, you see an item named Imported *Date*, where *Date* is today's date.

6. **Click the imported item.**

7. **Open the Sage Feeds folder.**

8. **Right-click the OPML Import - Feeds item, and then click Open in Tabs, as shown in figure 5.8.** Safari opens each RSS feed in its own tab, which enables Safari to see that these are feeds, not Web pages.

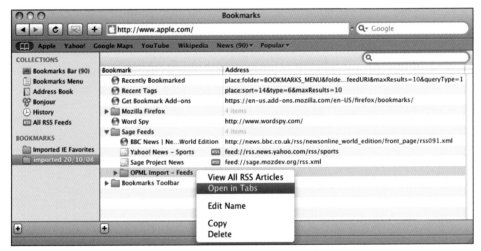

5.8 To tell Safari that the imported Sage items are RSS feeds, open them in tabs.

Okay, you're almost done. You complete the operation by following these steps to import the feeds into Mail:

1. **In Mail, choose File ⇨ Add RSS Feeds.** The Add RSS Feeds dialog box appears.

2. **Select the Browse feeds in Safari Bookmarks option.**

3. **In the Collections list, choose All RSS Feeds.**

4. **In the Name list, select the check box beside each feed you want to add, as shown in figure 5.9.**

5.9 Select the check box beside each RSS feed you want to read in Mail.

5. **Click Add.** Mail adds the feeds.

How Do I Work with Files, Folders, and Programs?

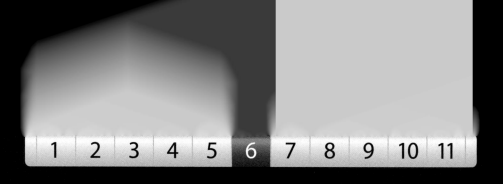

Now that you know a bit more about your Mac, you're familiar with the available applications, you've got a few day-to-day chores down pat, and you've coaxed your Windows data onto your Mac hard disk, you're well on your way to mastering your Mac. Your next challenge is to tackle files, folders, and programs, and this may be the most important one yet. After all, when you do something productive with your Mac, you're usually working with a file; when you store something on your Mac, you store it in a folder; and when you do *anything* on your Mac, you do it within a program.

Getting to Know Finder

Unlike any program you would have worked with on your Windows PC, your Mac's Finder program is always on. Finder starts automatically when you boot your Mac, it remains running throughout your Mac session, and it doesn't rest until you shut down your Mac. Finder is your Mac's always-ready, always-willing, and always-able companion for working with files, folders, and programs, and that means you'll be using Finder constantly throughout your Mac career. So it pays to take a second or three now and really get to know this application and what it can do.

Understanding the Finder layout

Finder is similar to Windows Explorer, and you use it to examine the contents of various types of objects, particularly the following:

- Folders
- Hard disks, CDs, DVDs, and other removable media
- Shared network folders
- Search results

That's a wide variety, but Finder handles them all with a remarkably and refreshingly simple interface. Figure 6.1 points out the highlights.

Genius

The buttons on the Finder toolbar appear only as icons by default, so you either have to memorize what they do, or you can hover the mouse pointer over an icon for a few seconds to see a description of it. Even better, tell Finder to display the name of each item under the icon: Right-click (or Control+click) the toolbar and then click Icon & Text.

Here's a summary:

- **Back/Forward.** You use these buttons to navigate the folders you've visited in the current Finder session (see "Navigating your Mac with Finder").
- **View buttons.** You use these buttons to change how the contents of the current folder are displayed (see "Changing the Finder view").
- **Quick Look.** Click this button to get a quick preview of the selected file (see "Taking a quick look at a file").

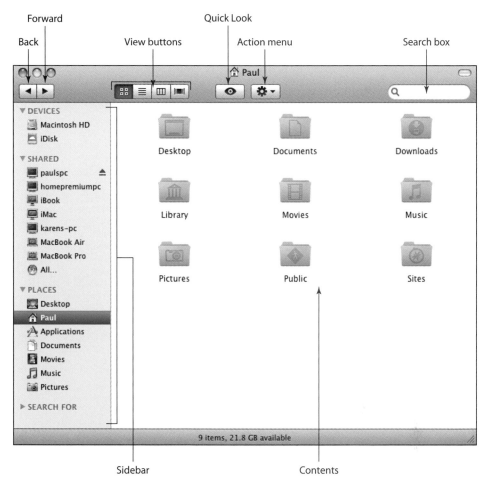

6.1 The main features of a typical Finder window

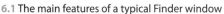

- **Action menu.** This menu offers quick access to some common commands associated with whatever object is currently selected.

- **Sidebar.** This pane offers a number of shortcuts to objects such as devices, network shares, and local folders (see "Working with Finder's Sidebar").

- **Contents.** The bulk of any Finder window is taken up by the contents, which shows (depending on the current view) the folders, subfolders, and files associated with the current Finder object.

- **Search box.** You use this box to run Spotlight searches from within Finder (see "Performing advanced Spotlight searches").

Genius

The Finder toolbar has lots of useful icons, but they're not the only ones available. You can customize the toolbar to remove any items you don't use, and to add ones you find more useful. Choose View⇨Customize Toolbar (or right-click — or Control+click — the toolbar and then click Customize Toolbar). Drag items you don't want off the toolbar, and drag items you do want onto the toolbar.

Navigating your Mac with Finder

Finder's main job is to show you your stuff: the documents, photos, music, and videos in your user account; the files and folders on a hard disk, optical disc, or memory card; and the contents of a shared network drive. Of course, before you can see what's *inside* something, you need to find your way *to* that something. Finder helps here, too, because it offers lots of ways to navigate your Mac. Here's a summary:

- **Drill down into subfolders.** If the current folder or drive has subfolders, double-click a subfolder to open it. Keep doing this to drill down into the subfolders (and sub-subfolders) of the current folder or drive.

- **Go up the folder levels.** To reverse course (that is, to navigate to the parent folder of the current subfolder), choose Go⇨Enclosing Folder, or press ⌘+Up Arrow.

Genius

An easy way to navigate your way through the folder hierarchy is to press ⌘+[to go up to the next folder in the hierarchy, and press ⌘+] to go reverse course and go back down into the hierarchy.

- **Choose a shortcut.** Your Mac offers menu and keyboard shortcuts to six of the most popular locations on your Mac. Pull down the Go menu and then choose one of the following (or just press the keyboard shortcut shown):

Computer	Shift+⌘+C
Home	Shift+⌘+H
Desktop	Shift+⌘+D
Network	Shift+⌘+K
Applications	Shift+⌘+A
Utilities	Shift+⌘+U

- **Choose a recent folder.** Your Mac maintains a list of the ten most recent folders (local folders or network shares) that you've visited. To return to one of those folders, choose Go ⇨ Recent Folders and then click the folder in the menu that appears.

Genius If other people have access to your Mac while you're logged in, you might not want those people to see the folders you've visited recently (for example, one of those folders might contain confidential information). To remove all items from the menu, choose Go ⇨ Recent Folders ⇨ Clear Menu.

- **Click something in the Sidebar.** The Sidebar offers one-click links to all kinds of useful locations. For more info, see "Working with Finder's Sidebar."

- **Click the Back and Forward buttons.** After you navigate to various places using Finder, click Finder's Back button (see figure 6.1) to retrace your steps. To reverse course and go back through the places in the order you visited them, click the Forward button, instead.

Working with Finder's Sidebar

The Sidebar pane that takes up the entire left side of any Finder window is one of the handiest innovations in recent OS X history. Depending on your setup, the Sidebar offers as many as two dozen icons, and each one gives you one-click access to a location on your Mac or on the network. The Sidebar is divided into four sections:

- **Devices.** This section contains icons for your Mac's hard disk (usually called Macintosh HD), your MobileMe iDisk, as well as for devices you connect to your Mac, such as an iPod or an iPhone.

- **Shared.** This section contains icons for some of the computers on your network. Click an icon to connect to that computer. If the remote computer has a user account with the same name and password as your account, you get connected automatically; otherwise, you're connected using the Guest account, which gives you only limited privileges. If you know the name and password of an account on the remote computer, click Connect As and then log in. Note, too, that clicking the All icon is the same as choosing Go ⇨ Network.

- **Places.** This section contains icons for popular destinations on your Mac, including your user account's Home folder, the Desktop, and the Applications folder.

- **Search For.** This section contains icons for several default Spotlight searches. You can also add your own searches to this section by creating a smart folder (see "Setting up a smart folder," later in this chapter).

Genius

If you find that you constantly have to scroll up or down to find things on the Sidebar, you can tighten up Sidebar's display by hiding sections that you don't use. Click the downward-pointing arrow to the left of the section name to hide the items in that section. To show the items, click the arrow again.

The Sidebar also gives you an easy way to eject a connected device or network computer. When you connect a device or connect to a network computer, the Sidebar adds an Eject icon to the right of the item; it looks like an upward-pointing arrow. For example, in the Sidebar shown in figure 6.2, you see the Eject icon beside Paul's iPod and Time Machine Backups in the Devices section, and beside paulspc and tabletpc in the Shared section. To cut one of these connections, click its Eject button.

6.2 Connected devices and computers show an Eject icon in the Sidebar.

Customizing the Sidebar

The Sidebar is a handy tool, for sure, but you can make it even handier by customizing it to suit the way you work. That is, you can configure the Sidebar to remove those icons that you never use, and to add icons for locations that you use frequently.

Adding an icon for a location to the Sidebar

If you have a folder or other location that you visit regularly, it may take you a few clicks to get there, particularly if you have to drill down into a bunch of subfolders to get there. You can't always rely on the folder showing up in the Recent Folders list, so you need to take the navigation bull by its digital horns and add an icon for the location to the Sidebar.

Here are the steps to follow:

1. **Use Finder to navigate to the item that contains the location you want to add to the Sidebar.**

2. **Click the icon for the location.**

3. **Choose File ⇨ Add to Sidebar, or press ⌘+T.** Your Mac adds an icon for the location to the Sidebar.

Another way to add a location to the Sidebar is to click and drag the item's icon and drop it inside the Sidebar.

Genius

153

Removing an icon from the Sidebar

To reduce clutter in the Sidebar and make it easier to navigate, you should remove any icons that you rarely or never use. You have three choices here:

- **Click and drag an icon off the Sidebar and then release it.**

- **Right-click (or Control+click) a Sidebar icon and then click Remove From Sidebar.**

- **Choose Finder ⇨ Preferences and then click the Sidebar tab, shown in figure 6.3.** Deselect the check box beside each item you no longer want in the Sidebar.

Changing the Finder view

Finder offers you several different configurations — or *views* — for displaying the contents of a folder, drive, or network share. These views give you some flexibility in how you see those contents, and each view is useful in different circumstances. There are four views in all:

6.3 In the Sidebar tab of the Finder Preferences, deselect the check box beside each item that you want removed from the Sidebar.

- **Icons.** Choose View ⇨ as Icons (or press ⌘+1 or click the Icons button in the toolbar). This view (see figure 6.4) shows each item as an icon and a label, arranged in rows. This is a good view to use if the folder or drive you're examining has lots of subfolders and files, or if the current location has lots of photos, because this view shows a preview of each photo as the file icon.

- **List.** Choose View ⇨ as List (or press ⌘+2 or click the List button in the toolbar). This view (see figure 6.5) displays the contents as a vertical list that shows, for each item, the icon, name, size, and other data. This is a good view to use if you want to see more information about each item, or if you want to sort the items. To sort, click a column header to get an ascending sort, and click the same header again to switch to a descending sort.

Genius

If you think the icons or the labels are too small, you can adjust their size. Switch to Icons view and then choose View⇨ Show View Options (or press ⌘+J). Click and drag the Icon Size slider to the right to set a larger size, and use the Text Size pop-up menu to choose a larger font size for the labels.

6.4 Finder's Icons view

6.5 Finder's List view

Genius By default, Finder's List view shows four columns: Name, Date Modified, Size, and Kind. To add more columns or to hide an existing column, switch to List view and then choose View ⇨ Show View Options (or press ⌘+J). In the Show Columns section, select the check box beside any column you want to add, and deselect the check box beside any column you want to hide.

- **Columns.** Choose View ⇨ as Columns (or press ⌘+3 or click the Columns button in the toolbar). This view (see figure 6.6) shows a series of columns. The rightmost column shows a preview of the currently selected item; the column second from the right shows the icon and name of each item in the current location; the next column to the right shows the contents of the current location's enclosing folder, and so on. This is a good view to use if you want to see a preview of one or more items in a location, or if you need to quickly navigate between items in the enclosing folder.

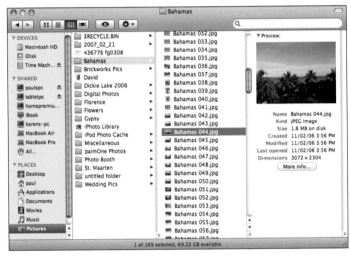

6.6 Finder's Columns view

- **Cover Flow.** Choose View ⇨ as Cover Flow (or press ⌘+4 or click the Cover Flow button in the toolbar). This view (see figure 6.7) shows a split screen, with a List view of the contents on the bottom, and a preview of the current item on the top. The preview includes a scroll bar so that you can easily navigate the items. This is a good view to use if you want to see previews of the items in the current location.

6.7 Finder's Cover Flow view

Genius

By default, Finder opens each location in whatever view is currently selected. However, you can configure your Mac to always open a specific location using a particular view. Navigate to the location and choose the view you want to use. Choose View ⇨ Show View Options (or press ⌘+J), and then select the Always Open in *View* check box, where *View* is the name of the view that you just chose.

Opening multiple Finder windows

Finder usually has only a single window open at a time, but there's nothing stopping you from opening multiple Finder windows. Why would you want to do such a thing? Lots of reasons:

- **You might want to work with the contents of two different folders throughout the day, and it's a hassle to constantly navigate from one to the other.**

- **You might want to compare the contents of two different folders.**

- **You might want to copy or move a file or folder from one location to another.** The easiest way to do that is to open one window for the current location, open a second window for the destination, click and drag the item from the original window, and then drop it inside the destination window.

Whatever the reason, creating a new Finder window is easier done than said: Choose File ⇨ New Finder Window, or press ⌘+N.

By default, when you open a new Finder window, that window displays your user account's Home folder. That's usually a good starting point, but you might prefer to see some other folder in your new Finder windows. To set this up, choose Finder ➪ Preferences, click the General tab, and then use the New Finder windows open pop-up menu to choose a folder.

Working with Files and Folders

When you emigrated from the land of Windows, one of the things you left behind was the concept of the disk drive letter. That's right: no more drive C:, A:, Z:, or whatever. In the Mac world, drives come with names such as "Macintosh HD" and "External Hard Disk." Okay, it's not exactly poetry, but it's a step up.

What you didn't leave behind in your Mac move was the more folder-and-file concept that's fundamental to all personal computing. Just like your Windows PC, your Mac uses folders to store files, so at least in this part of the Mac transition your learning curve is nearly flat. Nearly, but not quite: Your Mac has a few file and folder features and quirks that you won't find in Windows and that you need to know to get the most out of your Mac.

Taking a quick look at a file

When you're looking through a bunch of documents and you're wondering what's inside each file, the filename might help some, but that's not guaranteed. Now, to be sure about the contents of a file, you need to look inside the file. The usual way to do this is to double-click the file to open it in its default application. That works fine enough, but it seems like overkill if all you want to do is take a quick peek at the file, plus it's a hassle because now you've got to close the application when you're done gawking at the file. Repeat that over a dozen files or more, and you can kiss your productivity goodbye.

Fortunately, your Mac offers several methods for getting a peek at a file. For example, you saw in the previous section that the Columns and Cover Flow views offer file previews. Those are great for simple files such as photos, but for more complex files such as word-processing documents and presentations, you might want to see more of the file's contents. That may sound like a tall order, but it's not a problem for the Quick Look feature, which displays the contents of a file in a window without opening the file's default application. Your Mac gives you four ways to preview the selected file with Quick Look:

- **Quickest:** Press the Spacebar.

- **Somewhat quick:** Click the Quick Look icon in Finder's toolbar.

- **Somewhat slow:** Press ⌘+Y.

- **Slowest:** Choose File ➪ Quick Look.

Whichever method you use, your Mac displays the file in a preview window, as shown in figure 6.8. If the document has multiple pages (or slides or whatever), you can use the scroll bar to navigate the document.

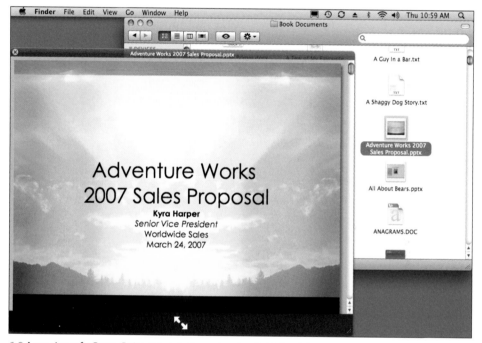

6.8 A preview of a PowerPoint presentation using the Quick Look feature

Genius

The Quick Look window stays on top of any other open window, and you can take advantage of this to quickly preview a bunch of files. Arrange your folder window and the Quick Look window so that you can see the files you want to preview, and then click the files in turn. As you click each file, the Quick Look window remains on-screen and shows a preview of the file. Note, too, that although not every type of file can be opened in Quick Look, you can add plugins for some file types; see www.quicklook plugins.com.

Renaming a file

You know all about renaming files in Windows, I'm sure. You select the file, then choose File ⇨ Rename (or press F2), type the new name, press Enter, and then move on to more productive pursuits. What could be simpler?

Unfortunately, renaming a file in OS X is not only *more complicated* than in Windows, it's actually a lot *harder* (or, at best, a lot less intuitive). That's because you can search the entire Finder interface from coast to coast and you won't find a Rename command anywhere in sight! It's not that your Mac doesn't allow file renaming, it's just that it makes you take a long and winding road to get it done:

1. **Select the file you want to rename.**

2. **Choose File ⇨ Get Info, or press ⌘+I.** The file's Info window appears, and this window shows a number of file details, including the file type, size, and its name and extension, as shown in figure 6.9.

3. **In the Name & Extension text box, edit the file name.**

4. **Close the Info window.**

Yeah, I know: *way* too much work! Fortunately, there's a much easier way:

1. **Select the file you want to rename and then press Return.** Yes, that's right: Return (this is the unintuitive part that I mentioned earlier). OS X adds a text box around the file name.

2. **Edit the filename and then press Return.**

6.9 The Info window shows detailed information about each file.

Creating a file alias

Most of the files you create on your Mac will happily reside in their original folders and you won't have any need to make copies of those files in other folders. However, what if you want to give people access to a copy of a file in, say, your Public folder? Or what if you use a photo on your Web site and you want a copy of the file to appear in both your Pictures folder and the folder you use to store your Web files?

The easiest way to accomplish this is to copy the original file (select it and press ⌘+C) and then paste it in the other folder (press ⌘+V). However, there are a couple of problems with this approach:

- **If you change the original file, you need to copy and paste the file all over again (and vice versa).**

- **The copy uses up disk space.** Although this isn't a big deal for most files, some images, songs, and videos can be tens or hundreds of megabytes, or even several gigabytes in size, so having copies of such files scattered throughout your Mac is wasteful. To help you avoid these problems, your Mac offers the *file alias*, which is a special type of file that does nothing but point to an original file. That is, if you double-click an alias, your Mac locates the original and opens it. This makes Mac aliases very similar to Windows shortcuts.

In other words, instead of copying a file to another location, you create an alias for the file in the other location, instead. Aliases solve both of the problems I mentioned earlier:

- **Because you're always working with the original file, the alias and the original can never have different content.**

- **No matter how large the original file, an alias takes up only between 100KB and 150KB.** That's tiny, so you're free to populate your Mac with as many aliases as you need (or more!).

There are two methods you can use to create an alias:

- **Select the original file and then choose File ⇨ Make Alias (or press ⌘+L).** OS X creates a new icon that uses the name of the original file with "alias" tacked on at the end.

- **Hold down Option and ⌘, click and drag the original file, and then drop it in the destination folder.** OS X creates a new icon that uses the name of the original file.

Notice that the second method creates the alias without appending the word "alias" to the filename. (The exception is when you create the alias in the same folder as the original file, in which case your Mac always adds "alias" to the filename to avoid having two files with the same name in the same folder.) That's a bit tidier, but how will you know the file is an alias? Just look at the icon. As you can see in figure 6.10, OS X staples a tiny arrow to the bottom-left corner of the icon, and that arrow brands the file as an alias.

6.10 You can identify any alias file by looking for the telltale arrow in the lower-left corner of the icon.

161

Note
If you need to rename or move the original file, but you only have the alias in front of you, right-click (or Control+click) the alias, and then click Show Original. Your Mac opens the folder containing the original file and selects the file. Don't worry: even if you rename or move the original, your Mac updates the alias so that it still points to the same file.

Genius
In some cases you may create a new file that you want to use instead of the original. Fortunately, you don't have to create a new alias, too. Instead, you can configure the existing alias to point to the new file. Right-click (or Control+click) the alias, click Get Info, click Select New Original, choose your new file, and then click Choose.

Creating a new folder

If you need a fresh folder to store your files, your Mac makes it easy. Open the containing folder and then use any of the following techniques:

- Choose File ⇨ New Folder.
- Press Shift+⌘+N.
- Right-click (or Control+click) an empty section of the folder and then click New Folder.

You then type the folder name and press Return.

Note
You can create a new folder just about anywhere on your Mac. The major exceptions are the System folder (open Macintosh HD to see the System folder), and the folders for other user accounts on your Mac.

If you find that you do this regularly, follow these steps to add a New Folder icon to Finder's toolbar:

1. **Choose View ⇨ Customize Toolbar.** Finder displays a list of toolbar icons.
2. **Click and drag the New Folder icon and drop it on the toolbar.**
3. **Click Done.**

Performing advanced Spotlight searches

It's probably not much of a stretch to describe Spotlight as one of the Mac's most successful features. It's handy, it's fast, it's accurate, and it's remarkably, even compulsively, useful, which makes it a rousing success in my books. I introduced you to Spotlight's barebones search capabilities in Chapter 3, but Spotlight has got tons of tricks up its electronic sleeve, and you simply can't use Spotlight to its full extent unless you know at least a few of these tricks.

When you type some text into the Spotlight search box, your Mac examines the contents of your files and returns those that include the text you typed. Scouring the contents of files is probably the most common search method you'll want to use, but Spotlight actually offers a lot more ways to search that give you access to some amazingly powerful search capabilities. You can use Spotlight to build complex searches that use file attributes (such as name, file type, audio bit rate, and many more), operators (such as Begins With for text and Is Greater Than for numbers), and Boolean logic (such as AND and OR).

You can do all this from the Spotlight search box, as I'll explain in a second. For now, take a look at how you can build these powerful searches using the Spotlight window:

1. **Open a Finder window:**

   - If you want to search your entire Mac, open any Finder window.

   - If you want to search within a specific folder, open a Finder window and then navigate to that folder.

2. **Choose File ⇨ Find, or press ⌘+F.** Your Mac displays the Spotlight window, as shown in figure 6.11.

6.11 You can use the Spotlight window to run powerful searches.

3. **In the Search section, click where you want to search.** The default is This Mac (your entire Mac), but you can also click the current folder (which appears in quotation marks), or Shared (which searches the shared folders in connected network computers).

4. **Click either Contents (to search within each file) or File Name (to search only the names of your files), and then type your search text in the Spotlight box.**

5. **Use the pane below Search — the one that shows two pop-up menus (with Kind and Any selected in figure 6.11) — to narrow your search by specifying a criterion.** The criterion uses the form *Attribute Operator Value*. Here are the details:

    ● **Attribute.** This is the file attribute you want to search. The default attribute is Kind, which refers to the file type (Folder, JPEG Image, Plain Text, and so on). You can also use the list to select a different attribute such as Last Modified Date. To see the complete list of more than 130 attributes, click the left pop-up menu and then click Other to open the dialog box shown in figure 6.12. Click the attribute you want to search on, and then click OK.

Select a search attribute:				
Attribute	**Description**	**In Menu**		
Album	Title for a collection of media, such as a record album	☐	
Alpha channel	Whether the image has an Alpha channel	☐	
Alternate display na...	Alternate names of the file	☐	
Altitude	The altitude of the item in meters above sea level, expre...	☐	
Aperture	Aperture setting of the camera when the picture was taken	☐	
Audiences	Who the document is intended for	☐	
Audio bit rate	Bit rate of the audio in the media	☐	
Audio encoding appl...	Name of the application that encoded the data in the au...	☐	
Author Email addresses	Email addresses for authors of this item	☐	
Authors	Authors of this item	☐	
Bits per sample	Number of bits per sample	☐	
Channel count	Number of channels in the file's audio data	☐	
City	City of the item	☐	

Cancel   OK

6.12 Spotlight offers more than 130 file attributes for your searches.

Note

If you want to run later searches using this attribute, add it to the Spotlight window's Attribute menu by selecting the In Menu check box associated with the attribute.

● **Operator.** Use this part of the criterion to determine how the attribute and the value (discussed next) relate to each other in the search. With some attributes (such as Kind), the operator is set and you can't change it. For the other attributes, you see a list of operators, and the ones you see depend on the attribute. For example, if the attribute is numeric (such as Audio Bit Rate), you see four operators: Equals, Is Greater Than, Is Less Than, and Is Not.

● **Value.** This is the value you want Spotlight to match when it searches your files. If the attribute can take on only a specific set of values, you see a list of those values; otherwise, you see a text box that you use to specify a search string, number, or date (depending on the attribute).

6. **To add another criterion, click the plus (+) icon on the right side of the Spotlight window.** You can add as many criteria as you want. Figure 6.13 shows the Spotlight window with a few criteria added.

6.13 The Spotlight window with a few criteria on the go.

7. **Repeat Step 6 until you find the file you're looking for.** Note that if you think a criterion is causing the search to fail, you can remove it by clicking the minus (-) icon to its right.

You'll probably use the Spotlight window for your most sophisticated searches, but it's also possible to harness all this search power in the Spotlight search box. You just need to know how to phrase your searches.

To specify a file attribute, use the following syntax:

attribute:value

165

Here, *attribute* is the name of the file attribute you want to search on, and *value* is the value you want to use. For example, if you're searching your music, you can use the following search string to match music where the Audio Bit Rate attribute is 128:

bitrate:128

If the value uses two or more words and you want to match the exact phrase, surround the phrase with quotation marks. For example, the following search string matches music where the Name attribute includes the phrase "rock me":

name:"rock me"

You can also refine your searches with the following operators:

> Matches files where the specified property *is greater than* the specified value. For example, the following code matches pictures where the Item Creation attribute is later than January 1, 2008:

  created:>1/1/2008

>= Matches files where the specified attribute *is greater than or equal to* the specified value. For example, the following code matches files where the Size attribute is greater than or equal to 10000 bytes:

  size:>=10000

< Matches files where the specified attribute *is less than* the specified value. For example, the following code matches pictures where the Modified attribute is earlier than December 31, 1999:

  modified:<12/31/1999

<= Matches files where the specified attribute *is less than or equal to* the specified value. For example, the following code matches files where the Audio Bit Rate attribute is less than or equal to 128 Kbps:

  bitrate:<=128

- Matches files where the specified attribute *is between (and including)* two values. For example, the following code matches files where the Last Opened attribute is between and including August 1, 2008 and August 31, 2008:

  lastused:8/1/2008-8/31/2008

For even more sophisticated searches, you can combine multiple criteria using Boolean operators:

AND Use this operator to match files that meet *all* of your criteria. For example, the following code matches files where the Item Creation attribute is later than January 1, 2008 and the Size attribute is greater than 1000000 bytes:

created:>1/1/2008 AND size:>1000000

OR Use this operator to match files that meet *at least one* of your criteria. For example, the following code matches music where the Genre attribute is either Rock or Blues:

genre:rock OR genre:blues

NOT Use this operator to match files that *do not meet* the criteria. For example, the following code matches pictures where the Kind attribute is not JPEG:

kind:NOT jpeg

Note The Boolean operators AND, OR, and NOT must appear with all-uppercase letters in your query.

How do you know which keywords correspond to each attribute? Well, that's the hard part. To help you out, Table 6.1 lists all of the file attributes that have a corresponding search keyword.

Table 6.1 Keywords Associated with Spotlight's Search Attributes

Attribute	Search Keyword(s)
Album	album
Alpha channel	alpha
Altitude	altitude
Aperture	aperture, fstop
Audiences	audience, to
Audio bit rate	audiobitrate, bitrate
Audio encoding application	audioencodingapplication
Author Email addresses	email, from
Authors	author, from, with, by
Bits per sample	bitspersample, bps

continued

Table 6.1 continued

Attribute	Search Keyword(s)
Channel count	channels
City	city
Codecs	codec
Color space	colorspace
Comment	comment
Composer	composer, author, by
Contact keywords	contactkeyword, keyword
Content created	contentcreated, created
Content Creator	creator
Content modified	contentmodified, modified
Contributors	contributor, by, author, with
Copyright	copyright
Country	country
Coverage	coverage
Created	created
Delivery type	delivery
Description	description, comment
Device make	make
Device model	model
Display name	displayname, name
Due date	duedate
Duration	duration
Editors	editor
Email addresses	email
Encoding software	encodingapplication
EXIF version	exifversion
Exposure mode	exposuremode
Exposure program	exposureprogram
Exposure time	exposuretime
File invisible	invisible
File label	label
File pathname	path
Filename	filename
Flash	flash

Attribute	Search Keyword(s)
FNumber	fnumber, fstop
Focal length	focallength
Fonts	font
General MIDI sequence	ismidi
Group	group
Headline	headline, title
Identifier	id
Instant message addresses	imname
Instructions	instructions
Instrument category	instrumentcategory
Instrument name	instrumentname
ISO speed	iso
Item creation	itemcreated, created
Key signature	keysignature, key
Keywords	keyword
Kind	kind
Last opened	lastused, date
Latitude	latitude
Layers	layer
Longitude	longitude
Lyricist	lyricist, author, by
Max aperture	maxaperture
Media types	mediatype
Metering mode	meteringmode
Modified	modified
Musical genre	musicalgenre, genre
Organizations	organization
Orientation	orientation
Owner	owner
Page height	pageheight
Page width	pagewidth
Pages	pages
Phone number	phonenumber
Pixel height	pixelheight
Pixel width	pixelwidth

continued

Table 6.1 continued

Attribute	Search Keyword(s)
Producer	producer
Profile name	profile
Projects	project
Publishers	publisher
Rating	starrating
Recipient Email addresses	email, to
Recipients	recipient, to, with
Recording date	recordingdate
Red eye	redeye
Resolution height	heightdpi
Resolution width	widthdpi
Rights	rights
Sample rate	audiosamplerate, samplerate
Security method	securitymethod
Size	size
Spotlight comment	spotlightcomment, comment
State or Province	state, province
Stationery	stationery
Streamable	streamable
Subject	subject, title
Tempo	tempo
Text content	intext
Theme	theme
Time signature	timesignature
Title	title
Total bit rate	totalbitrate
Track number	tracknumber
URL	url
Used dates	used, date
Version	version
Video bit rate	videobitrate
Where from	wherefrom
White balance	whitebalance
Year recorded	yearrecorded, year

Genius

To beef up Spotlight with even more metadata, you can download and install Spotlight plugins. See www.apple.com/downloads/macosx/spotlight/.

Setting up a smart folder

A *smart folder* is a kind of virtual folder where the contents depend on the criteria you specify, and your Mac adjusts the contents automatically as your files change. If by my use of the word "criteria" you guessed that smart folders are based on Spotlight searches, give yourself a gold star because that's exactly right. For example, suppose you're working on a long-term project for a customer named Penske, and you have Penske-related data all over your Mac: documents, spreadsheets, e-mail messages, Safari bookmarks, and so on. To gather all that disparate data into a single location, you could create a smart folder based on a full-Mac search of the word "Penske."

Now that you know how to run a sophisticated search using Spotlight, you're ready to create your own smart folders:

1. **In any Finder window, choose File ⇨ New Smart Folder, or press Option+⌘+N.** The New Smart Folder window appears.
2. **Set up the search criteria that define the data you want to appear in your smart folder.** See the section "Performing advanced Spotlight searches."
3. **Click Save.**
4. **Use the Save As text box to type a name for the smart folder.**
5. **Click Save.**

To open your smart folder, open any Finder window, display the Sidebar's Search For items, and then click your smart folder.

Working with Applications on Your Mac

Without applications, your new Mac is basically a large, expensive door stopper. A *good-looking* door stopper, to be sure, but a door stopper nonetheless. Fortunately, your Mac comes with quite a few applications installed, particularly if it came bundled with the iLife suite of programs. In the rest of this chapter, you learn how to add more applications, work with running applications, remove applications you no longer need, and much more.

Installing an application

The good news about installing applications on your Mac is that, at its worst, installing a Mac program is about the same as installing a Windows program, but at its best (which is much more of the time), installing a Mac program is almost laughably easy.

Before I explain, note that you have three ways to begin the installation:

- Insert the application's CD or DVD and the installation program begins automatically.
- Download the application from the Internet.
- Double-click a downloaded file that resides on a network share.

What happens next with the last two methods depends on the type of file you're dealing with:

- **Disk Image file (.dmg).** This is the most common type of download. A Disk Image file is a kind of virtual CD. That is, launching the file is just like inserting a disc: you get an icon on your desktop, the disk image appears in Finder's Sidebar in the Devices section, and the installation program starts automatically. When the install is done, you "eject" the disk image either by clicking the eject button in Finder or by dragging the desktop icon to the Trash.

- **Compressed file (.zip, .sit, .gz, or .tar.gz) or archive file (.tar).** These file types mean that all the program's installation files have been combined into a single download file. Most such files are compressed to speed up the download, and of these by far the most common is the .zip format. You double-click the downloaded file to see the installation files, and then you double-click the program that runs the installation.

Note

The ZIP format is the standard Mac compression format, but it's not the only one. If you download another compressed file type such as Stuffit Archive (.sit), Gzip Compressed Archive (.gz), or Tape Archive Gzip Compressed (.tar.gz), or if you download an archive file such as .tar, your Mac won't know what to do with the file. To fix this, you need a third-party application that can handle such formats. I recommend StuffIt Expander (see www.stuffit.com), which can expand and decode almost any file type that you're likely to come across.

Many Mac installations proceed in the fashion that you're no doubt used to from Windows: You run through a series of dialog boxes that let you choose your install options, and then the installer adds the application to your Mac. In some cases, however, installing the application requires that you do just one thing: Click and drag the application's icon from the install window, and then drop it on your Applications folder. That's it! Installing an application doesn't get any easier than that, and this is one of my favorite Mac features. Figure 6.14 shows an example of such an installer. In this case, all you do is click and drag the Fetch icon and drop it on the Applications folder. Nice!

Switching between running applications

If you've got two or more applications on the go (including Finder, which is always running), you need some way to switch from one application to another. The two most obvious

6.14 Some Mac applications install just by dragging the icon to the Applications folder.

methods are either to click inside an application's window, if you can see it, or to click the application's Dock icon. (Remember that OS X displays a blue dot below the Dock icon of each running application.)

Those techniques work well, but they're not often the handiest. For example, if your hands are near the keyboard, you might prefer to keep them there to make the switch. In that case, your Mac offers you two keyboard techniques for switching applications:

- **Press ⌘+Tab.** This technique switches between the current application and the application you used most recently.

- **Hold down ⌘ and tap the Tab key.** The first time you tap Tab, you see a menu that shows an icon for each running application, as shown in figure 6.15. With each subsequent press of the Tab key, OS X highlights the next icon in the menu. When the application you want is high-

6.15 Hold down ⌘ and tap the Tab key to cycle through the icons of your running applications.

lighted, release ⌘ to switch to that application. This technique is almost identical to the famous Alt+Tab program switching technique in Windows. Note, too, that if you prefer to cycle through the icons from right to left, hold down both Shift and ⌘ and then tap Tab.

Genius

● **Hold down Control and tap the F4 key.** This technique cycles through all the open windows in your running applications. For example, if you have two Safari windows open, you'll see both windows as you tap F4. When the application windows you want are on-screen, release Control to switch to those windows. This technique is similar to the famous Alt+Esc window-switching technique in Windows. If you want to cycle through the windows in the reverse order, hold down both Shift and Control and then tap F4. (Note that for all this to work, your Mac's keyboard must be configured to use F1 through F12 as standard function keys; see Chapter 1 for more info.)

On the other hand (literally!), if you're currently using the mouse, you might prefer a mouse-based technique for switching applications. That's no problem as long as you have a mouse with a scroll wheel in the middle:

Unfortunately, these techniques don't work with the scroll ball on Apple's Mighty Mouse.

Note

● **Tap the scroll wheel.** Use this technique to switch between the current application and the application you used most recently.

● **Press down the scroll wheel and tilt it to one side.** When you press and hold down the scroll wheel, you see the same menu of running application icons as you saw earlier in figure 6.15. Tilt the scroll wheel to the right to cycle through the icons left to right; tilt the scroll wheel to the left to cycle through the icons right to left. When the application you want is highlighted, release the scroll wheel to switch to that application.

If you have two or more windows open in a single application, hold down ⌘ and repeatedly press the backquote key (`) to cycle through the open windows. (Hold down Shift, as well, to cycle the windows in reverse.)

Genius

Hiding an application

If you've got a bunch of applications on the fly, your desktop can end up awfully messy. To reduce the clutter, you can remove an application from the desktop. If you won't need that application for a while, it's best just to quit the program to conserve your Mac's resources. Otherwise, a quick click of the application's Minimize button clears the application from the desktop and displays it as an icon on the right side of the Dock.

Actually, I should say that it clears the application's *window* from the desktop. If the application has other windows open, they remain in place, and you won't be much better off. Ideally, you need a quick way to hide *all* the open windows in an application. Fortunately, your Mac gives you *three* ways to do this:

- Switch to the application and then press ⌘+H.

- Right-click (or Control+click) the application's Dock icon and then click Hide.

- Hold down ⌘ (or both Shift and ⌘), tap the Tab key until the application you want to hide is highlighted in the icon menu, and then press H.

Managing multiple applications with Exposé

It's a rare computer user these days who works with only a couple of applications at a time. Instead, most of us have a veritable army of applications on the march: Finder, Safari, Mail, iTunes, iChat, Address Book, iCal, and who knows what else. Not only that, but in some of those applications you might have a platoon of windows on patrol: You might have two or three Safari windows open, three or four Finder windows open, and so on. What all this means is that most of us have Mac desktops that are stuffed to the edges with windows of various sizes and shapes, and locating the window you want becomes a major headache.

Instead of wasting your day "⌘+Tabbing" or "Control+F4ing" until your fingertips are numb, you should take advantage of one of the nicest features in all of OS X: Exposé. This utility is a window management program that temporarily shrinks all your running windows and then arranges them on your screen so that nothing overlaps. This lets you see at a glance what's in each open window, and then you can select the one you want with a quick click of the mouse.

Best of all, Exposé is ridiculously easy to use: Simply press F9. Exposé quickly shrinks and arranges all the nonminimized windows so that you can see each one, as shown in figure 6.16. You then click the window you want to use, and your desktop goes back to its previous state with your chosen window up front.

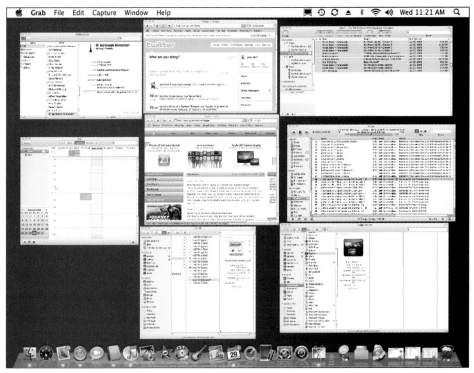

6.16 Press F9 to tell Exposé to arrange your desktop windows so that you can see each one.

Exposé Keyboard Inconsistencies

The Exposé keyboard techniques that I talk about in this section work on most keyboards but, unfortunately, not on all of them. For example, many Mac notebook keyboards don't support the standard Exposé keystrokes, and neither does the Apple Keyboard. If Exposé doesn't kick in when you press F9 (or when you press F10 or F11 to run Exposé's other features, described below), you still have other options.

First, consider configuring your Mac keyboard to use F1 through F12 as standard function keys, as I described in Chapter 1. Alternatively, there is an Exposé key you can use: F3. For F10 and F11 (or even F9, for that matter), you must also hold down the Fn key to run the Exposé features.

Finally, you can configure Exposé to use different keys altogether. Open System Preferences and click the Exposé and Spaces icon. In the Exposé and Spaces preferences, click Exposé and then use the All Windows, Application Windows, and Show Desktop pop-up menus to choose the keys you want to use to run the Exposé features.

That's a pretty cool trick, but Exposé is no one-trick pony. It actually has two other features that you'll use a lot:

- **Press F10 (or Fn+F10).** This tells Exposé to arrange just the open windows in the current application. To see the open windows in the rest of your running applications, tap the Tab key.

- **Press F11 (or Fn+F11).** This tells Exposé to clear all the windows from the desktop. This is one of Exposé's outstanding features because it gives you a super-fast way to see the desktop. Press F11 again to restore the windows to their former stations.

Managing multiple desktops with Spaces

Exposé is a great way to be the boss of desktop clutter, but your Mac offers another feature that lets you open as many applications as you want and avoid desktop clutter altogether! It sounds like pie-in-the-Mac-sky stuff. After all, if you open a bunch of applications, then by definition you must end up with a messy desktop, right? Yes, right, *if* you have only one desktop. However, your Mac offers a feature called Spaces that lets you set up not just a single desktop, but a whole herd of them — up to 16 in all! These are called *spaces* and they act as virtual desktops. The idea is that you configure each space with a single application that has multiple windows, or with multiple applications that are related in some way.

For example, you might have Safari running multiple open windows in one space, your communications applications (Mail, iChat, and so on) in a second space, applications related to a project in a third space, and media applications (iTunes, iPhoto, and so on) in a fourth space. Your Mac makes it easy to switch from one space to another, and you can easily drag windows between spaces.

Here are the steps to follow to enable and configure Spaces:

1. **Choose Apple ⇨ System Preferences.** The System Preferences window appears.
2. **Click Exposé and Spaces**. The Exposé and Spaces window appears.
3. **Click the Spaces tab.**
4. **Select the Enable Spaces check box.** System Preferences enables the rest of the controls, as shown in figure 6.17.

Note I suggest selecting the Show Spaces in menu bar check box. This adds an icon to the menu bar that shows the number of the current space, which helps you get oriented when you're just starting out with Spaces.

6.17 Select the Enable Spaces check box to begin configuring your spaces.

5. To increase the number or layout of the spaces, use the following techniques

- To add a row, click the Rows plus sign (+).

- To add a column, click the Columns plus sign (+).

- To remove a row, click the Rows minus sign (-) and then click OK.

- To remove a column, click the Columns minus sign (-) and then click OK.

6. To assign an application to a space, click + below the Application Assignments list, click an application (or click Other to choose a nonrunning application), and then use the associated Space list to choose which space you want to use. Figure 6.17 shows the Application Assignments list with a few applications added.

7. Adjust the keyboard and mouse shortcuts in the Keyboard and Mouse Shortcuts section if you feel like it.

Assuming you didn't mess around with the default Spaces keyboard shortcuts, here are the basic techniques to use with Spaces:

- **To cycle through your spaces:** Hold down Control and tap the Right Arrow key to cycle the spaces in ascending order; tap the Left Arrow key to cycle the spaces in descending order.

- **To switch to a specific space:** Press Control+*Space*, where *Space* is the number of the space you want to switch to. For example, Control+2 switches to space 2, and Control+0 switches to space 10. (If you have more than 10 spaces, you can't use this technique to switch to spaces 11 and up.)

- **To see all your spaces:** Press F8 to display thumbnail versions of all your spaces, as shown in figure 6.18. Click the space you want to switch to.

Note

As I described earlier with Exposé, many Apple keyboards assign a different feature to F8, so pressing that key may not activate Spaces on your Mac. In that case, you must press Fn+F8 instead, or map a different key to activate Spaces.

6.18 Press F8 to see thumbnail versions of your spaces.

- **To move a window from one space to another:** Press F8 to display the space thumbnails, click and drag the window you want to move, and then drop it inside the new space.

Quitting an application

Quitting an application seems like a no-brainer: Just click the red X in the upper-left corner of the application's window, right? Well, not always. Yes, sometimes this technique *does* quit the application, but in many Mac applications it just closes that window and leaves the application humming along. The only way to be sure you're quitting an application is to switch to that application and then use one of the following methods:

- Choose *Application* ⇨ Quit *Application*, where *Application* is the name of the program.
- Press ⌘+Q.
- Hold down ⌘ (or both Shift and ⌘), tap the Tab key until the application you want to quit is highlighted in the icon menu, and then press Q.

Running widgets using Dashboard

Your Mac comes equipped with about 20 or so mini-applications called *widgets* that perform very specific tasks such as showing the weather, displaying stock quotes, or making simple calculations. Instead of messing up your desktop with these widgets, OS X gives you a separate layer of screen real estate called Dashboard. When you invoke Dashboard, your Mac sends your desktop and its windows into the background, and brings Dashboard and its widget collection into the foreground, as shown in figure 6.19.

To invoke Dashboard, you have three choices:

- **Press F12.** (On Mac keyboards where F12 is mapped to a different function, either press F4 or press Fn+F12.)
- **Click the Dock's Dashboard icon.**
- **Click the scroll ball on Apple's Mighty Mouse.**

With Dashboard on-screen, you can interact with each widget, click and drag the widgets to new locations, and (in some cases) size the widget windows. To change a widget's settings, hover the mouse pointer over the lower-right corner of the widget; if you see a stylized "i" click it to open the settings.

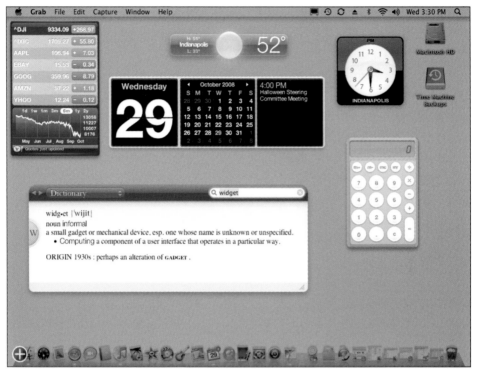

6.19 Dashboard displays your Mac's collection of running widgets.

To customize the collection of displayed widgets, follow these steps:

1. **Display Dashboard.**

2. **Click the plus sign (+) in the lower-left corner of the screen.** Your Mac displays the Widget Bar.

3. **Click and drag the widget you want to add, and drop it on the Dashboard in the position you prefer.**

Note

Apple has hundreds of widgets available on its Web site. To see them, display the Widget Bar and then click Manage Widgets and then click More Widgets. Your Mac uses Safari to open the Dashboard Widgets page. Locate the widget you want and then click Download.

4. **To remove a widget, click the X in the upper-left corner of the widget.**

5. **When you're done, click the X above the Widget Bar to close it.**

When you've finished your widget work, either click the desktop or press F12 to hide Dashboard.

Uninstalling an application

You saw earlier that installing Mac applications is generally pretty easy, and in some cases is almost *too* easy. That is, as former Windows users, we just have to laugh when all it takes to install an application is to merely drag an icon and drop it in the Applications folder!

Amazingly, that level of ease and convenience is also part of the Mac uninstall experience. That is, for 99 percent of all Mac applications, you follow this simple procedure:

1. **Open Finder.**

2. **Choose the Applications folder.**

3. **Click and drag the application's icon, and then drop it on the Dock's Trash icon.** Your Mac uninstalls the application.

Now *that* is easy!

Note

Very occasionally, a Mac application comes with an Uninstall program of its own. This usually means that the application has bits of itself scattered around your Mac's hard disk, so it's a good idea to use that program to uninstall the application. Note, too, that simply tossing an application into the Trash can sometimes leave unused libraries and preference files scattered about your hard disk, which isn't always a good idea. To ensure that your applications are fully uninstalled, use a third-party uninstaller, such as AppTrap (see http://konstochvanligasaker.se/apptrap/).

How Do I Connect and Work with Devices?

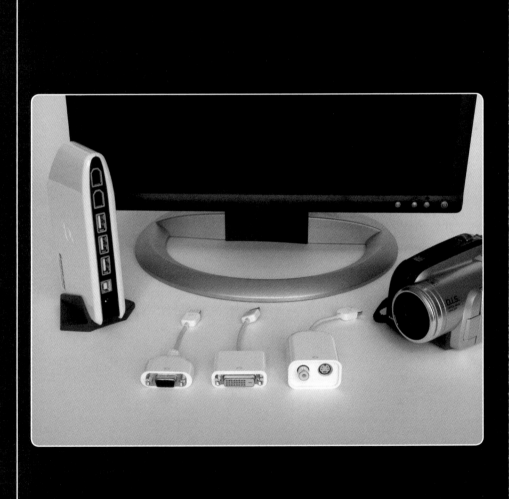

Windows is okay at the whole plug-and-play thing, but Macs take this to a whole new level. Got a new mouse? Just plug it into any free USB port and it's ready to use within seconds. Nice! Unfortunately, there are some devices that are more ornery and require a bit of extra effort on your part to get them connected and configured. In this chapter, I take you through a few such devices, including an iPod, iPhone, external display, digital camera, scanner, camcorder, printer, and Bluetooth devices.

Synchronizing with an iPod

Long gone are the days when the only thing you could fill up your iPod with was music. With modern iPods and the latest version of iTunes, you can cram your players not only with your favorite tunes, but also with music videos, audiobooks, movies, TV shows, podcasts, photos, contacts, calendars, and even games. Suddenly those once-massive 80GB iPods don't look so big anymore. Whatever your iPod's hard drive size, if you find yourself running out of space, the alternative isn't (necessarily) to go out and buy a bigger player. Instead, iTunes gives you lots of options for controlling what gets added to (and removed from) your iPod when you sync.

Genius

If iTunes doesn't fire up automatically when you connect your iPod, you can force it to do so. In iTunes, click your iPod in the Devices list, click the Summary tab, and then select the Open iTunes when this iPod is connected check box. Click Apply to put the setting into effect.

Synchronizing music and videos

iPods are digital music players at heart, so you probably load up your iPod with lots of audio content and, depending on the type of iPod you have, lots of music videos, too. To get the most out of your iPod's music and video capabilities, you need to know all the different ways you can synchronize these items. For example, if you'll be using your iPod primarily as a music player and it has far more disk capacity than you need for all of your digital audio, feel free to throw all your music onto the player. On the other hand, you may have an iPod with a limited capacity, or you may only want certain songs and videos on the player to make it easier to navigate. In such cases, you need to configure the iPod to sync only those songs and videos you want to play.

You can easily tell iTunes to toss every last song and video onto your iPod or just selected playlists. Follow these steps:

1. **In iTunes, click your iPod in the Devices list.**

2. **Click the Music tab.**

3. **Select the Sync music check box.** From this point, the options you select determine what is actually synchronized.

    - Select the Selected playlists option to choose specific playlists to be included, as shown in figure 7.1. If there are videos in any of the selected playlists you do not want synced, deselect the Include music videos check box.

- Select the Include music videos check box to include all music videos.

- Select the Display album artwork on your iPod if you want to see this artwork on your iPod.

4. **Click Apply.** iTunes syncs the iPod using the new settings.

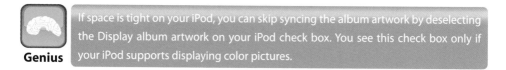

7.1 Select the Selected playlists option and then select the playlists you want to sync.

If you want to control the individual tracks that get synced to your iPod, you can manage your music and videos by hand. One way to do this is to use the check boxes that appear beside each track in your iTunes Music library.

Here's how you do it:

1. **In the Devices list, click your iPod.**

2. **Click the Summary tab.**

3. **Select the Sync only checked songs and videos check box.**

187

4. **Click Apply.** If iTunes starts syncing your iPod, click the Cancel button (the X icon that appears beside the Syncing iPod message).

5. **In the Library list, click Music.** If a track's check box is selected, iTunes syncs the track with your iPod. If a track's check box is deselected, iTunes doesn't sync the track with your iPod; if the track is already on your iPod, iTunes removes the track.

6. **In the Devices list, click your iPod.**

7. **Click the Summary tab.**

8. **Click Sync.** iTunes syncs just the checked tracks.

An alternative method is to drag tracks from the Music library and drop them on your iPod. Here's how this works:

1. **In the Devices list, click your iPod.**

2. **Click the Summary tab and select the Manually manage music and videos check box.** iTunes asks you to confirm.

3. **Click OK, click Apply, and then click Music.**

Genius

For maximum control over manual syncing, you can configure your iPod for syncing checked tracks *and* tracks that you drag and drop. In the Summary tab, select the Sync only checked songs and videos check box before you select the Manually manage music and videos check box.

4. **Select the tracks you want to sync.** For noncontiguous tracks, ⌘+click each track. For contiguous groups, Shift+click the first track, hold down Shift, and then click the last track.

5. **Click and drag the selected tracks to the iPod icon that appears in the Devices list and drop the selected tracks on the iPod icon.** iTunes syncs the selected tracks.

Synchronizing movies

It wasn't all that long ago when technology prognosticators and pundits laughed at the idea of people watching movies on a 2.5-inch screen. Who could stand to watch even a music video on such a tiny screen? The pundits were wrong, of course, because nowadays it's not at all unusual for people to use their iPods to watch not only music videos, but also short films, animated shorts, and even full-length movies.

The major problem with movies is that their file sizes tend to be quite large — even short films lasting just a few minutes weigh in at dozens of megabytes, and full-length movies are several gigabytes. Clearly there's a compelling need to manage your movies to avoid filling up your iPod and leaving no room for the latest album from your favorite band. If you have a video-friendly iPod, follow these steps to configure and run the movie synchronization:

1. **In iTunes, click your iPod in the Devices list.**

2. **Click the Movies tab.**

3. **Select the Sync movies check box.**

4. **Choose what movies you want to sync.** You have three options: All movies, X unwatched movies (where *X* is the number you select), or Selected. Use the Selected option to pick out the specific items you want to sync. Choose either movies or playlists in the list, and then select the check boxes for the items you want to sync. A blue bullet indicates the movie has not been viewed yet.

Note

A movie is unwatched if you haven't yet viewed it either in iTunes or on your iPod. If you watch it on your iPod, the player sends this information to iTunes when you next sync. This is one of the rare examples of information that gets sent to iTunes when you sync an iPod. If you watch a movie but you want to leave it on the iPod during the next sync, you need to mark the movie as new (that is, unwatched). In iTunes, choose the Movies library, Control+click (or right-click) the movie, and then choose Mark as New.

5. **Click Apply.** iTunes syncs the iPod using your new movie settings.

Genius

If you download a music video from the Web and then import it into iTunes (by choosing File ⇨ Import), iTunes adds the video to its Movies library. To display it in the Music library instead, open the Movies library, Control+click (or right-click) the music video, and then click Get Info. Click the Video tab and then use the Kind list to choose Music Video. Click OK. iTunes moves the music video to the Music folder.

Synchronizing TV show episodes

If the average video iPod is at some risk of being filled up by a few large movie files, it probably is at grave risk of being overwhelmed by a large number of TV show episodes. A single half-hour episode eats up approximately 250MB, so even a modest collection of shows consumes multiple gigabytes of precious iPod disk space.

This means it's crucial to monitor your collection of TV show episodes and keep your iPod synced with only the episodes you need. Fortunately, iTunes gives you a decent set of tools to handle this:

1. **In iTunes, click your iPod in the Devices list.**

2. **Click the TV Shows tab.**

3. **Select the Sync check box and choose an option from the drop-down list to specify the episodes you want to sync.**

Note

As with movies, a TV episode is unwatched if you haven't yet viewed it either in iTunes or your iPod. If you watch an episode on your iPod, the player sends this information to iTunes when you next sync. To mark a TV episode as unwatched, in iTunes choose the TV Shows library, Control+click (or right-click) the episode, and then choose Mark as New.

4. **Select one of these options.**

   - **All TV shows.** Select this option to sync all your TV shows with your iPod.

   - **Selected.** Select this option to sync specific TV shows with your iPod. Choose either TV shows or Playlists in the list, and then select the check boxes for the items you want to sync.

5. **Click Apply.** iTunes syncs the iPod using your new TV show settings.

Synchronizing podcasts

In many ways, podcasts are the most problematic of the various media you can sync with your iPod. Not that the podcasts themselves pose any concern. Quite the contrary: They're so addictive that it's not unusual to collect them by the dozens. Why is that a problem? Most professional podcasts are at least a few megabytes in size, and many are tens of megabytes. A large enough collection can put a serious dent in your iPod's remaining storage space.

All the more reason, then, to take control of the podcast-syncing process. Here's how you do it:

1. **In iTunes, click your iPod in the Devices list.**

2. **Click the Podcasts tab.**

3. **Select the Sync check box and choose one of these options from the drop-down menu.**

   • **All podcasts.** Select this option to sync all your podcasts with your iPod.

   • **Selected podcasts.** Select this option to sync specific podcasts with your iPod. Select the check boxes for the items you want to sync.

Note

A podcast episode is *unplayed* if you haven't yet played at least part of the episode either in iTunes or your iPod. If you play an episode on your iPod, the player sends this information to iTunes when you next sync. Even better, your iPod also lets iTunes know if you paused in the middle of an episode; when you play that episode in iTunes, it starts at the point where you left off.

Genius

To mark a podcast episode as unwatched, in iTunes choose the Podcasts library, Control+click (or right-click) the episode, and then choose Mark as New.

4. **Click Apply.** iTunes syncs the iPod using your new podcast settings.

Synchronizing photos

If your iPod can display photos (and all new iPods can), you can use iTunes to synchronize photos between your iPod and either your Pictures folder or iPhoto. Note that Apple supports a number of image file types — the usual TIFF and JPEG formats that you normally use for your photos — as well as BMP, GIF, JPG2000 or JP2, PICT, PNG, PSD, and SGI.

If you use your Mac to process lots of photos, and you want to take copies of some or all of those photos with you on your iPod, then you need to follow these steps to get synced:

1. **In iTunes, click your iPod in the Devices list.**

2. **Click the Photos tab.**

3. **Select the Sync photos from check box and choose an option from the drop-down menu.** In the Sync photos from list, you have three choices:

● **Pictures.** Choose this item to sync the images in your Pictures folder.

● **Choose folder.** Choose this command to sync the images contained in some other folder.

● **iPhoto.** Choose this item to sync the photos, albums, and events you've set up in iPhoto.

4. **Select the photos you want to sync.** The controls you see depend on what you chose in Step 4:

● **If you chose either Pictures or the Choose folder.** In this case, select either the All photos option or the Selected folders option. If you select the latter, select the check box beside each subfolder you want to sync, as shown in figure 7.2.

7.2 To sync photos from specific folders, choose the Selected folders option and then select the check boxes for each folder you want synced.

● **If you chose iPhoto.** In this case, you get three further options: Select the All photos and albums option to sync your entire iPhoto library; select the *X* events option, where *X* is one of the following values that determines the number of iPhoto events that get synced: All, 1 most recent, 3 most recent, 5 most recent, 10 most recent, or 20 most recent; select the Selected albums option and then select the check box beside each album you want to sync.

5. **If you selected either the Selected folders option or the Selected albums option, use your mouse to click and drag the folders or albums to set the order you prefer.**

6. **Click Apply.** iTunes syncs the iPod using your new photo settings.

Note iTunes doesn't sync exact copies of your photos to the iPod. Instead, it creates what Apple calls TV-quality versions of each image. These are copies of the images that have been reduced in size to match the iPod's screen size. This not only makes the sync go faster, but it also means the photos take up much less room on your iPod.

Synchronizing your address book and calendars

I don't know too many people who use their iPod as a PDA (personal digital assistant), and I'd bet not many people even know about the iPod's PDA features. I'm talking, of course, about the iPod's ability to display contact information — for each contact, you see the person's name, job title, company, work phone number, street address, and e-mail address, and optionally the contact's picture — and calendar data, including events and to-do lists.

Still, if you're traveling with your iPod and you need to look up a phone number or get reminded of some important event, why not embrace the technology? This is especially true when you can sync your iPod with contact data from your Mac's Address Book application, and calendar data from your Mac's iCal application.

Follow these steps to sync this data with your iPod:

1. **In iTunes, click your iPod in the Devices list.**

2. **Click the Contacts tab.**

3. **Select the Sync Address Book contacts check box and select an option.**

   - **All contacts.** Select this option to sync all your Address Book contacts.

   - **Selected groups.** Select this option to sync only those groups that have their check box selected.

4. **Select the Include contacts' photos check box if you have photos for some or all of your contacts.**

5. **Select the Sync iCal calendars check box and select an option to add the calendar data as well.** If you want to bypass syncing calendars, deselect the Sync iCal calendars check box and click Apply.

- **All calendars.** Select this option to sync all your iCal calendars.

- **Selected calendars.** Select this option to sync only those calendars that have their check box selected (see figure 7.3).

7.3 You can sync Address Book contacts and iCal calendars with your iPod.

6. **Click Apply.** iTunes syncs the iPod using your new contacts and calendars settings.

Synchronizing games

Listening to tunes is a great way to pass the time, but sometimes you need more to keep yourself occupied. If you find yourself in a long lineup or otherwise delayed without a book in sight, perhaps a rousing game of Tetris would interest you. Fortunately, that's a lot easier to do now that the iTunes Store is selling quite a few games designed for the iPod screen. You can get old favorites such as Pac-Man, Sonic the Hedgehog, Solitaire, Mahjong, and, yes, Tetris, as well as newer pastimes such as Sudoku, Lost, and Brain Challenge.

Once you purchase a game or three from the iTunes Store, follow these steps to sync them to your iPod:

1. **In iTunes, click your iPod in the Devices list.**

2. **Click the Games tab.**

3. **Select the Sync games check box and select an option.**

    ● **All games.** Select this option to sync all your games.

    ● **Selected games.** Select this option to sync only specific games. Click those you want to sync (a check box appears), as shown in figure 7.4.

4. **Click Apply.** iTunes syncs the iPod using your new games settings.

7.4 To sync specified games, select the Selected games option and then select the check boxes for each game you want synced.

195

Synchronizing with an iPhone

Synchronizing your Mac and your iPhone (or your iPod touch) is nearly identical to synchronizing your Mac and your iPod. Your iPhone stores much of the same types of data as the iPod, including music, photos, videos, TV shows, movies, Address Book contacts, and iCal calendars. The iPhone can also sync your Mac's Mail accounts, Safari bookmarks, and iTunes ringtones. As with an iPod, when you connect your iPhone, your Mac starts iTunes automatically and runs the synchronization.

Note

If you'd prefer that iTunes not start the iPhone sync automatically, click your iPhone in iTunes' Devices list, click the Summary tab, and then deselect the Automatically sync when this iPhone is connected check box.

Customizing the iPhone sync is nearly identical to customizing the iPod sync as described in the section "Synchronizing with an iPod," so I won't go into the details again. Here are the basic steps to follow to set up a custom iPhone sync:

1. **Connect your iPhone to your Mac, if you haven't yet done so.**

2. **In iTunes' Devices list, click your iPhone.**

3. **Click the Info tab.**

4. **If you want to sync with your Mac Address Book, select the Sync Address Book contacts check box, and then select either All contacts or Selected groups.**

5. **If you want to sync with your Mac calendars, select the Sync iCal calendars check box, and then select either All calendars or Selected calendars.**

6. **If you want to sync with your Mac e-mail accounts, select the Sync selected Mail accounts check box, and then select the accounts you want to sync.**

7. **If you want to sync with your Mac bookmarks, select the Sync Safari bookmarks check box.**

Genius

By default, if iTunes comes across data on the iPhone that's the same as data on your Mac, it does *not* replace the iPhone data. To change this, click the Info tab, scroll down to the Advanced section, and then select the check box beside each type of data you want iTunes to replace on the iPhone: Contacts, Calendars, Mail Accounts, or Bookmarks.

8. **Click the Ringtones tab.** If you want to sync with your Mac's iTunes ringtones, select the Sync ringtones check box, and then select either All ringtones or Selected ringtones.

9. **Click the Music tab.** If you want to sync with your Mac's iTunes music, select the Sync music check box, and then select either All songs and playlists or Selected playlists.

10. **Click the Photos tab.** If you want to sync with your Mac's photos, select the Sync photos from check box, choose a location (such as iPhoto), and then select the photos, events, or albums you want to sync.

11. **Click the Podcasts tab.** If you want to sync with your Mac's iTunes podcasts, select the Sync check box, choose which episodes you want to sync, and then select either All podcasts or Selected podcasts.

12. **Click the Video tab.**

    • **If you want to sync with your Mac's iTunes TV shows.** Select the Sync check box in the TV Shows section, choose what episodes you want to sync, and then select either All TV shows or Selected TV shows.

    • **If you want to sync with your Mac's iTunes movies.** Select the Sync movies check box, and then select the movies you want to sync.

13. **Click the Applications tab.** If you want to sync with your Mac's downloaded App Store applications, select the Sync check box and then select either All applications or Selected applications

14. **Click Apply.**

Using an External Display

If you have an extra external display — a monitor, television set, or projector — kicking around, you can connect it to your Mac in various scenarios:

• **As a new desktop monitor.** You can use the external display as a replacement for the monitor that came with your desktop Mac.

• **As a notebook alternative.** You can use the external display instead of the built-in monitor on your Mac notebook.

• **As a desktop extension.** You can use the external display to extend the desktop of your Mac. To do this with a Power Mac G5, you need to either add a second graphics card, or replace the existing graphics card with one that supports two monitors.

Fortunately, all of these connection types are plug-and-play (meaning once you plug in and turn on the external display, your Mac recognizes the new device right away). That's the good news. The bad news is that although using an external monitor is plug-and-play, the *plug* part isn't as straight-forward as you might like because there are many different ways to connect a Mac and a display. The next few sections provide you with the details you need to make things happen.

Understanding external display connections

To connect your Mac and an external display, you have to know the various ways these connec-tions can occur. For starters, you get familiar with the five main connector types: DVI, Mini-DVI, Micro-DVI, VGA, and video.

DVI connections

The standard video connection type on modern-day Macs is called DVI (digital video interface), which is now common on most LCD monitors and on some televisions and projectors. That sounds simple enough, and it is — on the Mac side. Unfortunately, external displays such as LCD monitors and televisions can use different DVI connectors. There are actually three types:

- **DVI-A.** This connector works with only analog signals (see figure 7.5).

7.5 A DVI-A connector

- **DVI-D.** This connector works with only digital signals and it comes in single-link and dual-link versions (see figure 7.6).

7.6 DVI-D single-link (left) and dual-link (right) connectors

DVI-I. This connector works with both analog and digital signals and comes in single-link and dual-link versions (see figure 7.7). Mac Pros, MacBook Pros, Mac Minis, and Power Mac G5s all use the DVI-I dual-link connector, as do some versions of the PowerBook G4.

Note What's the difference between single-link and dual-link? DVI uses a transmitter to send information along the cable. A single-link cable uses one transmitter, and a dual-link cable uses two transmitters. This means that dual-link connections are faster and offer a better signal quality than single-click connections.

7.7 DVI-I single-link (left) and dual-link (right) connectors

As you can see, each type of DVI connector uses a slightly different pin arrangement, so when you're matching your external display, DVI cable, and Mac, you need to make sure that they all use the same type of DVI connector.

Mini-DVI connections

The Intel-based iMac, the MacBook, and most 12-inch PowerBook G4s don't use regular DVI connectors. Instead, they use a different connec- tor called a Mini-DVI, shown in figure 7.8.

To connect your Mac's Mini-DVI port to a DVI port on an external dis- play, you must purchase at least the Apple Mini-DVI to DVI Adapter. I say *at least* because the Mini-DVI to DVI Adapter uses a DVI-D connec- tor. This is either good news or bad news depending on your external display port:

7.8 A Mini-DVI connector

 DVI-D port. This is good because it probably means you have a DVI-D cable, which connects to both the adapter and the dis- play. In this case, the adapter is all you need.

199

A dual-link DVI connector plugs into (and works with) a single-link DVI port. Unfortunately, the reverse isn't true: that is, you can't plug a single-link DVI connector into a dual-link DVI port. Note, too, that a DVI-D connector can plug into a DVI-I port, but a DVI-I connector won't fit into a DVI-D port.

- **DVI-I port.** This isn't so good because it probably means you have a DVI-I cable, and that cable won't fit the adapter's DVI-D connector. In this case, the adapter on its own won't cut it. To solve the problem, you either need to buy a DVD-D cable, or hunt down a DVI-D to DVI-I adapter so you can use your DVI-I cable.

Note

In high-tech cable and port connections jargon, a connector with pins is described as *male* and a connector with holes is described as *female*. The Apple Mini-DVI to DVI Adapter has a female DVI connector, which means you can't plug it directly into an external display's DVI port, given it is also female. In other words, you need to run a DVI cable — which is male on both ends — between the adapter and your external display.

Micro-DVI connections

The MacBook Air uses yet another type of connection for external displays. It's called Micro-DVI, and it's shown in figure 7.9 (it's the port on the right).

— Micro-DVI port

7.9 The MacBook Air comes with a Micro-DVI port for connections to external displays.

To connect MacBook Air's Micro-DVI port to a DVI port on an external display, use the Micro-DVI to DVI adapter that comes with the MacBook Air package. (If you can't find yours, you can buy one from the Apple Store or a Mac dealer for about $19.)

VGA connections

All CRT monitors and many LCD monitors and projectors come with a VGA connector, shown in figure 7.10.

To connect your Mac to an external display that offers only a VGA connector, you have two choices depending on your connector:

7.10 VGA connectors are standard on CRTs and common on LCDs.

- **DVI connector.** Get the Apple DVI to VGA Display Adapter.

- **Mini-DVI connector.** Get the Apple Mini-DVI to VGA Adapter.

- **Micro-DVI connector.** Get the Apple Micro-DVI to VGA Adapter.

Note Older Mac models such as the iMac G5, iBook, eMac, and some 12-inch PowerBook G4s come with a Mini-VGA port. To connect a VGA external display to any of these Macs, purchase the Apply VGA Display Adapter, which offers a Mini-VGA connector on one end and a VGA connector on the other.

Video connections

If your external display is a television or projector (or even a VCR), it likely has either a Composite (yellow RCA) connector or an S-Video connector; both are shown in figure 7.11.

To connect your Mac to an external display that only offers either Composite or S-Video connectors, you have two choices depending on your connector:

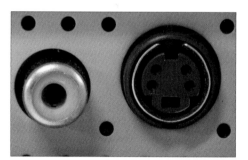

7.11 Composite (left) and S-Video (right) connectors are common on televisions, projectors, and VCRs.

- **DVI connector.** Get the Apple DVI to Video Adapter.

- **Mini-DVI connector.** Get the Apple Mini-DVI to Video Adapter.

- **Micro-DVI connector.** Get the Apple Micro-DVI to Video Adapter.

Setting the external display mode

The hard part about using an external display is getting the correct cables and adapters and ensuring they fit into the appropriate connectors on both your Mac and on the display. Once you've got that set, however, the rest is a breeze because as soon as you connect the external display and turn it on, your Mac recognizes it and starts using it. That's more like it!

How you use the external display depends on what you want to do with it. Your Mac gives you two choices:

- **Video mirroring.** This external display mode means that the same image that appears on the Mac's main or built-in display also appears on the external display. This is useful if you want to use a larger monitor to work with your Mac notebook, or if you want to show the desktop on a projector so that other people can see it.

- **Extended desktop mode.** This mode means that your Mac's desktop is extended onto the external display. This is useful if you need more screen real estate to display your programs. For example, you can have your main application open on one display and an application that you're monitoring — such as Mail, iChat, or Safari — on the other display.

To switch between these external display modes, follow these steps:

1. **Click System Preferences in the Dock.** The System Preferences window appears.

2. **Click the Displays icon.** The display preferences appear, and you see one set of preferences for each screen. Figure 7.12 shows the preferences for the main display, and a similar window appears for the secondary display.

3. **Click the Arrangement tab to select the external display mode.**
   - To turn on video mirroring, select the Mirror Displays check box.
   - To turn on extended desktop mode, deselect the Mirror Displays check box.

7.12 The preferences for the main display. A similar window appears with preferences for the secondary display.

4. **If you turned on extended desktop mode, use the objects in the Arrangement tab to configure the screen layout (see figure 7.13).** To set the relative screen positions, click and drag the screen icon to the positions you prefer. To set the location of the menu bar, click and drag the white strip to the screen you prefer.

7.13 Use the objects in the Arrangement tab to configure the screen layout in extended desktop mode.

Genius

After you connect your external display, you should calibrate the display so that the colors of images appear correctly. To calibrate a display, open System Preferences, click Displays, select the Color tab, and then click Calibrate. This launches the Apple Display Calibrator Assistant, which takes you step by step through the calibration process.

Connecting Imaging Devices

Your Mac is a graphics powerhouse, so you should take advantage of that power by connecting various imaging devices, including digital cameras, digital camcorders, and document scanners. Most of these devices connect without a hassle, but there are a few things to watch out for, and a few extra steps you need to follow to make sure each works as it should. In the next few sections, I take you through all this, as well as show you how to set up a camcorder or digital camera as a Webcam.

Connecting an imaging device

Connecting an imaging device to your Mac is mostly a straightforward bit of business that begins by attaching the device:

- **Digital camera.** Attach a USB cable to the camera and to a free USB port on your Mac.

- **Digital camcorder.** Attach a FireWire cable to the video camera and to a FireWire port on your Mac.

Caution

Most FireWire-compatible digital camcorders are compatible with Macs, but not all. For example, most Sony digital camcorders don't work with Macs. If you're looking to buy a camcorder, do some research on the Web to make sure the camera you want is Mac-friendly.

- **Scanner.** Attach a USB cable to the scanner and to a free USB port on your Mac. Note, too, that you must also install the software that came with the scanner. This installs the scanner device driver as well as the scanning application — sometimes called the TWAIN software — that operates the scanner.

For most digital cameras and camcorders, your Mac immediately connects to the device and perhaps even offers to download images (via iPhoto) or video (via iMovie). However, with some cameras and most scanners, you need to perform some extra steps to complete the connection:

1. **In Finder, choose Applications ⇨ Image Capture.** The Image Capture program appears.

2. **Choose Devices ⇨ Browse Devices (or press ⌘+B).** Image Capture displays a list of available devices.

3. **If necessary, double-click the branch containing the device you want to connect.** For example, to connect a scanner, open the TWAIN devices branch.

4. **Choose the device you want to work with.**

5. **If you're working with a scanner, select the Use TWAIN software check box to use the device's application to scan images rather than Image Capture.**

6. **Connect the device.**

   ● **OS X Leopard.** Select the check box in the device's Connected column.

   ● **Earlier versions of OS X.** Click the Connect button.

Connecting to a network imaging device

When you set up a network for your Macs, you might expect to share devices such as a printer and a DVD drive, but did you know that you can also share imaging devices? This is a great feature because it enables you to view and download a camera's pictures, import a camcorder's video, or operate a scanner, all without having any of these devices connected directly to your Mac, but to another Mac on your network. Follow these steps to connect to a shared imaging device:

1. **In Finder, choose Applications ⇨ Image Capture.** The Image Capture program appears.

2. **Choose Devices ⇨ Browse Devices (or press ⌘+B).** Image Capture displays a list of available devices.

3. **Double-click the Remote Image Capture devices branch.**

4. **Double-click the branch that contains the imaging device you need.**

5. **Choose the device you want to work with.**

6. **Connect the device.**

   ● **OS X Leopard.** Select the check box in the device's Connected column.

   ● **Earlier versions of OS X.** Click the Connect button.

Sharing an imaging device

If you have a digital camera, digital camcorder, or scanner connected to your Mac, you can share that device with your network pals.

How you go about this is quite a bit different in OS X Leopard than in earlier versions of OS X, so I'll treat them separately. First, here's how to do it in Leopard:

1. **In Finder, choose Applications ⇨ Image Capture.** The Image Capture program appears.

2. **Choose Devices ⇨ Browse Devices (or press ⌘+B).** Image Capture displays a list of available devices.

3. **Click Sharing.**

4. **Select the Share my devices check box.**

5. **For each device you want to share, select the check box in the device's Shared column.**

6. **Edit the Shared name if you feel like it.**

7. **If you want folks to enter a password to use the devices, select the Password check box and then type your password.**

8. **Click OK. The Image Capture Device Browser window now appears with a Shared column.**

Now here are the steps for sharing an imaging device in earlier versions of OS X:

1. **In Finder, choose Applications ⇨ Image Capture.** The Image Capture program appears.

2. **Choose Image Capture ⇨ Preferences.** The Image Capture Preferences dialog box appears.

3. **Click the Sharing tab.**

4. **Select the Share my devices check box.**

5. **Select the check box for each device you want to share.**

6. **Edit the Shared name, if so desired.**

7. **If you want to protect your devices with a password, select the Password check box and then type your password.**

8. **Click OK.**

Connecting a Printer

Nine times out of ten — it's probably more like 99 times out of 100 — connecting a printer to your Mac is a no-brainer: You plug it in to the USB port, turn it on, and presto! Your Mac and your printer have already become fast friends and you can start printing right away. How can you be sure? There are a couple of ways to tell:

- **In any application that supports printing, choose File ⇨ Print.** In the dialog box that appears, you should see your printer's name in the Printer list.

- **Click System Preferences in the Dock, and then click Print & Fax.** In the Print & Fax preferences that appear, you should see your printer's name in the Printers list.

Genius

One of the things that OS X does that can be impractical at times is set the default printer to whatever printer you used or added most recently. To fix this, choose System Preferences ⇨ Print & Fax, and then use the Default Printer list to choose the printer you want to use as the default.

Connecting a printer manually

What happens on those rare occasions when your Mac doesn't recognize your printer? In that case, you need to do a bit more legwork and install the printer manually. Here's how it's done:

1. **Connect and turn on the printer if you haven't done so already.**

2. **Click System Preferences in the Dock, click Print & Fax, and then click the + icon.** Your Mac displays the list of connected printers.

Note

You can also display the list of connected printers from any application that supports printing. Choose File ⇨ Printer, open the Printer list, and then select Add Printer.

3. **Choose your printer.**

   - If your printer shows up in the Printer Browser's list of available printers, simply choose it from the list.

   - If you don't see your printer in the list, you need to install the printer driver by hand as follows:

207

1   Insert the disc that came with your printer.

2   Choose Other in the Print Using list.

3   Open the printer disc (or the folder where you downloaded the printer driver), choose the printer driver, and then click Open.

4. **In the Print Using list, choose Select a driver to use and then choose your printer in the list that appears.**

5. **Click Add.** Your printer is now connected.

Genius

If you don't have a printer disc, or if the disc doesn't contain Mac drivers, visit the printer manufacturer's Web site and download the drivers you need. If you can't get drivers for the printer (annoyingly, many printer manufacturers don't bother writing Mac drivers), you may still be able to use the printer by choosing Generic PostScript Printer in the Print Using list.

Adding a shared network printer

If your Mac is part of a network, one of the big advantages you have is that you can connect a printer to one computer, and the other computers on the network can then use that computer for printing. That saves you big bucks because you don't have to supply each computer with its own printer.

To use a shared network printer, you must first add it to your Mac's list of printers. Follow these steps if the printer is shared on another Mac (see the next section for Windows printers):

1. **Click System Preferences in the Dock, click Print & Fax, and then click the + icon.** Your Mac displays the list of connected printers.

2. **In the Printer Browser's list of printers, select the shared printer you want to use.** There are two ways to recognize a shared printer.

   • **OS X Leopard.** The Kind column displays Bonjour Shared, as shown in figure 7.14.

7.14 In OS X Leopard, look for Bonjour Shared in the Kind column.

- **Earlier versions of OS X.** The Connection column displays Shared Printer.

3. **Click Add.** You can now use a shared network printer.

Adding a shared Windows network printer

If the shared printer you want to use is part of a Windows network, follow these steps to add it to your Mac's list of printers:

1. **Click System Preferences in the Dock, click Print & Fax, and then click the + icon.**
   Your Mac displays the Printer Browser.

2. **Display the list of Windows workgroups on your network.**
   - **OS X Leopard.** Click the Windows tab.
   - **Earlier versions of OS X.** Click More Printers and then use the top list to select Windows Printing.

3. **Choose the workgroup that contains the computer you want to work with.**

4. **Click the computer with the shared printer you want to add.**

5. **Log on to the Windows computer.**

6. **Click the shared printer you want to use.**

7. **In the Print Using list, choose Select a driver to use and then choose the printer in the list that appears.** Figure 7.15 shows an example.

8. **Click Add.** You can now use a shared printer on a Windows network.

7.15 You can add a shared printer from a Windows computer.

Connecting Bluetooth Devices

In theory, connecting Bluetooth devices should be criminally easy: You turn on each device's Bluetooth feature — in Bluetooth jargon, you make the devices *discoverable* — bring them within 33 feet of each other, and they connect without further ado. In practice, however, there's usually at least a bit of further ado (and sometimes plenty of it). This usually takes one or both of the following forms:

● **Making your device discoverable**. Unlike Wi-Fi devices that broadcast their signals constantly, most Bluetooth devices broadcast their availability only when you say so. This makes sense in many cases because you usually want to use a Bluetooth device such as a mouse or keyboard with only a single computer. By controlling when the device is discoverable, you ensure that it works only with the computer you want it to.

● **Pairing your Mac and the device.** As a security precaution, many Bluetooth devices need to be *paired* with another device before the connection is established. In most cases, the pairing is accomplished by your Mac generating an 8-digit *passkey* that you must then type into the Bluetooth device (assuming, of course, that it has some kind of keypad). In other cases, the device comes with a default passkey that you must enter into your Mac to set up the pairing. Finally, some devices set up an automatic pairing using an empty passkey.

Connecting a Bluetooth mouse or keyboard

Having a wireless mouse and keyboard is a blissful state because, with no cord to tie you down, it gives you the freedom to interact with your Mac from just about anywhere. Wi-Fi mice and keyboards are often cumbersome because they require a separate transceiver, and these tend to be large and take up a USB port. If your Mac already has Bluetooth, however, you don't need anything else to use a Bluetooth-compatible mouse or keyboard.

Follow these general steps to connect a Bluetooth mouse or keyboard:

1. **Click the Bluetooth status icon in the menu bar, and then choose Set up Bluetooth Device.** The Bluetooth Setup Assistant appears.

Note

You can also choose System Preferences ⇨ Bluetooth to open the Bluetooth window, and then click Set Up New Device. If the Bluetooth window shows that you already have at least one Bluetooth device set up, you start the Bluetooth Setup Assistant by clicking the + icon below the device list.

2. **Click Continue.** The Select Device Type dialog box appears.

3. **Select the option for the device you want to connect and then click Continue.** If the mouse or keyboard has an on/off switch, turn it on. If the mouse or keyboard has a separate switch or button that makes it discoverable, turn on that switch or press that button. When the Bluetooth Setup Assistant discovers the device, it displays the device name, as shown in figure 7.16.

7.16 When the Bluetooth Setup Assistant discovers a Bluetooth device, it displays the device name.

4. **Click Continue.** Your Mac connects with the mouse or keyboard. When your Mac connects with the keyboard, the Bluetooth Setup Assistant displays a passkey for the pairing, as shown in figure 7.17. Using the Bluetooth keyboard, type the passkey and then press Return.

5. **Click Quit and you are ready to use your Bluetooth mouse or keyboard.**

Note

When your Mac wakes from sleep mode, the Bluetooth mouse doesn't always respond right away. Wait a few seconds (usually no more than about 10 seconds) to give the mouse time to reestablish itself. Sometimes clicking the mouse helps it to reconnect right away.

211

7.17 To establish a pairing with a Bluetooth keyboard, you need to type a passkey on the keyboard.

Configuring your Bluetooth mouse and keyboard

When you connect a Bluetooth mouse and/or keyboard, in most cases you just go ahead and start mousing and typing. However, your Mac does give you a limited set of configuration options, and it also enables you to monitor the battery levels of these devices.

To change the configuration options, display the Keyboard & Mouse preferences by clicking the Dock's System Preferences icon, and then clicking the Keyboard & Mouse icon. From there click the Bluetooth tab, shown in figure 7.18.

You can use the Name text boxes to rename the devices, if desired. Or, use the Battery Level icons to monitor the current battery level for each device. You can also decide to have your Mac wake from sleep mode by tapping the keyboard or clicking the mouse. Simply select the Allow Bluetooth devices to wake this computer check box.

7.18 Use the Bluetooth tab to rename your device and monitor the battery level.

Connecting a Bluetooth headset

If you want to listen to music, headphones are a great way to go because the sound is often better than with the built-in Mac speakers, and no one else around gets subjected to Led Zeppelin at top volume. Similarly, if you want to conduct a voice chat, a headset (a combination of headphones for listening and a microphone for talking) makes life easier because you don't need a separate microphone, and at least one half of your conversation remains private. Add Bluetooth into the mix, and you've got an easy and wireless audio solution.

Follow these general steps to connect a Bluetooth headset:

1. **Launch the Bluetooth Setup Assistant.**

   - Click the Bluetooth status icon in the menu bar, and then choose Set up Bluetooth Device.

   - Choose System Preferences ⇨ Bluetooth to open the Bluetooth window, and then click Set Up New Device.

Note

If the Bluetooth window shows that you already have at least one Bluetooth device set up, you start the Bluetooth Setup Assistant by clicking the + icon below the device list.

2. **Click Continue.** The Select Device Type dialog box appears.

3. **Select the Headset option and then click Continue.** If the headset has a separate switch or button that makes the device discoverable, turn on that switch or press that button. Wait until you see the correct headset name appear in the list.

4. **Click Continue.** Your Mac connects with the headset and the Bluetooth Setup Assistant prompts you for the headset's default passkey to establish the pairing.

5. **See the headset document to get the passkey (it's often 0000); type the passkey and then click Continue.**

6. **Click Quit and the headset is ready to use.**

Using Bluetooth headphones for sound output

When you connect Bluetooth headphones, your Mac doesn't automatically use them as the default sound output device. If you want to listen to, say, your iTunes library without disturbing your neighbors, then you need to configure your Mac to use your headphones as the sound output device. Here's how:

1. **Click the System Preferences icon in the Dock.** The System Preferences window appears.

2. **Click the Sound icon.** The Sound preferences appear.

3. **Click the Output tab, and then select your Bluetooth headphones from the list.**

4. **Adjust the other sound settings as desired.**

Setting up a Bluetooth headset for voice chat

If you love to chat, typing messages back and forth is a fun way to pass the time. However, if you want to take things up a notch, you need to use iChat's voice chat capabilities, which enable you to have voice conversations with your buddies. When you connect to a Bluetooth headset, your Mac usually sets up the headset as the voice chat microphone, but it usually doesn't set up the headphones as the sound output device. Follow these steps to configure voice chat to use your Bluetooth headset:

1. **Click the Dock's iChat icon and choose iChat ⇨ Preferences from the menu that appears.**

2. **Click the Audio/Video tab.**

3. **Select your Bluetooth headset from the Microphone and Sound Output lists.**

Genius

If your buddies often tell you to stop shouting, even though you're using your normal voice, you'll need to make a quick volume adjustment. In the Audio chat window, you can click and drag the volume slider to the left. To set the global volume level, choose System Preferences ⇨ Sound and then click the Input tab. Click and drag the Input volume slider to the left to reduce the volume.

215

How Do I Perform Mac Maintenance?

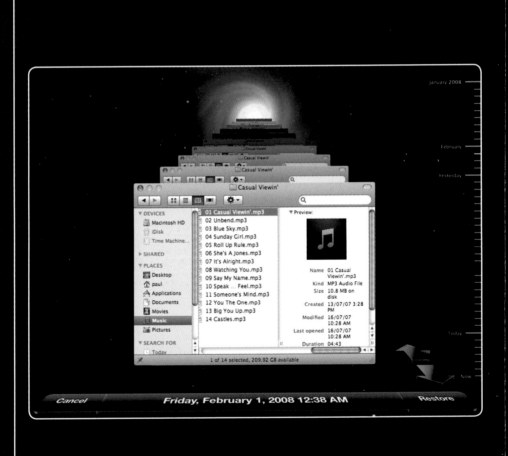

Unlike what you're probably used to with your old Windows computers, your Mac just works; and it is far less likely to head south on you than most. However, all computers are complex beasts, and your Mac is as complex as they come. Its excellent design and engineering ensure a mostly trouble-free operation, but it doesn't hurt to do a little preventative maintenance. The techniques addressed in this chapter help ensure your Mac and the precious data it holds are far less likely to run into trouble.

Routine Mac Maintenance

Get your maintenance chores off to a solid start by examining a few tasks that I describe as *routine*, meaning you ought to perform them regularly to help keep your Mac running smoothly.

Emptying the Trash

You might not give a whole lot of thought to the Trash icon that's a permanent resident on the right edge of the Dock. You delete something, your Mac dutifully tosses it into the Trash, and you move on with your life.

However, while you're busy with other things, the Trash is slowly expanding with each new deleted file or folder. After a while, the Trash might contain several *gigabytes* worth of data. What's the big deal, right? It's just the Trash for goodness sake! Ah, but the Trash is actually a folder on your Mac hard disk. (It's a hidden folder located at /Users/*You*/.Trash, where *You* is your user folder name.) So the more space the Trash takes up, the less space you have to store episodes of your favorite shows.

To see just how much space the Trash is occupying, follow these steps:

1. **Control+click (or right-click) the Trash icon in the Dock.**

2. **Click Open.** The Trash folder appears.

3. **Choose File ⇨ Get Info.** You can also click the Action icon and then click Get Info, or press ⌘+I. The Trash Info window appears.

4. **Read the Size value.**

In figure 8.1, you can see that the Trash contains a whopping 3.22GB of data.

So it makes sense to empty the Trash relatively often, perhaps once a month or once every two months, depending on how often you delete things. Here's the safe method of taking out the Trash:

8.1 The Trash Info window tells you how much hard disk space the Trash is currently using.

1. **Control+click (or right-click) the Trash icon in the Dock.**

2. **Click Open.**

Caution

Examining the contents of the Trash is crucial because once you empty the Trash, there's no turning back the clock — all those files are permanently deleted and there is nothing you can do to get any of them back.

3. **Examine the Trash files to make sure there's nothing important that you deleted by accident.**

4. **If you see a file that you don't want deleted, click and drag the file and drop it on the Desktop for now.** After you're done emptying the Trash, you can figure out where the rescued file is supposed to go.

5. **Choose Finder ⇨ Empty Trash.** You can also click the Empty button or press Shift+⌘+Delete. Your Mac asks you to confirm.

6. **Click OK.**

Now I don't know about you, but after being so careful about making sure I'm not permanently deleting anything important, it bugs me that my Mac asks if I'm sure I want to go through with it. Of course, I'm sure! Fortunately, there are a couple of ways to work around this.

The easiest is to hold down the Option key while you choose Finder ⇨ Empty Trash or click the Empty button. If your fingers are limber enough, you can also press Option+Shift+⌘+Delete.

A more long-term solution is to tell your Mac not to bother with the confirmation message at all. Here are the steps to follow to turn off this message:

1. **In any Finder window, choose Finder ⇨ Preferences.** The Finder Preferences window appears.

2. **Click the Advanced icon.**

3. **Deselect the Show warning before emptying the Trash check box, which is shown checked in figure 8.2.** Note, too, that if you have Leopard (OS X 10.5) you can also select the Empty Trash securely check box to force your Mac to always overwrite files with gibberish data when you remove them from the Trash.

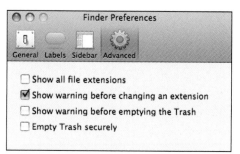

8.2 To get rid of your Mac's Trash confirmation prompts, deselect the Show warning before emptying the Trash check box.

Genius

Rather than try to remember to empty the Trash regularly, a program called Compost can do it for you. You can configure Compost to remove from the Trash any files that are older than a specified number of days or weeks. You can also set up Compost to impose a maximum size on the Trash, so you never have to worry about it taking over your hard disk. Download Compost from www.apple.com/downloads/macosx/system_disk_utilities/compost.html. Note that this is a free trial version that you can use for 30 days (after which you need to pay $19.95 to keep using the program).

Cleaning up your Desktop

The Mac Desktop is a handy place to store things, and most Mac users aren't shy about doing just that, so they end up with dozens of icons scattered around the Desktop. This isn't a terrible thing, to be sure, but it's not very efficient. Once you have more than, say, a dozen icons on your Desktop, finding the one you want becomes a real icon-needle-in-a-Desktop-haystack exercise.

So, periodically (say once every couple of weeks), you should tidy up your Desktop so that you can find things easily and keep the Desktop a useful tool. You can do a couple of things:

1. **Get rid of any icons you absolutely don't need on the Desktop.**

    - If you're still using the icon, move it to the appropriate folder in your user account.

    - If you don't need the icon anymore, off to the Trash it goes.

2. **Organize the remaining icons.**

    - If you don't care about the order of the icons, click the Desktop and then choose View ⇨ Clean Up. This lines up all the icons in neat columns and rows based on the Desktop's invisible grid.

    - If you want to organize the icons by name, click the Desktop and then choose View ⇨ Arrange By ⇨ Name (or press Control+⌘+1).

    - If you want to apply a label to related icons, Control+click (or right-click) the selection, and then click a label color. You can then sort the icon by label: Click the Desktop and then choose View ⇨ Arrange By ⇨ Label (or press Control+⌘+6).

Watching hard disk free space

Although it's true that hard disks are larger than ever these days, it's also true that files are getting larger, too. Music files are almost always multimegabyte affairs; a single half-hour TV show can usurp about 250MB, and movies can be three or four times as large. If you're not careful, it's easy to run out of hard disk space in a hurry.

To prevent that from happening, you should keep an eye on how much free space is left on your Mac's hard disk. One way to do this is to open any Finder window and click Macintosh HD (or any folder in Macintosh HD). As you can see in figure 8.3, Finder displays the amount of space in the status bar at the bottom of the open window.

8.3 Click Macintosh HD in any Finder window to display the hard disk's free space in the status bar.

Caution The Mac does most things right, but sometimes it's a bit brain-dead. For example, the Desktop icons only have so much room to display text, so the Macintosh HD icon might truncate the amount of free space. For example, if your Mac hard disk has a capacity of 232.57GB and you have 92.32GB free, the Macintosh HD icon displays this as follows: 232.57GB,...32GB free. To fix this, display the Desktop window and use the Text size menu to reduce the font size.

An even better way to keep your eyes peeled on the free hard disk space is to configure the Desktop to always show this information. Here's how:

1. **Click the Desktop.**

2. **Choose View ⇨ Show View Options.** You can also press ⌘+J. The Desktop window appears.

3. **Select the Show item info check box, as shown in figure 8.4.**

Finder now displays extra information under the name of each Desktop icon, such as the number of items in a folder and the dimensions of an image. In the case of the Macintosh HD icon, Finder shows the total size of the hard disk and the amount of free space, as shown in figure 8.5.

Deleting unneeded files

I mentioned earlier that a neglected Trash folder can eat up lots of hard disk real estate. If you're minding your Mac's hard disk and you find that you're running low on hard disk free space, you should empty the Trash as a first step. You should also uninstall any programs you no longer use.

Other than that, I also suggest periodically rummaging through the folders in your user account to look for documents, downloads, and other files that you don't need. Send these items to the Trash and, when you're done, empty the Trash to recover the disk space. However, you should also consider backing up your system before you start trashing a lot of files.

8.4 Select the Show item info check box.

8.5 The Macintosh HD icon now shows the total space and total free space.

Uninstalling unused applications

To free up some room on your Mac's hard disk, get rid of any installed applications that you no longer use. The great thing about uninstalling Mac software is that it's just so darn easy. If you've ever used Windows, you know that removing a program is a long, involved process that always requires a large number of mouse clicks. On your Mac, however, the uninstall process couldn't be simpler:

1. **In Finder, choose the Applications folder.** There's a chance the application you want to delete is in the Utilities folder, so you may need to choose that folder before continuing.

2. **Click and drag the folder of the application you want to get rid of, and then drop the folder on the Trash.**

Genius

Many applications also install files in your user account's Library/Application Support folder, or in the Macintosh HD/Library/Application Support folder. Check those locations and delete any folder that belongs to the application you removed. You can also use AppDelete (see www.apple.com/downloads/macosx/system_disk_utilities/appdelete.html) or AppTrap (see http://konstochvanligasaker.se/apptrap/) to remove the application and associated files.

Checking hard disk status

A hard disk can suddenly bite the dust thanks to a lightning strike, an accidental drop from a decent height, or an electronic component shorting out. However, most of the time hard disks die a slow death. Along the way, they almost always show some signs of decay, but a hard drive is hidden so how can you see these signs? Since about 1996, almost all hard-disk manufacturers have built into their drives a system called Self-Monitoring, Analysis, and Reporting Technology, or S.M.A.R.T. This system monitors a number of hard disk parameters, including spin-up time, drive temperature, drive errors, and bad sectors. It monitors these factors over time, so S.M.A.R.T. looks for signs of impending hard-disk failure, including the following:

- The spin-up time gradually slows.
- The drive temperature increases.
- The seek error rate increases.
- The read error rate increases.
- The write error rate increases.
- The number of bad sectors increases.
- An internal consistency check (called the cyclic redundancy check, or CRC) produces an increasing number of errors.

Other factors that might indicate a potential failure are the number of times that the hard drive has been powered up, the number of hours in use, and the number of times the drive has started and stopped spinning. S.M.A.R.T. uses a sophisticated algorithm to combine these attributes into a value that represents the overall health of the disk. When that value goes beyond some predetermined threshold, S.M.A.R.T. issues an alert that hard-disk failure might be imminent.

Although S.M.A.R.T. has been around for a while and is now standard, taking advantage of S.M.A.R.T. diagnostics originally meant using a third-party program. However, your Mac includes a component that can monitor S.M.A.R.T. status and alert you if there's a problem. Here's how to use it:

1. **Click Finder in the Dock.**
2. **Choose Applications ⇨ Utilities ⇨ Disk Utility.** The Disk Utility window appears.

3. **Click your Mac's hard disk in the list of drives.** Note that you must click the hard disk itself, not the Macintosh HD partition.

4. **Click the First Aid tab.**

5. **Read the S.M.A.R.T. Status value, as shown in figure 8.6.** This is located in the bottom part of the window, in the right-hand column.

8.6 Check your Mac hard disk's S.M.A.R.T. Status value.

If all is well, the S.M.A.R.T. Status value says Verified. If, instead, you see either About to Fail or, worse, Failing, perform an immediate backup and then replace the hard disk.

Verifying the hard disk

The S.M.A.R.T. diagnostics (discussed in the previous section) look for catastrophic errors — those that might cause the entire hard disk to go belly up. However, hard disks can also fall prey to smaller maladies that, although they won't cause the hard disk to push up the daisies, could cause it to behave erratically or even damage files.

For example, your Mac maintains what it calls a Catalog file, which is a file that stores the overall structure of the hard disk, including all the folders and files. If that file gets corrupted, it might mean that you or an application can no longer access a folder or file.

You should check your Mac's hard disk for these types of errors every month or so. Here's how:

1. **Click Finder in the Dock.**

2. **Choose Applications ⇨ Utilities ⇨ Disk Utility.** The Disk Utility window appears.

3. **Click Macintosh HD in the list of drives, and click the First Aid tab.**

4. **Click Verify Disk.** The Disk Utility begins the verification check, which takes several minutes.

5. **When the check is complete, read the results at the bottom of the window, as shown in figure 8.7.**

6. **There are two possible results.**

    ● **No problems.** Say "Whew!" and close the Disk Utility.

    ● **Problems.** You need to repair the hard disk, as described in Chapter 9.

8.7 Check the results of the Verify Disk operation.

Setting the software update schedule

One of the most important things you can do to keep your Mac in the pink is to update its system software and applications. Apple is constantly improving its software by fixing bugs, adding features, closing security holes, and improving performance. So your Mac software will always be in top shape if you install these updates regularly.

The good news is that your Mac checks for updates automatically. By default, your Mac does a weekly check, but you can change that if you'd prefer a shorter or longer schedule. Follow these steps:

1. **Click System Preferences in the Dock.** The System Preferences window appears.

2. **Click Software Update.** The Software Update window opens.

3. **Make sure the Check for updates check box is selected, as shown in figure 8.8.**

4. **Choose the frequency with which you want your Mac to check for new updates from the Check for updates list.** Your choices are Daily, Weekly, or Monthly.

8.8 Select the Check for updates check box and then use the list to choose the update frequency.

Updating software by hand

If you configure Software Update to check for updates weekly or monthly, there may be times when this frequency isn't what you want:

- If your Mac is turned off when the time for the next scheduled update occurs, your Mac skips that check.

- If someone tells you that an important update is available, you might not want to wait until the next schedule check to get that update.

For these and similar scenarios, you can grab your Mac by the scruff of its electronic neck and force it to check for updates. There are two ways you can do this:

- Click System Preferences in the Dock, click Software Update, and then click Check Now.
- Click the Apple icon in the menu bar and then click Software Update.

Genius

Software Update applies only to Apple software. If you have other software installed on your Mac, see if the applications come with update features and, if so, make regular use of them. For Microsoft Office, for example, run the Microsoft AutoUpdate application (in Finder, choose Applications ⇨ Microsoft AutoUpdate).

Cycling your Mac notebook battery

If you have a MacBook Pro, MacBook Air, MacBook, or other notebook Mac, your computer comes with an internal battery that enables you to operate the computer without an electrical outlet. The battery also serves as a backup source of power should the electricity fail.

Older notebooks used rechargeable nickel metal hydride (NiMH) or nickel cadmium (NiCad) batteries. The NiMH and NiCad types are being phased out because they can suffer from a problem called the *memory effect*, where the battery loses capacity if you repeatedly recharge it without first fully discharging it.

Most of the latest Mac notebooks have rechargeable lithium-ion (Li-ion) batteries. (The exception is the MacBook Air, which uses a lithium-polymer battery.) Li-ion batteries are lighter and last longer than NiMH and NiCad batteries and, most importantly, Li-ion batteries don't suffer from the memory effect.

However, to get the most performance out of your Mac notebook's battery, you need to cycle it. *Cycling* a battery means letting it completely discharge and then fully recharging it again. To maintain optimal performance, you should cycle your Mac's battery once a month or so.

More Mac Maintenance

In addition to maintenance tasks that you should perform frequently to keep your Mac in fighting form, there are other maintenance chores you can run. If you really want to get your Mac in tip-top shape, perform the tasks outlined in the following sections from time to time.

Removing login items

When you start your Mac, lots of behind-the-scenes tasks get performed to set up the computer for your use. One of these tasks is that your Mac checks the list of items that are supposed to start automatically when you log in to your user account. These items are usually applications, but they can also be files, folders, and shared network locations. Appropriately, these items are called *login items*.

Most login items are added by applications because they need some service running right from the get-go. Typical examples include

- **iTunesHelper.** iTunes uses this application to detect when an iPod is connected to the Mac.

- **Transport Monitor.** A Palm's HotSync Manager uses this application to detect when a Palm PDA is connected to the Mac.

- **Microsoft AU Daemon.** Microsoft Office uses this application to check for available updates to the Office software.

As you can see, login items are usually quite important. However, not all login items are vital. For example, a login item might be associated with an application you no longer use, or it might open a file or folder that you no longer need at startup. Whatever the reason, these unneeded login items only serve to slow down your Mac's startup and to consume extra system memory. Therefore, you should check from time to time your user account's login items and remove those you no longer need.

Follow these steps to remove a login item:

1. **Click System Preferences in the Dock.** The System Preferences window opens.
2. **Click Accounts.** The Accounts preferences window opens.
3. **Click the lock icon, if the lock is closed.** If the lock icon is open, skip to Step 5.
4. **Type the name and password of an administrator account and then click OK.**
5. **Click the Login Items tab.** You see a list of login items, as shown in figure 8.9.
6. **Click the login item you want to remove.**
7. **Click the minus sign (-).** Your Mac removes the login item.
8. **Click the lock icon to prevent further changes in the Accounts preferences window.**

8.9 The Login Items tab shows a list of your user account's login items.

Erasing your hard disk's free space

If you regularly deal with files that contain private, sensitive, or secure data, I mentioned earlier that even if you delete those files and then empty the Trash, the files remain on the disk for an indeterminate amount of time. A person who steals or gains physical access to your computer and has the appropriate disk recovery software can easily recover those files.

Genius

What about sensitive files that you haven't deleted? To protect those, you need to encrypt the contents of your hard disk using your Mac's FileVault encryption technology. Click System Preferences in the Dock, click the Security icon, and then click FileVault. Click Set Master Password to create a master password for your Mac. When that's done, click Turn On FileVault. Note that if you forget your master password, you'll lose access to all your data! Therefore, write down the master password and store it in a secure off-site location (such as a safety deposit box).

You can use Leopard's Empty Trash Securely feature (choose Finder ⇨ Preferences ⇨ Advanced) to improve security by writing gibberish data over the files. You might think this would be pretty darn secure, but it turns out that professional disk-recovery experts with high-end tools can *still* recover at least parts of the original files!

So is keeping deleted files secure an impossible goal? Fortunately, the answer is a resounding "No!" because your Mac comes with a great tool that can write over deleted files multiple times, thus ensuring that they can never be recovered. The tool is called Erase Free Space, and it's something you should run from time to time to ensure the security of any deleted files that contain important data. Here are the steps to follow:

1. **Click Finder in the Dock.**

2. **Choose Applications ⇨ Utilities ⇨ Disk Utility.**

3. **Click Macintosh HD in the list of drives.**

4. **Click the Erase tab.**

5. **Click Erase Free Space.** The Disk Utility displays the Erase Free Space Options dialog box, shown in figure 8.10.

6. **These options determine the number of times the hard disk free space gets overwritten.** Select the option you want to run.

   - **Zero Out Deleted Files.** This option writes over the free space once. This is the quickest option, but it provides the least security and it will be possible for a sophisticated user to recover some of the data.

   - **7-Pass Erase of Deleted Files.** This option writes over the free space seven times. This means the erasure takes seven times as long as the Zero Out option, but it gives you a highly secure (that is, government-grade) erasure. This is the option that's the best blend of convenience and security.

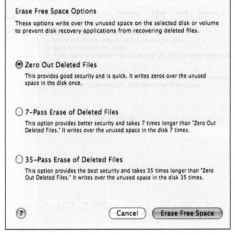

8.10 Use the Erase Free Space Options dialog box to choose the number of times the hard disk free space gets overwritten.

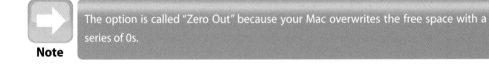

Note The option is called "Zero Out" because your Mac overwrites the free space with a series of 0s.

● **35-Pass Erase of Deleted Files.** This option writes over the free space 35 times. This means the erasure takes 5 times as long as the 7-Pass option and 35 times as long as the Zero Out option. It's likely that this will take a day or so to complete, but it gives you the highest possible security (military-grade).

7. **Click Erase Free Space.**

Cleaning your Mac inside and out

Your Mac is a beautiful piece of technology, no doubt about it, but in the long run it's only as good looking as it is clean. Unfortunately, computers never stay clean for very long: Screens get fingerprints on them; keyboards collect crumbs and other particles; mice get grimy; and, unless you've got some kind of heavy-duty air purifier on the job, all computer parts are world-class dust magnets.

To keep your Mac looking sharp, you should give it a thorough cleaning every so often (how often depends on your own cleanliness standards and outside factors such as how dusty your room is). The most frequent object of your cleaning duties will be the exterior, which you can do following these general steps:

1. **Turn off and unplug the Mac and the LCD monitor.**

2. **Use a soft, dry, clean cloth to wipe any excess dust from the screen, keyboard, and mouse.** If your Mac came with a cloth, use that cloth to do the wiping. If your components are still dirty (fingerprints, smudges, and so on), continue with the remaining steps.

3. **Take a soft, clean cloth and dampen it with water.** Be sure to merely dampen the cloth because you don't want there to be any excess water that might drip off the cloth.

Caution Never spray water or any other liquid onto an LCD screen. The liquid could seep into the monitor (or, in the case of the iMac and Mac notebooks, into the computer case) and damage the electronics.

4. **Use the damp cloth to wipe the screen and other components.**

5. **If you see any dust buildup around your Mac's ports, use a vacuum with a soft brush attachment to suck up the dust.** While you have the vacuum handy, use it on your keyboard as well to suck up any dust or other particles that have settled in between (and even below) the keys.

Genius

If water seems too low-tech of a solution (pun intended), give Klear Screen a try. It comes in an Apple version (that's recommended by Apple itself), and the kit contains iKlear, an antistatic screen polish, and a soft chamois cloth. See www.klear-screen.com for more info.

The outside of your Mac may be nice and shiny now, but there's a good chance you can't say the same for the inside. The inside? You bet. Your Mac has interior fans that serve to flow air through the system and keep it cool. There's usually an intake fan that brings in cool air from the outside of the case, and an exhaust fan that blows out hot air from inside the case. Unfortunately, in most environments the intake fan brings in lots of junk along with the outside air: mostly dust, but also human hair, pet hair, carpet fibers, and whatever else might be hanging around at ground level. Most of this grime takes up residence inside the case, which can be very bad for your Mac's health:

- Dust collects on electrical connections, which can make those connections unreliable.

- A component that's covered in dust retains more heat, which could cause it to perform erratically or even to fail because of overheating.

- The excess heat that dusty components generate causes your overall system to run hotter. This can make your system louder (because the fans have to work harder to cool the system) and can shorten the lifespan of crucial components such as the processor.

Dust, clearly, is a bad thing. So once every six months or so, you may want to consider opening up your Mac's case and giving the machine's innards a good cleaning. There are two ways to do this:

Caution

Please note that opening up your Mac's case will void your warranty, so you will want to think carefully before doing this.

- **Canned air.** This is a can of air under pressure, and you use it to blow away dust and other debris. I'm not a huge fan of this method because all it tends to do is blow the dust back into the air where it will simply settle elsewhere. However, it's often useful for getting to dust in areas where a vacuum can't reach.

- **Vacuum.** Be sure to use an attachment that has soft bristles to avoid damaging any of the sensitive electronics inside your Mac. If you want to take things up a notch, get a computer vacuum, which has attachments specifically designed for cleaning computers. If you want to go whole hog, get an electronics vacuum that has an antistatic feature (and a hefty price tag, too).

Preparing for Trouble

If, as the old saying has it, an ounce of prevention really is worth a pound of cure, then I suggest that your general state of mind when working with your Mac be what I call *ounce-of-prevention mode*. This means that you should assume that at some point your Mac will have a serious problem, and so you should be prepared to handle it. Performing regular backups, as I discuss in the section "Backing Up Your Mac," is a great start, but I also believe Mac users need to do two other things: create a secondary user account with default settings and create a secondary boot device.

Creating a secondary user account

Your Mac lets you define multiple accounts, but if you're the sole user of the computer, then you don't need another account, right? True, but having a secondary account around is actually a useful troubleshooting device, as long as you don't customize, tweak, or in any way hack your Mac using that account. The idea is that you want the other user account to be pure in the sense that it uses only the default settings. That way, if your Mac starts acting up, you can log in to the secondary account and see if the problem persists. If it doesn't, then you know the problem is almost certainly related to any user-specific settings you applied in your main account.

Here are the steps to follow to set up a secondary user account on your Mac:

1. **Click System Preferences in the Dock.** The System Preferences window appears.

2. **Click the Accounts icon.**

3. **Click the lock icon, enter your Mac's administrator credentials, and then click OK.**

4. **In the New Account list, choose Administrator.**

5. **Use the Name text box to enter the account name.** For example, enter your full name.

6. **Use the Short Name text box to enter a short version of the account name.** For example, enter your first name (or some variation if you're already using your first name for your main account).

7. **Use the Password and Verify text boxes to type a secure password for the account.** Figure 8.11 shows the dialog box filled in so far.

8.11 Use this dialog box to set up your Mac with a secondary administrator account for troubleshooting.

233

Caution

Because you're creating an all-powerful administrator account, it's really important that you give this account a secure password. The password should be at least eight characters long with a mix of uppercase and lowercase letters, numbers, and symbols. Click the key icon beside the Password text box to check the strength of your password (a good password turns the Quality bar all green).

8. **Use the Password Hint text box to type a hint about your password, just in case you forget it.**

9. **Click Create Account.**

10. **Click the lock icon to prevent changes.**

Creating a secondary boot device

If you want to paint the exterior of your house or wash the outside windows, you can't do either job from inside your house. This is analogous to performing certain troubleshooting tasks with your Mac, such as repairing the hard disk (described in Chapter 9). You can't fix the disk while the Mac operating system is using it. Instead, you have to "step outside" of the Mac hard disk to repair it. How do you do that? By creating a secondary boot device that you can boot to instead of the internal Mac hard disk.

There are a number of ways to do this, but the following are the most common:

- **Your Mac OS X Install DVD.** This is the easiest option, given you don't have to create anything, but it's also the slowest.

- **Another Mac connected by a FireWire cable.** You can start the other Mac in FireWire target disk mode, as described in Chapter 9, and then boot to that Mac.

- **A second internal hard disk.** This is a suitable route if you have a Mac Pro, which can accommodate more than one hard disk.

- **An external FireWire or USB hard disk.** This is probably the best way to go if you have a Mac that can't take a second internal hard disk.

For the latter two options, you need to insert your Mac OS X Install DVD and install Mac OS X to the other drive. If you're going the external drive route, however, you need to set up the drive with a bootable partition. First, follow these steps to see if the drive is already bootable:

1. **Connect the external drive, if you haven't done so already.**

2. **In Finder, choose Applications ➪ Utilities ➪ Disk Utility.** The Disk Utility window opens.

3. **Click the external hard disk.** Note that you need to click the hard disk itself, not a partition on the disk (such as the External HD partition shown in figure 8.12).

4. **Click the Partition tab.** You see a window similar to the one shown in figure 8.12.

8.12 Click the external drive and then click the Partition tab to check the drive's bootable status.

Examine the Partition Map Scheme value in the bottom-right corner of the window. There are three main possibilities:

- **GUID Partition Map.** This value tells you the drive is bootable only on an Intel-based Mac.

- **Apple Partition Map.** This value tells you the drive is bootable on a PowerPC-based Mac or as a nonboot drive on an Intel-based Mac.

- **Master Boot Record.** This value tells you the drive is bootable on a Windows-based PC.

If you see Master Boot Record or some other value not in the previous list, then you need to repartition the drive to make it bootable on your Mac. Here are the steps to follow:

1. **In the Volume Scheme list, choose 1 Partition.**

2. **Use the Name text box to specify a name for the partition.**

3. **Click Options.** The dialog box shown in figure 8.13 appears.

Caution

Repartitioning erases all the data on the drive. So if you have any important stuff on the drive, copy it to a safe location before proceeding.

4. **Select the partition scheme option you want to use.** For an Intel-based Mac, select GUID Partition Table; for a PowerPC-based Mac, select Apple Partition Map.

5. **Click OK.**

6. **Click Apply.** Disk Utility warns you that this will erase all the data on the disk.

7. **Click the Partition button.** Disk Utility partitions and then formats the drive. When Disk Utility is done, it remounts the drive, so you might see a prompt from Time Machine asking if you want to use the drive for backups.

8. **Click Cancel.**

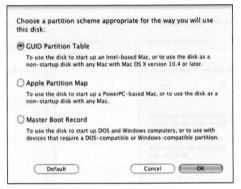

Choose a partition scheme appropriate for the way you will use this disk:

⦿ GUID Partition Table
To use the disk to start up an Intel-based Mac, or to use the disk as a non-startup disk with any Mac with Mac OS X version 10.4 or later.

○ Apple Partition Map
To use the disk to start up a PowerPC-based Mac, or to use the disk as a non-startup disk with any Mac.

○ Master Boot Record
To use the disk to start up DOS and Windows computers, or to use with devices that require a DOS-compatible or Windows-compatible partition.

(Default)   (Cancel)   (OK)

8.13 Select the partition scheme you want to use.

If you're using either an external hard disk or a second internal hard disk as your secondary boot device, you now need to follow the steps in Chapter 9 for reinstalling Mac OS X. In this case, however, you are not reinstalling Mac OS X on your main hard disk, you are installing a copy for the first time on your secondary boot device. That is, when you get to the Select a Destination window, click the external or second internal hard disk and then continue the installation.

Backing Up Your Mac

The data you create on your Mac is as precious as gold not only because it's yours, but mostly because it's simply irreplaceable. Macs are reliable machines, but they do crash and all hard disks eventually die, so at some point your data will be at risk. To avoid losing that data forever, you need to back up your Mac, early and often.

Configuring Time Machine

If your Mac runs Leopard (OS X 10.5), backing up your data has never been easier. That's because Leopard introduced Time Machine to the world. Time Machine is a backup application that's unlike anything you've seen before in the Mac world:

- The initial Time Machine backup includes your entire Mac.

- Time Machine runs another backup every hour, and this backup includes just those files and folders that you've changed or created since the most recent hourly backup.

- Time Machine runs a daily backup that includes only those files and folders that you've changed or created since the most recent daily backup.

- Time Machine runs a weekly backup that includes only those files and folders that you've changed or created since the most recent weekly backup.

All of this is completely automated, so Time Machine is a set-it-and-forget-it deal, which is exactly what you want in a backup application. However, Time Machine doesn't stop there: It also keeps old backups:

- It keeps the past 24 hourly backups.

- It keeps the last month's worth of daily backups.

- It keeps all the weekly backups until the backup location gets full, at which point it begins deleting the oldest backups to make room for more.

Keeping these old backups is what gives Time Machine its name. That is, it enables you to go back in time and restore not just a file, but also a *version* of a file. For example, say on Monday you created a document and added some text, and then spent Tuesday editing that text. If on Friday you realize that during Tuesday's edits you deleted some of the original text that you'd now give your eyeteeth to get back, there's no problem: Simply restore the version from Monday.

237

Time Machine is so simple and so potentially useful that you really ought to make it part of your backup toolkit. If there's a downside to Time Machine, it's that it only backs up to a second hard disk that is connected to your Mac (which is usually an external USB or FireWire hard disk, but it can also be a second internal hard disk). You can't, say, back up to a network folder. (If you want to back up to a network, then you need to get Apple's new Time Capsule device; see www.apple.com/timecapsule.)

When you first connect an external USB or FireWire hard disk, Time Machine sits up and takes notice, and it most likely displays the dialog box shown in figure 8.14. If you want to use the hard disk for your Time Machine backups, click Use as Backup Disk; otherwise, click Cancel to move on without configuring anything.

8.14 Time Machine usually asks if you want to use a freshly connected hard disk as the backup disk.

If you didn't set up an external hard disk as the Time Machine backup disk, or if you want to use a different external disk as the backup disk, you can choose the disk by hand, as shown in the following steps:

1. **Click the System Preferences in the Dock.**

2. **Click Time Machine.** If you've never set up a backup disk, the dialog box in figure 8.15 appears.

3. **Click Set Up Time Machine.** The Time Machine preferences window appears.

4. **Click Choose Backup Disk.** Time Machine displays a list of the hard disks on your system that you can use for backups, as shown in figure 8.16.

5. **Click the hard disk you want to use.**

6. **Click Use for Backup.** If the hard disk has data on it, or if it has never been formatted, Time Machine warns you that it must erase (that is, format) the disk.

8.15 You see this dialog box if you've never configured Time Machine with a backup disk.

8.16 Use this dialog box to choose which hard disk you want Time Machine to use for its backups.

7. **Click Erase.** If you want to save the hard disk's data first, click Choose Another Disk, copy the drive data to another location, and then repeat this procedure.

When you get back to the Time Machine preferences window, you see that the Time Machine setting is set to ON, and the application immediately begins a 120-second countdown to the next backup. (If you don't want the backup to run right away, click the X icon beside the countdown.)

Note If you're using an external hard disk for the Time Machine backups, remember that you have to leave the hard disk connected to your Mac and powered on for the backups to work.

When you launch Time Machine preferences from now on, it shows you the current status (ON or OFF), how much space is left on the backup disk, and the dates and times of your oldest and most recent backups, as shown in figure 8.17.

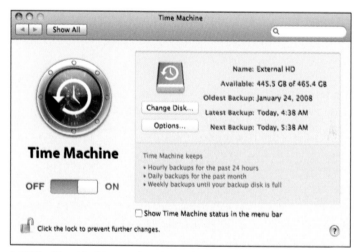

8.17 The Time Machine window shows the backup device, its free space, and the dates of your oldest and newest backups.

The more data you have, the longer the initial backup takes. If you have data that you don't want included in your backups — for example, recorded TV shows that you'll delete after watching them — it's a good idea to exclude the folders or files. Here's how it's done:

1. **In the Time Machine window, click Options.** Time Machine displays a list of items to exclude from the backups. (At first, this list includes the hard disk that Time Machine is using for the backups, which just makes sense.)

2. **Click the plus sign (+).**

3. **Choose the folder or file that you want to exclude from the backups.**

4. **Click Exclude.** Time Machine adds the folder or file to the Do not back up list, as shown in figure 8.18.

5. **Follow Steps 2 through 4 to exclude any other folders and files that you don't want backed up.**

6. **Click Done.**

Do not back up:	
External HD	19.9 GB
Recorded TV Shows	2.1 GB

+   −   Total Included: 18.6 GB

☑ Back up while on battery power
☑ Warn when old backups are deleted

(?)   (Cancel)   (Done)

8.18 You can tell Time Machine to exclude certain folders or files from the backups.

Genius

If you exclude any items while a backup is running, Time Machine cancels the current backup and reschedules it. If you'd really prefer that the backup run right away, click Change Disk, choose None, and then click Stop Backing Up. Click Change Disk again, choose the hard disk you're using for backups, and then click Use for Backup. Time Machine then runs the backup after the 120-second countdown.

Backing up your hard disk to a disk image

If you're using a version of Mac OS X earlier than Leopard, or if you'd rather back up your Mac to something other than another hard disk (such as a network folder), then you need a different backup strategy. One possibility is to create an *image* of your Mac's hard disk. A disk image is an exact copy of the disk. If your Mac hard disk gets corrupted, you can restore it from the disk image and you'll be back on your feet in no time.

Follow these steps to create a disk image for your Mac's hard disk:

1. **Click Finder in the Dock.**

2. **Choose Applications ⇨ Utilities ⇨ Disk Utility.**

3. **Click Macintosh HD, as shown in figure 8.19.**

8.19 Choose Macintosh HD to make an image of your hard disk.

4. **Click the New Image icon in the tool-bar.** The New Image from Folder dialog box appears, as shown in figure 8.20.

5. **Use the Save As text box to type a name for the disk image.**

6. **Choose the location where you want the disk image saved.** For example, choose a shared folder on another computer on your network.

7. **In the Image Format drop-down list, choose compressed.**

8. **If you don't want other people to be able to read the contents of the image, choose 128-bit AES encryption in the Encryption list.**

9. **Click Save.** Disk Utility creates the disk image.

8.20 Use the New Image from Folder dialog box to name the disk image, set its location, and set its format.

Caution

The image file will be about the same size as the total used space on the hard disk. Therefore, be sure to choose a location that has enough free space to hold the image file.

Note

Creating a disk image is a slow process that can take an hour or more, depending on the size of your Mac's hard disk.

Backing up your files to a DVD

Another useful backup strategy is to back up your files to a DVD disc. The advantage here is that you can take the disc with you, so you have access to your files while you're away from your Mac. This also enables you to store the DVDs offsite for extra security.

You back up files to a DVD (or a CD) by first creating a *burn folder*, which is a special folder that contains aliases of whatever folders or files you add to it. You can then burn that folder to the disc to complete the backup. Follow these steps:

1. **Choose a location for the burn folder.**

   • If you want to place the burn folder on the Desktop, click any empty part of the Desktop. This is probably the best place for the burn folder because it's usually the easiest place to drag and drop files.

   • If you want to place the burn folder in some other folder, use Finder to open that folder.

2. **Choose File ⇨ New Burn Folder.** Your Mac creates a new burn folder.

3. **Type a name for the burn folder and then press Return.**

4. **Use Finder to locate a folder or file you want to burn.**

5. **Click and drag the folder or file and then drop it on the burn folder.** Your Mac creates an alias for the folder or file within the burn folder.

6. **Repeat Step 5 to add all the folders and files you want to burn.**

7. **Double-click the burn folder to open it.** Figure 8.21 shows an example of a burn folder.

Genius

Make sure you don't add more files to the burn folder than can fit on the disc: 700MB for a CD, 4.7GB for a single-layer DVD, and 8.5GB for a double-layer DVD. To see the size of the items currently in the burn folder, double-click the burn folder to open it, and then examine the Minimum Disc Size value in the status bar (see figure 8.21).

8.21 A burn folder ready for burning to disc.

8. **Insert a writable DVD (or CD).** The burn folder interface appears.

9. **Click the Burn button.** The dialog box shown in figure 8.22 appears.

10. **Use the Disc Name text box to type a name for the disc.**

11. **Use the Burn Speed list to choose the burn rate.** If you have trouble burning, try again using a slower rate.

12. **Click Burn.** Your Mac burns the folders and files to the disc.

8.22 Specify a name and write speed for the burn.

Restoring files using Time Machine

If you delete a file by accident, you can always open the Trash to drag it back out. However, there are plenty of situations where recovering a file just isn't possible.

● You delete the file and then empty the Trash.

● You overwrite the file with another file of the same name. If you notice the problem right away, you can choose Edit⇨Undo or press ⌘+Z to undo the file operation. But if you don't notice until later, you're stuck.

243

- Your hard disk develops a problem that corrupts the file.

- You make and save substantial edits to the file.

The good news is that if you've had Time Machine on the job for a while, you can probably go back in time, locate a version of the file, and then restore it to its original location. Time Machine even lets you keep the existing file if you still need the newer version. Note that I'm talking here about files, but you can also recover folders and even your entire hard disk.

Follow these steps to restore data from your Time Machine backups:

1. **Use Finder to choose the folder you want to restore, or the folder that contains the file you want to restore.** If you want to restore your entire hard disk, choose Macintosh HD in the Sidebar.

2. **Click the Time Machine icon in the Dock.** The Time Machine interface appears, as shown in figure 8.23.

8.23 Use the Time Machine interface to choose which version of the folder or file you want to restore.

Genius

In many cases, it's faster to run a Spotlight search on the name of the folder or file you want to restore. In the search results, click the folder or file.

3. **Navigate to the version you want by using any of the following techniques (the date and time of the backup appear at the bottom of the screen).**

   - Click the top arrow to jump to the earliest version; click the bottom arrow to return to the most recent version.

   - Hold down the ⌘ key and click the arrows to navigate through each of the backups, from the earliest to most recent, one version at a time.

   - Use the timeline on the right side to click a specific version.

   - Click the version windows. These appear on the screen as stacked windows with the title bar showing for each version. The window in front is the most recent. The window in the back is the earliest version.

4. **Click the file and click Restore to restore a file.** Time Machine copies the version of the folder or file back to its original location. If the location already contains a folder or file with the same name, you see the dialog box shown in figure 8.24.

8.24 This dialog box appears if the restore location already has a folder or file with the same name.

5. **Click one of the following buttons.**

   - **Keep Original.** Cancels the restore and leaves the existing folder or file as is.

   - **Keep Both.** Restores the folder or file and keeps the existing folder or file as is. In this case, Time Machine restores the folder or file and adds the text (original) to the folder or file name.

   - **Replace.** Click this button to overwrite the existing folder or file with the restored folder or file.

245

Restoring your system

If disaster strikes and you can't start your Mac, you need to restore your system to an earlier state when it was working properly. You can do this using either Time Machine or a disk image.

To recover your system from a Time Machine backup, follow these steps:

1. **Insert the Mac OS X Installation DVD.**

2. **Turn on or restart your Mac.**

3. **Hold down C while your Mac is restarting.** You can release C when you see the Apple logo. Your Mac boots to the Mac OS X Install DVD.

4. **Select a language for the install.** The Install Mac OS X application appears.

5. **Choose Utilities ⇨ Restore System From Backup.** The Restore Your System window appears.

6. **Click Continue.** The Select a Backup Source window appears.

7. **Click the hard disk that contains your Time Machine backups.**

8. **Click Continue.** The Select a Backup window appears.

9. **Click the backup you want to use for the restore.**

10. **Click Continue.** The Select a Destination window appears.

11. **Click Macintosh HD.**

12. **Click Restore.** Install Mac OS X begins restoring your system.

To recover your system using a disk image, follow these steps:

1. **Follow Steps 1 through 5 in the previous set of steps.** You should be at the Install Mac OS X application window.

2. **Choose Utilities ⇨ Disk Utility.** The Disk Utility window appears.

3. **Click the Restore tab.**

4. **Beside the Source box, click Image.**

5. **Choose your disk image and then click Open.**

6. **Click and drag Macintosh HD from the left pane and drop it inside the Destination text box, as shown in figure 8.25.**

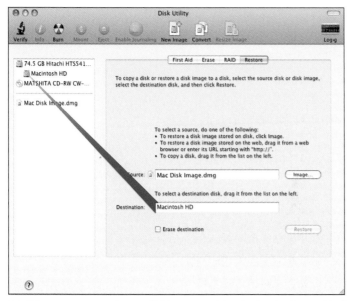

8.25 The restore source is your disk image, and the destination is your Mac's hard disk.

7. **Click Restore.** Disk Utility asks you to confirm.

8. **Click Restore.** Disk Utility begins restoring your system.

How Can I Solve Mac Problems?

Macintosh HD

Verify Info Burn Unmount Eject Enable Journaling New Image Convert Resize Image Log

74.5 GB SAMSUNG HS082HB
Macintosh HD

First Aid   Erase   RAID   Restore

If you're having trouble with the selected disk:
- Click Repair Disk. If the repair fails, back up and erase the disk.
- If Repair Disk is unavailable, click Verify Disk. If the disk needs repairs, start up from your Mac OS X installation disc, and then choose Utilities > Disk Utility.

If you have a permissions problem with a file installed by the Mac OS X installer, click Repair Permissions.

☑ Show details   Clear History

Verify and Repair disk Macintosh HD
Checking HFS Plus volume.
Checking Extents Overflow file.
Checking Catalog file.
Checking multi-linked files.
Checking Catalog hierarchy.
Checking volume bitmap.
Checking volume information.
The volume Untitled 1 appears to be OK.
Mounting Disk

1 HFS volume checked
No repairs were necessary

Verify Disk Permissions   Verify Disk
Repair Disk Permissions   Repair Disk

Mount Point : /   Capacity : 63.9 GB (68,585,259,008 Bytes)
Format : Mac OS Extended (Journaled)   Available : 45.3 GB (48,618,745,856 Bytes)
Owners Enabled : Yes   Used : 18.6 GB (19,966,513,152 Bytes)
Number of Folders : 143,810   Number of Files : 570,921

As a former Windows user, you know all about computer problems, unfortunately. In fact, I'll bet that it was Windows' seemingly endless litany of woes that drove you to switch to the Mac. That was a good move because you'll find that Mac problems are refreshingly, even blissfully, rare. The reason for such rarity is a simple one: Software developers and device manufacturers only have to build their Mac products for machines made by a single company. This really simplifies things, and results in fewer problems. Not, however, *no* problems. Even in the Mac world, applications and devices sometimes behave strangely or not at all. In this chapter, I give you some general troubleshooting techniques for tackling both software and hardware glitches.

General Software Troubleshooting Techniques

One of the ongoing mysteries that all Mac users experience at one time or another is what might be called the now-you-see-it-now-you-don't problem. This gremlin plagues you for a while and then mysteriously vanishes without any intervention on your part. (It also tends not to occur when you ask a nearby user or someone from the IT department to look at it.) When this happens, most people just shake their heads and resume working, grateful to no longer have to deal with the problem.

Tracking down the problem

Unfortunately, most computer ills don't just disappear. For more intractable problems, your first order of business is to track down the source of the glitch. There's no easy or set way to go about this, but it can be done if you take a systematic approach. Over the years, I've found that the best approach is to ask a series of questions designed to gather the required information and/or to narrow down what might be the culprit:

- **Did you get an error message?** Unfortunately, most computer error messages are obscure and do little to help you resolve a problem directly. However, error codes and error text can help you down the road, either by giving you something to search for in an online database or by providing information to a tech support person. Therefore, you should always write down the full text of any error message that appears. If the application offers to send an error report to the company that developed the program, be sure to read the report (even if you don't bother sending it in).

Genius

If the error message is lengthy and you can still use other programs on your Mac, don't bother writing down the full message. Instead, while the message is displayed, press Shift+⌘+3 to place an image of the current screen on the desktop.

- **Is there an error message in the Console?** If an error occurs behind the scenes, you don't see anything on-screen to tell you that something's amiss. However, there's a good chance that your Mac made a note of the error as a Console message. To check, open Finder and choose Applications ⇨ Utilities ⇨ Console. You should check both the Console log (choose File ⇨ Open Console Log; see figure 9.1) and the system log (choose File ⇨ Open ⇨ System Log). The Console window tends to be a bit of a mess, so it's hard to know what to look for. For starters, check the Sender column for the name of the program you think might be causing the problem. Also, only look at those messages that were written around the time that the problem occurred.

Time	Sender(PID)	Message
9/3/08 10:00:35 PM	com.apple.launchd[1]	(com.apple.backupd-wake[40310]) Exited with exit code: 1
9/4/08 5:07:08 AM	com.apple.launchd[1]	(com.apple.backupd-wake[40351]) Exited with exit code: 1
9/4/08 11:49:31 AM	com.apple.launchd[1]	(com.apple.backupd-wake[40436]) Exited with exit code: 1
9/4/08 12:01:42 PM	com.apple.launchd[1]	(org.samba.smbd[40423]) Stray process with PGID equal to this dead job: PID 40424 PPID 1 smbd
9/4/08 5:39:26 PM	_eUpdateCheck[40528]	Checking for updates
9/4/08 5:40:35 PM	com.apple.launchd[1]	(org.samba.smbd[40507]) Stray process with PGID equal to this dead job: PID 40508 PPID 1 smbd
9/4/08 5:40:47 PM	com.apple.launchd[1]	(org.samba.smbd[40514]) Stray process with PGID equal to this dead job: PID 40515 PPID 1 smbd
9/4/08 5:41:28 PM	com.apple.launchd[72]	([0x0-0x739739].SoftwareUpdateCheck[40528]) Exited with exit code: 102
9/4/08 5:41:28 PM	_eUpdateCheck[40528]	no Internet connection
9/4/08 5:41:28 PM	_ernelEventAgent[34]	KernelEventAgent: sysctl_queryfs: No such file or directory
9/4/08 5:46:24 PM	com.apple.launchd[1]	(org.samba.smbd[40553]) Stray process with PGID equal to this dead job: PID 40554 PPID 1 smbd
9/4/08 5:46:24 PM	com.apple.launchd[1]	(org.samba.smbd[40553]) Stray process with PGID equal to this dead job: PID 40555 PPID 1 smbd
9/4/08 5:57:54 PM	com.apple.launchd[1]	(org.samba.smbd[40560]) Stray process with PGID equal to this dead job: PID 40561 PPID 1 smbd
9/4/08 5:57:54 PM	com.apple.launchd[1]	(org.cups.cups-lpd) Unknown key: SHAuthorizationRight
9/4/08 5:57:54 PM	com.apple.launchd[1]	(org.samba.nmbd) Throttling respawn: Will start in 10 seconds
9/4/08 5:58:05 PM	com.apple.launchd[1]	(org.samba.nmbd) Throttling respawn: Will start in 10 seconds
9/4/08 6:04:10 PM	com.apple.launchd[72]	([0x0-0x738738].com.apple.systempreferences[40516]) Stray process with PGID equal to this dead job: PID 40541 PPID 1 SCHelper

31 messages from 9/3/08 10:00:35 PM to 9/4/08 6:09:48 PM

9.1 You can use the Console utility to check for error messages.

- **Did you recently change any application settings?** If so, try reversing the change to see whether doing so solves the problem. If that doesn't help, check the software developer's Web site to see whether an upgrade or patch is available. Otherwise, you could try uninstalling and then reinstalling the program.

- **Did you recently install a new program?** If you suspect a new program is causing system instability, restart your Mac and try operating the system for a while without using the new program. (If the program has any login items that load at startup, be sure to deactivate them, as described in Chapter 8.) If the problem doesn't reoccur, the new program is likely the culprit. Try using the program without any other programs running. You should also examine the program's README file (if it has one) to look for known problems and possible workarounds. It's also a good idea to check for a version of the program that's compatible with your version of OS X. (For example, some new versions of Mac applications don't play well with Leopard (OS X 10.5.) Again, you can also try reinstalling the program. Similarly, if you recently upgraded an existing program, try uninstalling the upgrade.

Note
One common cause of program errors is having one or more program files corrupted because of hard disk errors. Before you reinstall a program, try repairing the Mac's hard disk, as described later in this chapter.

- **Did you recently install a new device?** If you recently installed a new device or if you recently updated an existing device driver, the new device or driver might be causing the problem. Run through the general hardware troubleshooting techniques later in this chapter.

- **Did you recently install any updates?** It's an unfortunate fact of life that occasionally updates designed to fix one problem end up causing another problem. You can't uninstall a software update, so your only choice is to restore your Mac to a previous version, as described in Chapter 8.

- **Did you recently change any System Preferences?** If the problem started after you changed your Mac's configuration, try reversing the change. Even something as seemingly innocent as activating a screen saver can cause problems, so don't rule anything out.

Performing basic software troubleshooting steps

Figuring out the cause of a problem is often the hardest part of troubleshooting, but by itself it doesn't do you much good. When you know the source, you need to parlay that information into a fix for the problem. I discussed a few solutions in the previous section, but here are a few other general fixes you need to keep in mind:

- **Close all programs.** You can often fix flaky behavior by shutting down all your open programs and starting again. This is a particularly useful fix for problems caused by low memory or low system resources.

- **Log out.** Logging out clears the memory and so gives you a slightly cleaner slate than merely closing all your programs. Pull down the Apple menu and choose Log Out *User*, where *User* is your Mac username, or press Shift+⌘+Q to log out quickly.

- **Restart your Mac.** If there are problems with some system files and devices, logging off won't help because these objects remain loaded. By restarting your Mac, you reload the entire system, which is often enough to solve many problems. Various ways of restarting your Mac are discussed later in this chapter.

Monitoring your Mac to look for problems

If your Mac feels sluggish or an application is behaving erratically, what might the problem be? Perhaps the processor is busy with other tasks; perhaps your Mac is running low on memory; or perhaps there's a problem with the hard disk. It could be any of these things, but the only way to tell is to look under the hood, so to speak, and monitor these aspects of your Mac.

Your Mac's monitoring tools are useful troubleshooters, but they're also good for acquainting you with your Mac. Monitoring things like the processor and memory usage regularly (not just when you have a problem) helps you get a feel for what's normal on your Mac, which then helps you better diagnose your Mac when you suspect a problem.

Monitoring CPU usage

The CPU (central processing unit or just processor) is the chip inside your Mac that acts as the computer's control and command center. Almost everything you do on your Mac and almost everything that happens within your Mac goes through the CPU. It is, in short, a pretty darned important component, and it pays to keep an eye on how much your Mac's CPU is being taxed by the system. If your Mac feels less responsive than usual, or if a program has become very slow, it could be because the CPU is running at or near full speed.

To see if that's the case, you can use Activity Monitor, which gives you a list of everything that's running on your Mac and tells you, among other things, what percentage of the CPU's resources are being used. Follow these steps to get started:

1. **Click Finder in the Dock.** The Finder window opens.

2. **Choose Applications ⇨ Utilities ⇨ Activity Monitor.**

3. **Click the CPU tab.**

Figure 9.2 shows the Activity Monitor window. The bulk of the window is taken up by a list of running programs, which Activity Monitor calls *processes*. A process is a running instance of an executable program. All the applications you have running are processes, of course, but so too are all the behind-the-scenes programs that your Mac and your applications require to function properly.

By default, Activity Monitor shows the processes that are associated with your user account: the applications you've launched, your user account's login items, and other programs that your Mac started when you logged in. However, this is by no means a complete list of the running processes. You can use the Show pop-up menu to display a different set of processes. Here are the most important items in the Show list:

- **My Processes.** Displays the default list of processes, as shown in figure 9.2.

- **All Processes.** Displays a complete list of all the running processes.

- **Active Processes.** Displays just those processes that are currently or have recently used the CPU.

- **Inactive Processes.** Displays just those processes that are running but haven't used the CPU in a while.

Process ID	Process Name	User	CPU	# Threads	Real Memory	Virtual Memory	Kind
314	Activity Monitor	paul	3.2	5	12.87 MB	968.78 MB	Intel
95	AirPort Base Station A...	paul	0.0	1	2.84 MB	890.35 MB	Intel
101	ATSServer	paul	0.0	2	2.98 MB	632.92 MB	Intel
102	Dock	paul	0.7	4	10.77 MB	928.10 MB	Intel
106	Finder	paul	0.1	9	25.38 MB	982.84 MB	Intel
204	Grab	paul	0.8	9	26.60 MB	986.92 MB	Intel
113	iTunes Helper	paul	0.0	2	2.41 MB	859.00 MB	Intel
72	launchd	paul	0.0	3	524.00 KB	585.74 MB	Intel
33	loginwindow	paul	0.0	3	5.32 MB	866.49 MB	Intel
300	mdworker	paul	0.0	4	2.14 MB	598.80 MB	Intel
104	pboard	paul	0.0	1	588.00 KB	586.63 MB	Intel
108	Quick Look Server	paul	0.0	7	9.75 MB	901.14 MB	Intel
99	Spotlight	paul	0.0	2	4.19 MB	861.08 MB	Intel
105	SystemUIServer	paul	0.1	8	8.51 MB	904.21 MB	Intel
100	UserEventAgent	paul	0.0	2	2.37 MB	589.21 MB	Intel

CPU | System Memory | Disk Activity | Disk Usage | Network

CPU Usage

% User: 6.52
% System: 3.51
% Nice: 0.00
% Idle: 89.97

Threads: 207
Processes: 50

9.2 You can use Activity Monitor to keep an eye on your Mac's CPU usage.

- **Windowed Processes.** Displays just those processes associated with running programs that you can see in the Dock (that is, the programs with open windows you can interact with).

- **Selected Processes.** You can use this item to display specific processes. For example, if you want to watch certain processes, you'd choose them and then choose Selected Processes.

Genius

The processes appear alphabetically by name, but you can change that order by clicking any column header. For example, to sort the processes by CPU usage, click the CPU column header. (This gives you an ascending sort; click the header again to get a descending sort.)

Whichever processes you display, the list itself is divided into a number of columns that give you information about the resources that each process is using. Here's a summary:

- **Process ID.** This column shows the process identifier, a unique numerical value that your Mac assigns to the process while it's running.

- **Process Name.** This is the name (usually the executable filename) of the process. You also see the icon for each windowed process.

- **User.** This value tells you the name of the user or service that launched the process.

- **CPU.** This is the key column for you in this section. The values here tell you the percentage of CPU resources that each process is using. If your system seems sluggish, look for a process that is consuming all or nearly all of the CPU's resources. Most programs monopolize the CPU occasionally for short periods, but a program that is stuck at 100 (percent) for a long time most likely has some kind of problem. In that case, try shutting down the program or process, as described later in this chapter.

- **Threads.** This value tells you the number of threads that each process is using. A *thread* is a program task that can run independently of and (usually) concurrently with other tasks in the same program, in which case the program is said to support *multithreading*. Multithreading improves program performance, but programs that have an unusually large number of threads can slow down the computer because it has to spend too much time switching from one thread of execution to another.

- **Real Memory.** This value tells you approximately how much memory the process is using. This value is less useful because a process might genuinely require a lot of memory to operate. However, if this value is steadily increasing for a process that you're not using, it could indicate a problem, and you should shut down the process, as described later in this chapter.

Genius

You can control how often Activity Monitor refreshes its data. Choose View ➪ Update Frequency, and then choose Very Often (Activity Monitor refreshes the data twice per second); Often (Activity Monitor refreshes the data every second); Normally (Activity Monitor refreshes the data every 2 seconds; this is the default); or Less Often (Activity Monitor refreshes the data every 5 seconds).

- **Virtual Memory.** This value shows the total amount of virtual memory that each process is using. Your computer can address memory beyond what is physically installed on the system. This nonphysical memory is called *virtual memory,* and it's implemented by using a piece of your hard disk that's set up to emulate physical memory. Again, seeing a steady increase in this value for a process that you're not using could be a sign of a problem, and you should shut down the process, as described later in this chapter.

- **Kind.** This column shows you what type of CPU the process is programmed to run on: Intel or PowerPC.

- **CPU Time.** Display this column by choosing View ⇨ Columns ⇨ CPU Time. It shows the total time, in days, hours, minutes, and seconds, that the process has used the CPU since the process was launched. If you see another process that seems to have used an inordinate amount of CPU time (for example, hours of CPU time when all other processes have used only minutes or seconds of CPU time), it could mean that the process is frozen or out of control and should be shut down, as described later in this chapter.

The bottom-left part of the Activity Monitor window shows the CPU totals. For the percentage of CPU usage, you see separate percentages for User (processes running under your user account), System (processes that your Mac is using), Nice (processes that have had their priority changed), and Idle (the amount of resources available to the CPU, as a percentage of the total).

You want to monitor what percentage of the CPU is currently being used, but it's a hassle to always switch to Activity Monitor to check this. An easier way is to configure the Activity Monitor Dock icon as a graph that shows the current state of the CPU usage value. To do this, choose View ⇨ Dock Icon ⇨ Show CPU Usage. Figure 9.3 shows what it looks like.

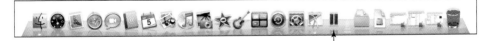

Activity Monitor icon

9.3 You can configure the Activity Monitor Dock icon as a graph that shows the current CPU usage.

Changing Your Priorities

The priority of a process determines how much scheduling time the CPU gives to it: A higher-priority process runs faster (because it gets more CPU time), and a lower-priority process runs slower. By default, all processes are given the same priority. However, if you want to try changing a process priority (for example, to make the process run faster), choose Finder ⇨ Applications ⇨ Utilities ⇨ Terminal. In the Terminal window, enter the following command: **sudo renice *priority Process ID.***

Here, replace *priority* with a value between –20 (highest priority) and 20 (lowest priority); replace *Process ID* with the process identifier number of the process you want to work with. You'll need to enter an administrator's password for this to work.

Monitoring memory usage

Memory is the lifeblood of any computer, and your Mac is no different. If your system runs low on memory, everything slows to a crawl, and programs may fail mysteriously. You can use Activity Monitor to examine how much real and virtual memory each running process is using. However, the total amount of memory being used is important, as well. To see that, you must click the System Memory tab in the Activity Monitor window, as shown in figure 9.4.

Process ID	Process Name	User	CPU	# Threads	Real Memory	Virtual Memory	Kind
314	Activity Monitor	paul	1.9	5	13.93 MB	969.48 MB	Intel
95	AirPort Base Station A...	paul	0.0	1	2.84 MB	890.35 MB	Intel
101	ATSServer	paul	0.0	2	2.98 MB	632.92 MB	Intel
102	Dock	paul	0.6	3	10.76 MB	927.56 MB	Intel
106	Finder	paul	0.0	8	25.21 MB	981.33 MB	Intel
204	Grab	paul	0.0	9	23.24 MB	980.16 MB	Intel
113	iTunes Helper	paul	0.0	2	2.41 MB	859.00 MB	Intel
72	launchd	paul	0.0	3	524.00 KB	585.74 MB	Intel
33	loginwindow	paul	0.0	3	5.32 MB	866.49 MB	Intel
300	mdworker	paul	0.0	4	2.14 MB	598.80 MB	Intel
104	pboard	paul	0.0	1	588.00 KB	586.63 MB	Intel
108	Quick Look Server	paul	0.0	7	9.75 MB	901.14 MB	Intel
99	Spotlight	paul	0.0	2	4.19 MB	861.08 MB	Intel
105	SystemUIServer	paul	0.0	8	8.51 MB	904.21 MB	Intel
100	UserEventAgent	paul	0.0	2	2.37 MB	589.21 MB	Intel

CPU   System Memory   Disk Activity   Disk Usage   Network

Free:	1.47 GB	VM size:	33.04 GB
Wired:	274.91 MB	Page ins:	103.65 MB
Active:	214.92 MB	Page outs:	0 Bytes
Inactive:	31.76 MB	Swap used:	0 Bytes
Used :	521.60 MB		2.00 GB

9.4 You can use Activity Monitor's System Memory tab to track how your Mac is using memory.

The pie chart shows how your Mac is currently allocating your computer's RAM, and the total amount of RAM available appears below the pie chart. These four types of RAM appear as

- **Free.** This is the number of megabytes that are currently available for processes. As this number gets lower, system performance slows because your Mac may reduce the memory used by each process. If this number (plus the Inactive number, described in this section) drops very low (a few megabytes), use the Activity Monitor to see if a process is using excessive amounts of memory. Otherwise, you may need to add RAM to your system.

- **Wired.** This is the number of megabytes that must stay in RAM and can't be stored on disk in virtual memory.

257

- **Active.** This is the number of megabytes that is currently being stored in RAM and is being used by processes.

- **Inactive.** This is the number of megabytes that is currently being stored in RAM and is no longer being used by processes. All of this data has also been paged out to virtual memory, so the RAM is available for another process to use.

Besides these four types of RAM, the System Memory tab also displays five other values:

- **Used.** This is the total number of megabytes of information currently being stored in RAM. It's the sum of the Wired, Active, and Inactive values.

- **VM size.** This is the size, in gigabytes, of the virtual memory cache on the hard disk.

- **Page ins.** This is the amount of data that the system has read in from virtual memory. If this number grows quite large, it means your Mac's performance is not what it could be because the system must retrieve data from the relatively slow hard disk. You need to shut down some running programs or processes, or add RAM.

- **Page outs.** This is the amount of data that the system has had to write to the hard disk virtual memory to free up real memory. This value is likely 0 most of the time, but it's okay if it's not. However, if it starts to get large (hundreds of megabytes) in a short time, then it likely means that your system doesn't have enough real memory for the programs you're running.

- **Swap used.** This is the size of the *swap file*, which is the area of virtual memory that your Mac is actually using. So even though the entire virtual memory cache may be 25 or 30GB, the swap file is (or should be) vastly smaller. It should actually be 0 most of the time, but it may grow to a few megabytes. If you see it grows to hundreds of megabytes over a short period, then your Mac likely doesn't have enough RAM for the programs you're running.

Genius

On almost all Macs, you can solve most memory problems simply by adding more RAM to the system. Unfortunately, this isn't an option with the MacBook Air because the memory chips are soldered to the motherboard, which means they can't be replaced or upgraded.

Monitoring hard disk activity

Having enough RAM is crucial for system stability, but everything in RAM was originally stored on the hard disk. This means that it's nearly as important to monitor your hard disk activity. The crucial thing here is how often your system asks the hard disk to read data from the disk and write data to the disk:

● **Reading data from the hard disk.** Hard disks are extremely fast and they read data from the disk all the time. However, a hard disk is still relatively slow compared to RAM, so if the hard disk has to read data excessively, it slows down your system. Excessive disk reading is most often a sign that your hard disk is defragmented.

Genius

Your Mac's files don't easily get defragmented (that is, broken into smaller chunks and spread around the hard disk). This is probably why your Mac doesn't come with a disk-optimization utility to fix defragmentation. Defragmenting can happen, however, so to fix it you need a program such as iDefrag from Coriolis Systems (www.coriolis-systems.com), which costs $34.95, but there's a demo version that defrags up to 100MB.

● **Writing data to the hard disk.** If your hard disk is writing data back to the disk excessively, it's usually a sign that your Mac doesn't have enough RAM for all the programs you're running. Try shutting down a few programs.

So if you quite often get the spinning wait cursor (the rainbow-colored spinning cursor that appears when the system is taking its sweet time to complete some task), excessive disk reads and writes could be the culprit. To check, run Activity Monitor (in Finder, choose Applications ⇨ Utilities ⇨ Activity Monitor) and then click the Disk Activity tab, shown in figure 9.5.

○ ○ ○			Activity Monitor				
● ⓘ ●				My Processes	▼	Q▼ Filter	
Quit Process Inspect Sample Process				Show		Filter	

Process ID	Process Name	User	CPU	# Threads	Real Memory	Virtual Memory	Kind
314	Activity Monitor	paul	2.1	5	13.95 MB	969.14 MB	Intel
95	AirPort Base Station A..	paul	0.0	1	2.84 MB	890.35 MB	Intel
101	ATSServer	paul	0.0	2	2.66 MB	629.92 MB	Intel
102	Dock	paul	0.6	3	10.76 MB	927.56 MB	Intel
106	Finder	paul	0.0	8	25.20 MB	979.14 MB	Intel
204	Grab	paul	2.4	9	23.44 MB	978.01 MB	Intel
113	iTunes Helper	paul	0.0	2	2.41 MB	859.00 MB	Intel
72	launchd	paul	0.0	3	524.00 KB	585.74 MB	Intel
33	loginwindow	paul	0.0	3	5.32 MB	866.49 MB	Intel
300	mdworker	paul	0.0	4	2.14 MB	598.80 MB	Intel
104	pboard	paul	0.0	1	588.00 KB	586.63 MB	Intel
108	Quick Look Server	paul	0.0	7	9.75 MB	901.14 MB	Intel
99	Spotlight	paul	0.0	2	4.19 MB	861.08 MB	Intel
105	SystemUIServer	paul	0.0	8	8.51 MB	904.21 MB	Intel
100	UserEventAgent	paul	0.0	2	2.37 MB	589.21 MB	Intel

CPU	System Memory	Disk Activity	Disk Usage	Network

Peak: 101.02 KB/sec

Reads in:	10748	Data read:	305.86 MB
Writes out:	5590	Data written:	101.13 MB
Reads in/sec:	0	Data read/sec:	0 Bytes
Writes out/sec:	0	Data written/sec:	0 Bytes

○ IO   ● Data

9.5 You can use Activity Monitor's Disk Activity tab to track how frequently your Mac's hard disk is reading and writing data.

There's lots of data here, but you only need to monitor two values:

- **Reads in.** This tells you the number of times per second the hard disk is reading data.

- **Writes out.** This tells you the number of times per second the hard disk is writing data.

These values should be 0 most of the time, but they do jump up occasionally when you use your Mac. If you see these numbers jump up and stay up for an extended period, then you know you have a problem.

Checking for software updates

When Apple or a third-party software developer prepares an update to a program, they often include new features, support for new technologies, performance boosts, and security enhancements. However, the vast majority of items in a software update are fixes that squash bugs, provide more stability, and make the program more compatible with existing hardware.

In other words, if you're having consistent trouble with a program, chances are that other people have been having the same problem, the software developer knows about the problem, and they've taken steps to fix it. This means that installing the most-recent update for the application can be the cure you've been seeking.

You have two ways to check for software updates:

- **For Apple software.** Pull down the Apple menu and choose Software Update.

- **For other software developers.** Go to the company's Web site. First find your program's product page and check out the latest version number. If it's later than the version you have, see if you're eligible for a free (or at least cheap) upgrade. Otherwise, go to the site's support pages and look around to see if a patch or other update is available for your application.

Bypassing your login items

It's always possible that flaky system behavior could be caused by one of your login items. To find out, it's possible to log in without loading any of your login items (this is called a *safe login*). If the problem goes away, you're a step closer to locating the culprit.

First, follow these steps to log in without your login items:

1. **Pull down the Apple menu and choose Log Out *User*, where *User* is your user name.** You can also press Shift+⌘+Q. Your Mac asks if you're sure.

2. **Click Log Out.** Your Mac logs you out and displays the login screen.

3. **Choose your user account (if necessary) and type your password.**

4. **Hold down the Shift key and then click Log In.** Your Mac logs you in without loading any of your login items.

5. **When you see the Desktop, release the Shift key.**

If the problem goes away, you can be fairly certain that a login item is the cause. From here, disable the login items one at a time (as described in Chapter 8) until you find the one that's the source of your woes.

Deleting a program's preferences file

A *preferences file* is a document that stores options and other data that you've entered using the application's Preferences command. One of the most common causes of application flakiness is a preferences file that's somehow become damaged or corrupted (for example, its data is written with the wrong syntax). In that case, you can solve the problem by deleting (or moving) the preferences file so that the application has to rebuild it. On the downside, this may mean that you have to reenter some preferences, but that's usually a fairly small price to pay for a stable application.

Preferences files use the .plist filename extension. In most cases, the filename uses the following general format: com.*company*.*application*.plist.

Here, *company* is the name of the software company that makes the application, and *application* is the name of the program. Here are some examples:

com.apple.iTunes.plist

com.microsoft.Word.plist

com.palm.HotSync.plist

Follow these steps to delete an application's preferences file.

1. **Quit the application if it's currently running.**

2. **In Finder, choose your user name and then choose Library ⇨ Preferences.**

3. **Locate the application's preferences file.** If you can't find the preferences file, choose Macintosh HD ⇨ Library ⇨ Preferences and see if it appears in that folder.

Genius

Unfortunately, not every preferences file uses the com.*company.application*.plist format. If you can't find the preferences file you're looking for, type either the company name or the program name in the Search box.

4. **Click and drag the preferences file and drop it in another location.** The desktop is probably the best spot for this. Note that if the application has multiple preferences files, you should move all of them to the new location.

5. **Run the application and see if the problem persists.**

   ● **Problem resolved.** The preferences file was the source after all, so go ahead and move it to the Trash from the location you chose in Step 4. You need to reenter your preferences.

   ● **Problem remains.** The preferences file wasn't the culprit after all. Quit the application and move the preferences file back to the Preferences folder from the location you chose in Step 4.

Reinstalling Mac OS X

If worse comes to worst and your Mac won't start or if it's just completely unstable, you need to bite the bullet and reinstall the operating system. As you see in the following steps, it's possible to have your data and settings transferred to the new installation using the Archive and Install option. However, if you still have access to the system, it's a good idea to make backups of your documents, just in case something goes wrong during the transfer. Chapter 8 addresses various ways to back up your files.

Genius

If you have a small hard disk, it may not have enough room for the reinstallation because the Archive and Install option moves all the old OS X System files to a separate folder called Previous System. In that case, the only way to reinstall OS X is to erase your hard disk and start from scratch (this is called the Erase and Install option). This means that if you don't back up your data, you lose it forever.

With that done, follow these steps to reinstall OS X:

1. **Insert the Mac OS X Installation DVD.**

2. **Turn on or restart your Mac.**

3. **Hold down C while your Mac is restarting.** You can release C when you see the Apple logo. Your Mac boots to the Mac OS X Install DVD.

4. **Select a language for the install and then press Return.** The Install Mac OS X application appears.

5. **Click Continue.** The license agreement appears.

6. **Click Agree.** The Select a Destination window appears.

7. **Click Options.** This opens the dialog box that contains the installation options, as shown in figure 9.6.

8. **Select the Archive and Install option, select the Preserve Users and Network Settings check box, and then click OK.** Remember that if your hard disk doesn't have enough room for Archive and Install, you must select the Erase and Install option, instead. You are returned to the Select a Destination window.

9. **Click Macintosh HD, as shown in figure 9.7.**

10. **Click Continue.** The Installer lets you know that it's ready to install Mac OS X.

11. **Click Install.** The program begins installing Mac OS X.

○ Upgrade Mac OS X
Upgrades an earlier version of Mac OS X.

● Archive and Install
Moves existing System files to a folder named Previous System, then installs a new copy of Mac OS X. This option is only available for volumes with Mac OS X already installed.

☑ Preserve Users and Network Settings
Imports existing user accounts, their home folders, and your network settings into the new system. You will skip the Setup Assistant when installation is complete.

○ Erase and Install
Completely erases the destination volume then installs a new copy of Mac OS X.

Format disk as: Mac OS Extended (Journaled)

Cancel   OK

9.6 Use this dialog box to select the Archive and Install option.

Install Mac OS X

Select a Destination

- Introduction
- License
- Select Destination
- Installation Type
- Install
- Finish Up

Select a destination volume to install the Mac OS X software.

Macintosh HD
95.9GB (77.9GB Free)

Installing this software requires 4.7GB of space.

You have selected to move the files in the System folder on this volume to a folder named "Previous System," then install a new version of Mac OS X.

Options...   Go Back   Continue

9.7 Select Macintosh HD as the install destination.

263

General Hardware Troubleshooting Techniques

If you're having trouble with a device attached to your Mac, the good news is that a fair chunk of hardware problems have a relatively limited set of causes, so you may be able to get the device back on its feet by attempting a few tried-and-true remedies that work quite often for many devices. The next few sections take you through these generic troubleshooting techniques.

First steps to troubleshooting hardware

If it's not immediately obvious what the problem is, your Mac hardware troubleshooting routine should always start with these very basic techniques:

- **Check connections, power switches, and so on.** Some of the most common (and some of the most embarrassing) causes of hardware problems are the simple physical things, such as devices being unplugged or disconnected. So your first troubleshooting steps should concentrate on the obvious: making sure that a device is turned on; checking that cable connections are secure; and ensuring that insertable devices (such as USB devices) are properly inserted. For example, if you can't access the Internet or your network, make sure your network's router or wireless access point is turned on and, if you have a wired connection, make sure the network cable between your Mac and your router is properly connected.

- **Replace the batteries.** Wireless devices such as keyboards and mice really chew through batteries, so if either one is working intermittently or not at all, always try replacing the batteries to see if that solves the problem.

- **Turn the device off and then on again.** You *power cycle* a device by turning it off, waiting a few seconds for its innards to stop spinning, and then turning it back on again. You'd be amazed how often this simple procedure can get a device back up and running. Of course, not all devices have an on/off switch, but this technique works very well for devices such as external displays, printers, scanners, routers, switches, modems, external hard disks and DVD drives, many USB and FireWire devices, and some wireless devices such as mice and keyboards. Many wireless mice have a reset button on the bottom, whereas some keyboards — notably the Apple Bluetooth keyboard — have an on/off switch. USB and FireWire devices often get their power directly from the USB or FireWire port. Power cycle these devices by unplugging them and then plugging them back in.

- **Close all programs.** If you have lots of programs going, device drivers (the little programs that enable Mac OS X to communicate with devices, and vice versa) may get weird because there isn't enough memory or other resources. You can often fix flaky behavior by shutting down all your open programs and starting again.

- **Log out.** Logging off serves to clear the memory by shutting down your programs, but it also releases much of the stuff your Mac has loaded into memory, thus creating a slightly cleaner palette than just closing your programs. To log out, pull down the Apple menu and choose Log Out *User*, where *User* is your Mac username, or just press Shift+⌘+Q.

- **Reset the device's default settings.** If you can configure a device, then perhaps some new setting is causing the problem. If you recently made a change, try returning the setting back to its original value. If that doesn't do the trick, most configurable devices have some kind of "Restore Default Settings" option that enables you to quickly return the device to its factory settings.

- **Upgrade the device's firmware.** Some devices come with *firmware*, a small program that runs inside the device and controls its internal functions. For example, all routers have firmware. Check with the manufacturer to see if a new version exists. If it does, download the new version and then see the device's manual to learn how to upgrade the firmware.

Restarting your Mac

If a hardware device is having a problem with some system files, logging off your Mac won't help because the system files remain loaded. By rebooting your Mac, you reload the entire system, which is often enough to solve many computer problems. You reboot your Mac by pulling down the Apple menu, choosing Restart, and then clicking Restart in the dialog box that appears.

Power cycling your Mac

For problem devices that don't have a power switch — basically, anything inside your Mac, including the display on your iMac or Mac notebook — restarting your Mac might not resolve the problem because the devices remain powered up the whole time. You can power cycle these devices as a group by power cycling the Mac:

1. **Close all running applications.**

2. **Pull down the Apple menu and choose Shut Down.** Your Mac asks you to confirm.

3. **Click Shut Down.** Your Mac shuts down the system.

4. **Once your Mac is off, wait for 30 seconds to give all devices time to spin down.**

5. **Turn your Mac back on.**

Forcing the issue: Making a stuck Mac restart or shut down

If things go seriously awry on your Mac, you may find that you can't do *anything*: Your applications are frozen. You can bang away at the keyboard all you want but nothing happens; the mouse pointer doesn't even budge when you move the mouse. That's a major-league lockup you've got there, and your only recourse is to force your Mac to restart or shut down.

⊙ **Forcing your Mac to restart.** Hold down the Control and ⌘ keys and then press the power button.

⊙ **Forcing your Mac to shut down.** Press and hold the power button until your Mac shuts off.

Caution

As you might expect, forcing your Mac to restart or shut down doesn't give you any graceful way to close your running applications. This means that if you have unsaved changes in any open documents, you lose those changes. Therefore, it's a good idea to make sure your Mac is frozen and not just in a temporary state of suspended animation while it's waiting for some lengthy process to finish. If you're not sure, wait 5 minutes before forcing the restart or shutdown.

Restarting your Mac in Safe Mode

Login items — programs that run automatically when you log in to your Mac — can cause system problems by using up resources and creating memory conflicts. However, they're not the only behind-the-scenes components that can make your system wonky. Other processes used by your Mac and by your applications can run amok and cause trouble. To see whether such a process is at the root of your problem, you can perform a Safe Boot: starting your Mac in Safe Mode, which means that it doesn't load most of those behind-the-scenes components. If the problem still persists even in Safe Mode, you know it's not caused by a hidden process. If the problem does go away, it's a bit harder to deal with because there's no way to disable individual components. So, you may need to reinstall Mac OS X, as described earlier.

Follow these steps to perform a Safe Boot:

1. **Pull down the Apple menu and choose Shut Down.** Your Mac asks if you're sure.

2. **Click Shut Down.** Your Mac logs you out and then shuts off.

3. **Press the power button to turn your Mac back on.**

4. **Hold down the Shift key until you see the Apple logo**. Your Mac loads with only a min-imal set of components. When you get to the login screen, you see the words "Safe Boot."

Note

Although you might think it would take your Mac less time to load without all those extra components, the opposite is actually the case: your Mac takes quite a bit lon-ger to start up in Safe Mode. If you want to know why, see the following page: http:// docs.info.apple.com/article.html?artnum=107392.

5. **Log in to your Mac.** Check to see if the problem is still present. If it is, continue with the troubleshooting techniques in the following sections.

Restarting your Mac using a secondary boot device

You can use a secondary boot device to boot your Mac when you need to troubleshoot or repair your main Mac hard disk. How you boot to this device depends on the device you're using:

⊙ **Another Mac connected by a FireWire cable.** Connect the cable, restart the good Mac (that is, not the Mac that you want to troubleshoot or repair), and hold down T until you see the FireWire icon. That Mac is now in *FireWire target disk mode*. Restart the Mac that you want to troubleshoot and hold down Option until you see the Apple icon. This invokes the Startup Manager, which displays icons for the hard disks of both Macs. Double-click the icon for the secondary Mac (the icon has the FireWire logo on it) to boot to that Mac. When the secondary Mac's desktop appears, you see an icon for the hard disk of the Mac you want to troubleshoot.

Genius

Another way to restart the other Mac in target disk mode is to click System Preferences in the Dock, click the Startup Disk icon, and then click Target Disk Mode.

Note

To exit target disk mode, shut down the Mac you're troubleshooting, and then turn off the Mac that's in target disk mode.

● **Your Mac OS X Install DVD.** Insert the DVD, restart your Mac, and hold down C until you see the Apple icon.

● **A second internal hard disk or an external FireWire or USB hard disk.** Connect the external drive (if necessary), restart your Mac, and hold down Option until you see the Apple icon. When the Startup Manager appears, double-click the icon for the secondary hard disk.

Running the Apple Hardware Test

If your Mac is running erratically, is locking up at random times, or is causing your applications to behave strangely, there are a number of things that could be wrong with the computer's memory, hard disk, processor, or some other internal component. To help you see whether faulty hardware is the source of these ills (and not faulty software), you can run the Apple Hardware Test. This program performs a thorough check of your system's innards to see if anything's amiss. If it finds a problem, it lets you know what component is acting up and it gives you an error code. However, Apple Hardware Test doesn't fix the problem. Instead, you're supposed to provide the error code to someone who knows what they're doing, and they ought to have enough information to fix the error.

On most Macs, the Apple Hardware Test isn't installed on the Mac. Instead, it's a separate program that resides on the Mac OS X Install Disc 1 that comes with each new Mac. (It's the gray disc.) You can't copy it to your Mac or run it directly from the disc. Instead, you need to reboot your Mac with the disc inserted. Follow these steps:

1. **Insert Mac OS X Install Disc 1 into your Mac.**

2. **Pull down the Apple menu and choose Restart.** Your Mac asks you to confirm the restart.

3. **Click Restart.** Your Mac shuts down and then restarts.

4. **When the Mac restarts, hold down D.** You see the Apple Hardware Test window.

5. **Click the language you prefer to use and then press Return.** The Apple Hardware Test opens.

6. **Select the Perform extended testing check box, as shown in figure 9.8.**

7. **Click Test or press T.** Apple Hardware Test begins testing your Mac, which takes a while. If Apple Hardware Test detects a problem, information about the problem appears in the Test Results area.

8. **Make a note of any problems found, particularly any error codes related to each issue.**

9. **Click Restart.**

Apple Hardware Test Version 3A131

About | Hardware Tests | Hardware Profile

Apple Hardware Test can perform hardware testing of your Macintosh.

To perform the tests, click on the "Test" button or press the "T" key.

Apple Hardware Test is a diagnostic tool for detecting problems with your computer's hardware components.

The tests performed will help determine if you have a hardware problem or a software problem.

If the test results determine that a hardware problem does not exist, consult the manual and/or Help (system) that came with your computer for further troubleshooting.

Estimated time to complete: 2 hours or longer, depending on the amount of memory installed.

Test

☑ Perform extended testing (takes considerably more time).

Test Results

Ready for testing.

Restart | Shut Down

9.8 Use the Apple Hardware Test to look for malfunctioning devices on your Mac.

Note Performing the extended tests could take between one and two hours, so only run this test when you won't need your Mac for a while. You might be tempted to run just the regular tests, which take only a couple of minutes. However, if you're having problems, the extended test is better because it delves much more deeply into your hardware.

Repairing the hard disk

If your Mac won't start, or if an application freezes, it's possible that an error on the hard disk is causing the problem. To see if this is the case, you need to repair the hard disk using your Mac's Disk Utility program. How are you supposed to do that if you can't even start your Mac? Good question! The answer is that you need to start your Mac using a secondary boot device (which is explained earlier in the chapter). You then run Disk Utility from that device, and that enables you to repair your main hard disk. Note, too, that even if you can start your Mac, you still need to boot to the secondary device because you can't repair the main hard disk while your Mac is using it.

269

Caution It's important to note you should *never* repair a hard disk without first backing up that hard disk. A failed disk repair can actually *destroy* the disk and make the data inaccessible, so play it safe and back up your data.

Follow these steps to repair your hard disk:

1. **Restart your Mac using a secondary boot device.**

2. **Launch the Disk Utility.**

   - If you booted to an external hard disk, or to a Mac in target disk mode, open Finder and choose Applications ➪ Utilities ➪ Disk Utility.

   - If you booted to the Mac OS X Install DVD, when you get to the Mac OS X Installer screen, choose Utilities ➪ Disk Utility.

3. **Choose Macintosh HD, which is the hard disk you want to repair.**

4. **Make sure the First Aid tab is selected, as shown in figure 9.9.**

9.9 You can repair your Mac's hard disk by running Disk Utility from a secondary boot device.

5. **Click Repair Disk**. Disk Utility verifies that the disk is sound and fixes any problems that it finds.

Genius

Ideally, Disk Utility reports that "The volume Macintosh HD appears to be OK." In the worst-case scenario, Disk Utility reports that it found errors, but it can't fix them. In that case, you need to turn to a more heavy-duty solution: a third-party disk repair application. I recommend these two: DiskWarrior (www.alsoft.com) and TechTool Pro (www.micromat.com). Note: At the time of this writing, software publisher Alsoft had not released a compatible version of DiskWarrior for Mac OS X 5.1 Leopard. Check with the software publisher for updates.

Repairing disk permissions

All the files on your Mac have *permissions* applied to them. Permissions are a collection of settings that determine what users or groups of users can do with each file. For example, if a file implements read-only permissions, it means that all users can only read the contents of the file and can't make any changes to the file or delete it. For things such as system files, particular permissions are set during installation and shouldn't ever be changed. If a system file's permissions *do* happen to change, it can cause all kinds of problems, including program lockups and flaky system behavior.

Fortunately, your Mac's Disk Utility has a feature that enables you to repair permissions for many of the files on your system. Here's how it works:

1. **If you can't start your Mac, boot using a secondary device.** Otherwise, boot your Mac normally.

2. **Launch the Disk Utility.**

   - If you booted to an external hard disk, or to a Mac in target disk mode, open Finder and choose Applications ⇨ Utilities ⇨ Disk Utility.

   - If you booted to the Mac OS X Install DVD, when you get to the Mac OS X Installer screen, choose Utilities ⇨ Disk Utility.

3. **Choose Macintosh HD, which is the hard disk with the permissions you want to repair.**

4. **Make sure the First Aid tab is selected.**

5. **Click Repair Disk Permissions**. Disk Utility repairs the permissions.

Genius

It's a good idea to repair permissions after every application install because there's always a chance that an installer program may change some system file permissions to something other than what Apple wants or expects for those files.

How Can I Share Data Between Mac OS X and Windows?

You may have left your Windows PC behind, but that doesn't necessarily mean you've left Windows behind. For example, you might still use a Windows machine for certain tasks; you might have a mix of Mac and Windows computers on your network; you might have to exchange documents with people who use Windows; or you might want to synchronize data between your Mac and a Windows PC. Whatever the scenario, if you find yourself straddling both the Mac and Windows worlds, at some point you're going to have to share data between those worlds, and this chapter shows you the best methods to do just that.

Sharing Data over a Network

All networks have multiple layers of communication, and the details of those layers are usually of interest only to networking geeks. However, I'd like to mention in passing an important networking layer used by all Microsoft networks: Server Message Block (SMB). It's via SMB that Windows PCs can share folders on the network and access folders that other Windows PCs have shared. In a very real sense, SMB *is* the network.

SMB's central role in Windows networking is good news for you as a Mac user because all versions of OS X support SMB natively. This means that you can use your Mac not only to view Windows shares, but also to open and work with files on those shares (provided, of course, that you have permission to access a share and that OS X has an application that's compatible with whatever file you want to work with).

SMB not only lets your Mac see shares on the Windows network, it also can let Windows PCs see folders shared by the Mac.

Making a wireless network connection

Most modern Macs come with an Ethernet port, which you can use to run a network cable from your Mac to a network router or switch. (The exception is the MacBook Air, which wears its wireless heart on its sleeve by not having an Ethernet port, so you have to network wirelessly.) However, all new Macs come with a built-in AirPort wireless networking card (the card is an option on the Mac Pro), which enables the Mac to connect to Wi-Fi (Wireless Fidelity) networks. This is useful if your desktop Mac resides in a different room than your router or switch, or if you want to roam around with your notebook Mac.

Here are the steps to follow to connect your Mac to a wireless network:

1. **In the menu bar, click the AirPort status icon.** Your Mac displays a list of available wireless networks, as shown in figure 10.1.

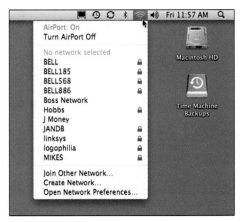

10.1 Click the menu bar's AirPort icon to see a list of wireless networks within range of your Mac.

Note

In the AirPort list, wireless networks that display the lock icon are secure networks protected by a password. To connect to such a network, you need to know the password.

2. **Choose the network you want to join.** If the network is password-protected, your Mac prompts you for the password, as shown in figure 10.2.

3. **Type the password.** If the password is long or complex, you can be sure that you're typing it correctly by selecting the Show password check box. If you're in a public area, it's a good idea to make sure no one can see the exposed password.

The network "logophilia" requires a WPA password.

Password: ●●●●●●●●●●●

☐ Show password
☑ Remember this network

Cancel   OK

10.2 Most wireless networks are protected by a password.

4. **If you want your Mac to automatically connect to this network the next time it comes within range, select the Remember this network check box.**

5. **Click OK.** Your Mac connects to the wireless network.

Connecting to a Windows PC

OS X support for connecting to shared Windows folders is turned on by default, so connecting your Mac to a Windows PC on your network and selecting a shared folder requires no prep work on your part.

How you go about making the connection depends on whether your Mac "sees" the Windows PC. To check this, switch to Finder and then do one of the following:

- In the Sidebar, open the Shared section and look for an icon for the Windows PC.

- Choose Go ➪ Network (or press Shift+⌘+K) and use the Network window to look for an icon for the Windows PC.

If you see an icon for the Windows PC, click the icon and then click Connect As to display the dialog box shown in figure 10.3. Select the Registered User option, type a username and password of an account on the Windows PC, select the Remember this password in my keychain check box, and then click Connect.

Note

If you don't know the username and password of an account on the Windows PC, select the Guest option, instead. This gives you read-only access to the Windows PC's shared folders.

Your Mac then presents you with a list of the shared folders on the Windows PC, as shown in figure 10.4. Click the shared folder you want to work with, and then click OK.

If your Windows PC doesn't show up in the Network window, first make sure it's turned on and not in sleep mode. If you still don't see it, follow these steps to make the connection:

1. **In Finder, choose Go ⇨ Connect to Server (or press ⌘+K).** The Connect to Server dialog box appears.

2. **In the Server Address text box, type smb://*WindowsPC*, where *WindowsPC* is the name of the Windows computer you want to connect to.** See figure 10.5 for an example.

3. **Click Connect.** Your Mac prompts you for the credentials of a user account on the Windows PC.

4. **Type a username and password of an account on the Windows PC, select the Remember this password in my keychain check box, and then click Connect.** Your Mac displays a list of the Windows PC's shared folders.

5. **Click the shared folder you want to use, and then click OK.**

Enter your user name and password to access the file server "tabletpc".

Connect as: ○ Guest
⦿ Registered User

Name: Paul

Password: •••••••••

☑ Remember this password in my keychain

Cancel | Connect

10.3 When you connect to the Windows PC, you need to provide a username and password for an account on the PC.

Select the volumes to mount:

My Documents
My Videos
Paul
SharedDocs

Cancel | OK

10.4 After you connect to the Windows PC, choose the shared folder you want to access.

Connect to Server

Server Address:
smb://paulspc | + | ☉

Favorite Servers:

? | Remove | Browse | Connect

10.5 If you don't see the Windows PC in Finder, use the Connect to Server command to connect to the PC directly.

Note You're not stuck with using only the shared folder that you chose when you made the initial connection to the Windows PC. To work with a different shared folder, switch to Finder, click the Windows PC in the Sidebar's Shared section, and then click the shared folder you want to use.

Sharing your Mac on a Windows network

The steps in the previous section assumed that you wanted to access a Windows shared network folder from your Mac. However, if your Mac has data of interest to Windows users, you'll need to set things up so that those Windows users can see that data. You do that by sharing one or more folders on your Mac in such a way that Windows PC can see and access them.

This feature isn't turned on by default on your Mac, so you need to follow these steps to turn it on:

1. **Choose Apple ⇨ System Preferences (or click the System Preferences icon in the Dock).** The System Preferences appear.

2. **Click the Sharing icon.** The Sharing preferences appear.

3. **In the list of services, select the File Sharing check box.**

4. **Click Options.**

5. **Select the Share files and folders using SMB check box, as shown in figure 10.6.**

6. **Select the check box for each user account to which you want to give access.**

7. **Click Done.**

8. **To share a folder, click the + icon under Shared Folders in the Sharing preferences, select the folder, and then click Add.**

9. **Click the folder in the Shared Folders list, click + under Users, select a user, and then click Add.**

☐ Share files and folders using AFP
  File Sharing: Off

☐ Share files and folders using FTP
  Warning: FTP logins and data transfers are not encrypted.

☑ Share files and folders using SMB
  When you enable SMB sharing for a user account, you must enter the password for that account. Sharing with SMB stores this password in a less secure manner.

On	Account
☐	Karen
☑	Paul

⑦   (Done)

10.6 To share your Mac with Windows PCs, deselect AFP sharing and select SMB sharing.

10. **Click a user in the Users list, and then click the permission level you want to assign from the drop-down menu.** You have four choices: Read & Write, Read Only, Write Only (Drop Box), or No Access.

11. **Repeat Steps 9 to 11 to share other folders and set other user permissions.** Figure 10.7 shows the Sharing preferences with several folders and users.

10.7 The Sharing preferences with Windows Sharing activated and several folders shared

One way to access the Mac shares from a Windows PC is to enter the share address directly using either the Run dialog box or Windows Explorer's Address bar. You have two choices:

*IP**user*

*Computer**user*

Here *IP* is the IP address shown in the Sharing window (shown in figure 10.7 as //192.168.0.90), *Computer* is the Mac's computer name (shown in figure 10.7 as iMac), and in both cases *user* is the username of the account enabled for Windows Sharing (shown in figure 10.7 as Paul). For example, I can use either of the following addresses to access my Mac:

\\192.168.0.90\paul

\\iMac\paul

Accessing a Mac via Vista

If you have trouble logging on to your Mac from Windows Vista, the problem is likely caused by Vista's use of NT LAN Manager version 2 (NTLMv2) authentication, which doesn't work properly when negotiated between some versions of Vista and some versions of OS X. To fix this, on the Vista PC, press Windows Logo+R (or select Start, All Programs, Accessories, Run), type **secpol.msc**, and click OK to open the Local Security Policy snap-in. Open the Security Settings, Local Policies, Security Options branch. Double-click the Network Security: LAN Manager Authentication Level policy, change the authentication level to Send LM & NTLM-Use NTLMv2 Session Security If Negotiated, and then click OK.

If your version of Vista doesn't come with the Local Security snap-in (it's not available in Home and Home Premium), open the Registry Editor (press Windows Logo+R, type **regedit**, and click OK), and navigate to the following key:

HKEY_LOCAL_MACHINE\SYSTEM\CurrentControlSet\Control\Lsa\

Change the value of the LMCompatibilityLevel setting to 1.

Alternatively, run Windows Explorer on your Windows PC, open your workgroup, and look for the icon that has the same name as the Mac's computer name. Double-click that icon.

Unless you're logged on to Windows with the same username and password as the Mac, you're prompted for the username and password of the Mac account that you enabled for Windows Sharing. For the username, use the form *Computer\UserName*, where *Computer* is the name of your Mac and *UserName* is the name of the Windows Sharing account.

Sharing Documents with Windows Users

One common experience that new Mac users have is to play around with their Mac for a time, really enjoy how easy the Mac makes things, and then wonder why in the name of Steve Jobs isn't *everyone* using a Mac? Although it's true that the Mac's share of the personal computer market has risen dramatically in the past few years, it's also true that Windows still dominates that market. This means that most of the people you deal with will still be using Windows, but that's no big deal to you, right? Not necessarily. If you have to share documents with a Windows user, it becomes a very big deal, indeed, because you want to be able to read and edit Windows documents sent your way, and you want Windows users to be able to read and edit the Mac documents you send them. The next few sections take you through a few issues related to sharing documents with Windows users.

Understanding file compatibility

File compatibility between Mac and Windows is often problematic because almost all files are associated with a particular application, and as you've seen there isn't always a Mac equivalent for a Windows program (and vice versa). For example, if a Windows user sends you a copy of an Access database, there's not much you can do with the file itself because there's no Mac equivalent for Microsoft Access. (Although as you see later in this chapter you can still connect to the Access database by using special software.) The associated application is determined by the file's extension, so a filename ending with .doc is a Microsoft Word document, a .xls file is a Microsoft Excel workbook, and so on.

How do you know if you have a Mac program that's compatible with a particular document? The easiest way to tell is to right-click (or Control+click) the document in Finder, and then click Open With. If you see <None> in the list that appears (see figure 10.8), it means your Mac doesn't have an application that's associated with the file extension. If, instead, you see one or more applications in the list, you can click the application you want to use to open the file.

10.8 If you see <None> when you click Open With, it means your Mac doesn't have an application that's compatible with the file.

Note

In the Open With list, the application at the top of the list is the default application associated with the file type. This means that when you double-click the document, your Mac opens it using the default application.

This isn't an issue with many standard file formats supported by multiple applications both on the Mac and in Windows. For example, Rich Text Format (.rtf) is a standard word-processing format that's supported by probably every word-processing application available. On your Windows PC, you could open RTF documents using WordPad or Word, whereas on your Mac you can open RTF files using TextEdit, Word, Page, or any number of other applications (see figure 10.9).

10.9 Many standard file formats, such as RTF, are compatible with multiple applications both on the Mac and on Windows.

Text files (.txt), Web page files (.htm or .html), and many media files (.jpg, .png, .mp3, and so on) are standard formats compatible with applications for both Mac and Windows.

Sharing Microsoft Office documents

If the people you work with want to share Microsoft Office files — Word documents, Excel workbooks, or PowerPoint presentations (but, as I've said, *not* Access databases) — and you've got some version of Office installed on your Mac, you're in luck. Microsoft Office documents almost always travel seamlessly between Mac and Windows, and no conversion is necessary to work with these files on either system. I said "almost always" because there are, as usual, a few exceptions to the rule:

- The most important consideration is backward compatibility. All versions of Office are backward compatible with any previous version of Office, which means that you can use your version of Office to open any document created with any earlier version of Office. What you want to avoid here is forward compatibility (or incompatibility, I guess), where you're faced with a document that uses the updated file format from a later version of Office. For example, if you're running Office 2004 for the Mac, you won't be able to read any documents created using the new formats supported by Office 2007 (or Office 2008 for the Mac), such as .docx, .xlsx, and .pptx. If that happens, ask your colleague to save the document in an earlier format, such as Office 2003.

Genius You may not be able to open Office 2008 or Office 2007 files directly in Office 2004, but you can do it indirectly by using Microsoft's Open XML File Format Converter (see www.microsoft.com/downloads/details.aspx?FamilyId=2A8D9A3B-B8A4-43B6-82A6-A2E7D16AE11D).

- The more complex the document is, the more likely it is that some of the document's fancier objects and formatting won't survive the transition from one system to another.

- If the Office document you're working with includes fonts that you don't have on your Mac, you won't see those fonts and, instead, your Mac will substitute some existing font. (The substitution happens only on the Mac. If you later open the file in Windows — even if you saved changes to the file on the Mac — you still see the original font.) Note, however, that the Windows versions of Word and PowerPoint enable you to embed fonts in the file, which means you'll be able to see those fonts on your Mac even if you don't have them installed. If it's important that you see the original fonts on your Mac, then embed the fonts using the following techniques:

  - **Word:** Choose Office ⇨ Word Options (in Word 2007) or Tools ⇨ Options (in earlier versions), click the Save tab, and then select the Embed fonts in the file check box. Click OK.

  - **PowerPoint:** Choose Office ⇨ PowerPoint Options (in PowerPoint 2007) or Tools ⇨ Options (in earlier versions), click the Save tab, and then select the Embed fonts in the file check box. Click OK.

- If an Office document contains Visual Basic for Applications (VBA) macros and you're using Office 2008 for the Mac, which doesn't support VBA macros (boo!), you see the dialog box shown in figure 10.10 when you open the file. You may occasionally want to strip out the macros by clicking Open and Remove Macros, but that's probably presumptuous if you're sharing the document, so click Open, instead. This means that Office 2008 opens the document normally, but you don't have access to its macros.

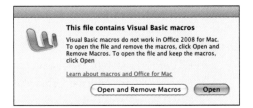

This file contains Visual Basic macros

Visual Basic macros do not work in Office 2008 for Mac. To open the file and remove the macros, click Open and Remove Macros. To open the file and keep the macros, click Open

Learn about macros and Office for Mac

[Open and Remove Macros] [Open]

10.10 You see this dialog box if you open an Office document with macros in Office 2008 for the Mac.

Genius In Word and PowerPoint you can control which fonts your Mac uses to substitute for the missing font. Open the Word or PowerPoint preferences, click the Compatibility tab, and then click Font Substitution.

Connecting to an Access database

I mentioned earlier that there's not much you can do directly with a Microsoft Access database because there's no Mac application that opens an Access database. However, the key word here is "directly." If all you want is to interact with the Access data, there is a way to connect to the database from either Excel for the Mac or from FileMaker Pro (version 6 or later). A company called Actual Technologies (www.actualtechnologies.com) makes an Open Database Connectivity (ODBC) driver for the Mac that enables Excel and FileMaker Pro to connect to any Access database (including Access 2007 files) and interact with the data. It costs $29.95, but a trial version is available for download.

Note The trial version is fully functional, but it's crippled: it returns only the first three records for any query.

Creating an Access data source

Once you've installed the ODBC driver, follow these steps to set up an Access database *data source*, which is the information required to connect to that Access database:

1. **In Finder, choose Applications ⇨ Utilities ⇨ ODBC Administrator.** The ODBC Administrator utility appears.

2. **Choose who you want to be able to use the data source:**

   - **Just you.** If you're the only user on your Mac, or if you have multiple users and you want only your account to connect to the Access database, click the User DSN tab.

   - **All users.** If you want every user account on your Mac to be able to connect to the Access database, click the System DSN tab. If you go this route, you must also click the lock icon and then enter an administrative password to continue.

3. **Click Add.** The Choose a Driver dialog box appears.

4. **Click Actual Access and then click OK.** The Create a New Data Source to an Access Database dialog box appears.

5. **Click Continue.**

6. **Use the Name text box to type a name for the data source.**

7. **Click Choose.** The Choose a File dialog box appears.

8. **Click the Access database and then click Choose.**

9. **Click Continue.** The Enter the Database Information dialog box appears.

10. **Click Continue.** The Conclusion dialog box appears.

11. **Click Done and then click Cancel.**

Note

In the Conclusion dialog box, it's a good idea to click the Test button to test the connection to the Access database. If you see the message "Test completed successfully," you know the data source is set up correctly. Otherwise, you need to go back and change some settings. (For example, make sure the Access database is accessible from Finder.)

The new data source appears in the ODBC Administrator window, as shown in figure 10.11.

```
         ODBC Administrator
  ⊙ ⊙ ⊙

   User DSN   System DSN   Drivers   Tracing   Connection Pooling   About

   Name        Description          Driver                        Add...
   Northwind   Access 2007 Database  Actual Access
                                                                  Remove

                                                                  Configure...




   An ODBC System data source stores information about how to connect to the indicated data
   provider. A System data source is visible to all users and processes on this machine.

                                                           Revert    Apply
   🔓 Click the lock to prevent further changes.
```

10.11 The ODBC Administrator with a data source for an Access database

With your Access data source in place, you can now use either Excel for the Mac or FileMaker Pro to connect to the Access database.

Connecting to an Access database using FileMaker Pro

Here are the steps to follow to connect to your Access database using FileMaker Pro

1. **Choose File ⇨ Open (or press ⌘+O).** The Open File dialog box appears.

2. **In the Show list, choose ODBC Data Source.** The Select ODBC Data Source dialog box appears.

3. **Choose your Access data source and then click Continue.** FileMaker Pro prompts you for a username and password.

4. **Enter the database login data, if necessary (if not, leave the text boxes blank), and then click OK.** The SQL Query Builder appears.

5. **Build your query.** I won't go into the details (because this isn't a FileMaker Pro book), but the basic idea is to choose a table, choose a column, click Insert into SQL Query, and then repeat as needed. Use the WHERE tab to set criteria, and use the ORDER BY tab to sort the data.

6. **Click Execute.** FileMaker Pro prompts you to create a new file.

7. **Use the Save As text box to name the file, and then click Save.** FileMaker Pro connects to the Access database, runs the query, and then displays the data, as shown in figure 10.12.

10.12 FileMaker Pro showing data extracted from an Access database

Connecting to an Access database using Excel

Here are the steps to follow to connect to your Access database using FileMaker Pro:

1. **Choose Data ⇨ Get External Data ⇨ New Database Query.** Excel launches Microsoft Query and displays the iODBC Data Source Chooser dialog box.

2. **Choose your Access data source and then click OK.** Microsoft Query displays a new query window.

3. **Build your query.** I won't go into the details (because this isn't an Excel book), but the basic idea is to double-click a table, double-click a column to add it to the query, add sort options and criteria, and then repeat as needed.

4. **Click Return Data.** Excel prompts you to select a location for the data.

5. **Choose a location and then click OK.** Excel connects to the Access database, runs the query, and then displays the data, as shown in figure 10.13.

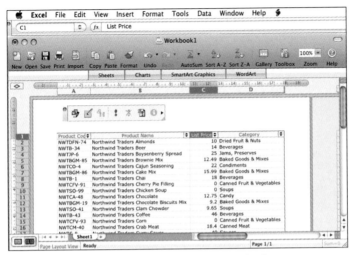

10.13 Excel showing data extracted from an Access database.

Synchronizing Data Between Mac OS X and Windows Using MobileMe

When you go online, you take your life along with you, of course, so your online world becomes a natural extension of your real world. However, just because it's online that doesn't mean the digital version of your life is any less busy, chaotic, or complex than the rest of your life. Apple's MobileMe service is designed to ease some of that chaos and complexity by automatically syncing your most important data — your e-mail, contacts, calendars, and bookmarks. However, the syncing itself may be automatic, but getting it set up is not, unfortunately. This rest of this chapter shows you what to do.

A bit about MobileMe

These days, the primary source of online chaos and confusion is the ongoing proliferation of services and sites that demand your time and attention. What started with Web-based e-mail has grown to a Web site, a blog, a photo-sharing site, online bookmarks, and perhaps a few social networking sites, just to consume those last few precious moments of leisure time. You might be sitting in a chair, but you're getting run ragged anyway!

A great way to simplify your online life is to get a MobileMe account. For a Basic Membership fee ($99 per year currently), or a Family Pack membership, which consists of one main account plus four subaccounts ($149 per year currently), you get a one-stop Web shop that includes e-mail, an address book, a calendar, a Web Gallery for sharing photos, and a generous 20GB of online file storage (40GB with the Family Pack). The price is, admittedly, a bit steep, but it really is convenient to have so much of your online life in one place.

Note

If you don't want to commit any bucks before taking the MobileMe plunge, you can sign up for a 60-day trial that's free and offers most of the features of a regular account. Go to www.apple.com/mobileme and click the Free Trial button.

The Web applications that make up MobileMe — Mail, Contacts, Calendar, Gallery, and iDisk — are *much* nicer and much more functional than their .Mac predecessors. That's the "Me" side of MobileMe (because the Web applications are housed on Apple's me.com site), but that's not the big news with MobileMe. The real headline generator is the "Mobile" side of MobileMe. What's *mobile* is simply your data, particularly your e-mail accounts, contacts, calendars, and bookmarks. That data gets stored on a bunch of me.com-networked servers, which collectively Apple calls the *cloud*. When you log in to your MobileMe account at me.com, you use the Web applications to interact with that data.

That's pretty mundane stuff, right? What's revolutionary here is that you can let the cloud know about all the other devices in your life: your Mac, your work PC, your notebook, your iPhone, and your iPod Touch. If you log in to your MobileMe account and, say, add a new appointment, the cloud takes that appointment and immediately sends the data to all your devices. Fire up your Mac, open iCal, and the appointment's there; switch to your Windows PC, click Outlook's Calendar folder, and the appointment's there; tap Calendar on your iPhone's Home screen and, yup, the appointment's there, too.

This works if you change data on any of your devices. Move an e-mail message to another folder on your Mac, and the same message is moved to the same folder on the other devices and on your MobileMe account; modify a contact on your Windows PC, and the changes also propagate everywhere else. In each case, the new or changed data gets sent to the cloud, which then sends the data to each device, usually in a matter of seconds. This is called *pushing* the data, and the new MobileMe applications are described as *push e-mail*, *push contacts*, and *push calendars*.

With MobileMe, you never have to worry about entering the same information into all of your devices. With MobileMe, you won't miss an important meeting because you forgot to enter it into the calendar on your work computer. With MobileMe, you can never forget data when you're traveling because you've got up-to-the-moment data with you at all times. MobileMe practically organizes your life for you; all you have to do is show up.

Note If you've used e-mail, contacts, and calendars in a company that runs Microsoft Exchange Server, you're no doubt used to push technology because Exchange has done that for a while through its ActiveSync feature. MobileMe push is a step up, however, because you don't need a behemoth corporate server to make it happen. Apple calls MobileMe "Exchange for the rest of us."

Understanding MobileMe device support

MobileMe promises to simplify your online life, but the first step to that simpler existence is to configure MobileMe on all the devices that you want to keep in sync. The next few sections show you how to configure MobileMe on various devices, but it's important to understand exactly which devices can do the MobileMe thing. Here's a summary:

- **iPhone or iPod Touch.** MobileMe works with any iPhone or iPod Touch that's running version 2.0 of the device software.

- **Mac.** You must be running OS X 10.4.11 or later. To access the MobileMe Web applications, you need either Safari 3 or later, or Firefox 2 or later.

- **Windows XP.** You must be running Windows XP Service Pack 2 or later. To access the MobileMe Web applications, you need Internet Explorer 7 or later, Safari 3 or later, or Firefox 2 or later. For push e-mail you need either Outlook Express or Outlook 2003 or later; for push contacts, you need either Windows Address Book or Outlook 2003 or later; for push calendar, you need Outlook 2003 or later.

- **Windows Vista.** Any Vista version will work with MobileMe. To access the MobileMe Web applications, you need Internet Explorer 7 or later, Safari 3 or later, or Firefox 2 or later. For push e-mail you need either Windows Mail or Outlook 2003 or later; for push contacts, you need either Windows Contacts or Outlook 2003 or later; for push calendar, you need Outlook 2003 or later.

Setting up your MobileMe account on your Mac

If you want to keep your Mac in sync with MobileMe's push services, you need to add your MobileMe account to the Mail application and configure your Mac's MobileMe synchronization feature.

First, here are the steps to follow to get your MobileMe account into the Mail application:

1. **In the Dock, click the Mail icon.** The Mail application appears.

2. **Choose Mail ⇨ Preferences to open the Mail preferences.**

3. **Click the Accounts tab.**

4. **Click +.** Mail displays the Add Account dialog box.

5. **Type your name in the Full Name text box.**

6. **Type your MobileMe e-mail address in the Email Address text box.**

7. **Type your MobileMe password in the Password text box.**

8. **Leave the Automatically set up account check box selected.**

9. **Click Create.** Mail verifies the account info and then returns you to the Accounts tab with the MobileMe account added to the Accounts list.

Setting up MobileMe synchronization on your Mac

Now you need to configure your Mac to make sure MobileMe sync is activated, and that your e-mail accounts, contacts, and calendars are part of the sync process. Follow these steps to set your preferences:

1. **Click the System Preferences icon in the Dock.** Your Mac opens the System Preferences window.

2. **In the Internet & Network section, click the MobileMe icon.** The MobileMe preferences appear.

3. **Click the Sync tab.**

4. **Select the Synchronize with MobileMe check box.** Your Mac enables the check boxes beside the various items you can sync, as shown in figure 10.14.

5. **In the Synchronize with MobileMe list, choose Automatically.**

6. **Select the check box beside each data item you want to sync with your MobileMe account, particularly the following push-related items:**

   - Bookmarks
   - Calendars
   - Contacts
   - Mail Accounts

7. **Click the Close button.** Your Mac is now ready for MobileMe syncing.

10.14 Select the Synchronize with MobileMe check box and then select the items you want to sync.

Configuring your MobileMe account on your Windows PC

MobileMe is happy to push data to your Windows PC. However, unlike with a Mac, your Windows XP or Vista machine wouldn't know MobileMe if it tripped over it. To get Windows hip to the MobileMe thing, you need to configure it to work with your Windows PC.

Here are the steps to follow:

1. **On the Windows PC that you want to configure to work with MobileMe, select Start ⇨ Control Panel to open the Control Panel window.**

2. **Double-click the MobileMe Preferences icon.** If you don't see this icon, first open the Network and Internet category. If you still don't see it, it means you haven't yet installed a version of iTunes that also comes with the MobileMe Preferences icon. You need to install the latest version of iTunes (at least 7.7). The MobileMe Preferences window appears.

3. **Use the Member Name text box to type your MobileMe member name.**

4. **Use the Password text box to type your MobileMe password.**

5. **Click Sign In.** Windows signs in to your account.

6. **Click the Sync tab.**

7. **Select the Sync with MobileMe check box and then choose Automatically in the Sync with MobileMe list, as shown in figure 10.15.**

8. **Select the Contacts check box, and then use the Contacts list to select the address book you want to sync.**

9. **Select the Calendars check box, and then use the Calendars list to select the calendar you want to sync.**

10. **Select the Bookmarks check box, and then use the Bookmarks list to select the Web browser you want to sync.**

11. **To run the sync, click Sync Now.**

12. **If you see the First Sync Alert dialog box, choose Merge Data and then click Allow.**

13. **Click OK.**

10.15 Select the Synchronize with MobileMe check box and then select the items you want to sync.

How Can I Run
Windows on My Mac?

Despite your best efforts to leave the Windows world behind, you may find that Windows just keeps rearing its big old head. It might be data that you can't work with because your Mac doesn't have the right application, or it might be just a favorite game that has no Mac version and that you're loath to give up. Whatever the reason, if you find that you can't get Windows out of your life, why not bring Windows into your Mac? As you see in this chapter, there are several ways that you can run Windows on your Mac, and so get the best of both worlds.

Why Run Windows?

Unlike in those ubiquitous Apple commercials where a Mac and a PC are always together, these two worlds don't often collide in real life. The planet is divided (albeit rather unequally) into Mac and Windows camps, and it's a rare user who has a foot in both. Rare, yes, but nonexistent, no. The Mac and Windows worlds do intersect, and here are just a few examples:

- **No Mac version of the software you need.** Thanks to the popularity of Windows, the vast majority of software developers create programs for Windows, so that operating system has by far the largest collection of available applications. Because many developers don't bother creating Mac versions of their programs, often there's no Mac equivalent of a particular type of software. In that case, you need Windows in order to run one of those non-Mac programs.

- **The Mac equivalent just isn't the same for you.** If you use Windows at work, or if you used to run Windows at home, you might have a favorite Windows program that doesn't have a Mac version. Yes, there may be Mac applications that do something similar, but you really like the version you were using on Windows. In that case, you need Windows in order to install and run that program.

- **Better gaming opportunities.** If you like to play games, you probably already know that the Mac isn't a great gaming platform. Windows is very game-friendly, however, and not only do most games run better under Windows than under Mac, but many (perhaps even most) of the best games don't have Mac versions. In that case, you need Windows for the optimum gaming experience.

- **Access to the full Office suite.** If you're an Office user, you already know that the Mac version of Office doesn't come with Outlook (it has Entourage, instead) or the Access database program. If you really need to use either or both of these programs, you need Windows in order to install Office 2007, Office 2003, or some other version of Office for Windows.

- **Viewing the Windows Internet platforms.** If you develop content for the Web, it's crucial to know what your content looks like on all the most popular platforms. And given Windows is the most popular operating system in the world, you'd be remiss in your duties if you didn't fire up your site (or whatever it is) using the Windows versions of Internet Explorer, Safari, and Firefox. In that case, you need Windows in order to view your content in these programs.

In all these examples, you probably only need to use Windows every now and then, or just for short periods each day. Buying a separate PC to run Windows will set you back hundreds of dollars (at least), which is more than likely wasteful for something that you won't be using all that often. On the other hand, of the three methods for running Windows on your Mac that I talk about in this chapter, one (Boot Camp) comes free with Mac OS X 10.5 (Leopard) and the others (Parallels Desktop and VMware Fusion) cost just $79.99 at the time of this writing. (In all cases, you also need a copy of either Windows XP Service Pack 2 or later, or Windows Vista, so be sure to add that into your budget.) Either way, running Windows on your Mac is much more economical than using a separate PC, and you don't have to clutter your desk with multiple monitors, keyboards, and mice!

Dual-Boot or Virtualization (or Both!)?

When you run Windows on a Mac, Windows itself doesn't "know" that it's operating on Mac hardware. It "sees" an Intel processor, and all the other hardware components in your Mac — memory, hard drive, video card, DVD drive, and so on — aren't fundamentally different from the same components on a pure Windows PC. However, Windows (like any operating system) does insist that it have complete control over the computer. Before you decide how to go forward, you should know how the Mac's operating system (OS X) relinquishes control (or *appears* to relinquish control) because this defines how you use Windows and whether OS X and Windows can share data. You can dual-boot, go the virtualization route, or even do both.

- **Dual-boot.** To *dual-boot* your Mac means to configure it with two different operating systems — Mac OS X and Windows — running on two separate sections (called *partitions*) on your Mac's hard drive. When you start your Mac, you have a choice to boot into either OS X or into Windows. If you choose to boot into OS X, your Mac runs exactly as it does now. If you choose to boot into Windows, instead, for all intents and purposes your Mac turns into a Windows PC. That is, you see the Windows desktop, Windows has control of the hardware, and your Mac OS is nowhere in sight. You use Apple's Boot Camp software (which comes with Mac OS 10.5 Leopard) to set up a dual-boot configuration with Windows.

- **Virtualization.** This method refers to running Windows on your Mac in a *virtual machine*: a software environment that simulates a physical computer. In this scenario, you boot into Mac OS X as usual, and then you run Windows essentially as an application in its own window. This virtual machine is configured in such a way that Windows is fooled into thinking that it's controlling an actual PC. Several virtualization applications are available, including the following:

  - Parallels Desktop (www.parallels.com)
  - VMware Fusion (www.VMware.com/mac)

- VirtualBox (www.virtualbox.org)

- Q (www.kju-app.org/kju)

- iEmulator (www.iemulator.com)

- WinTel (www.openosx.com/wintel)

So which method should you choose? That depends on a number of factors, including price, performance, compatibility, and data sharing.

You should dual-boot OS X and Windows if

- **Your budget is tight.** Apple's Boot Camp dual-boot software comes free with Leopard, whereas many of the third-party virtualization programs are commercial products that you have to pay for.

- **You want maximum performance.** Dual-booting into Windows means that Windows gets to use all of the Mac's hardware resources, particularly the memory and processor. This means that Windows running on the Mac is just as fast as Windows running on a comparably equipped PC. Virtual machines share RAM and the processor with Mac OS X, so Windows performance suffers a bit as a result.

Note

It's important to note that the performance hit when Windows is running in a virtual machine isn't onerous. That is, Windows runs at perhaps 80 to 90 percent of its top speed when it's running in a virtual machine.

- **You want maximum compatibility.** Dual-booting into Windows means that Windows gets direct access to the Mac's hardware components, so Windows should recognize most if not all of those components and install the appropriate device drivers to work properly with them. When Windows is running in a virtual machine, however, it often installs only generic drivers for the virtual devices, and it may not recognize any other hardware on the system.

On the other hand, you should use virtualization to run Windows if

- **You want easier access to Windows.** Having to reboot your Mac every time you need to use Windows is a major hassle. With virtualization, however, you can make Windows available all the time, and you can switch between OS X and Windows as easily as you can switch from one running application to another.

- **You want to run other versions of Windows.** Boot Camp supports only Windows XP Service Pack 2 (or later) and Windows Vista. Most virtualization applications support these Windows versions as well as older versions such as Windows 2000, Windows NT, and Windows 98.

- **You want to easily share data between OS X and Windows.** With Boot Camp, you can access files on your Windows partition when you're working in OS X, but you can't access OS X files while working with Windows. Also, you can't cut or copy data from an application running in one operating system and paste that data into an application running in the other operating system. Sharing data is usually much more straightforward under virtualization. To share files, you can either turn on Windows Sharing in OS X, or you can use the virtualization software's sharing feature (such as Parallel Desktop's Shared Folders command). Also you can cut or copy data in Windows and then paste that data into a Mac application (and vice versa).

Still not sure which method to use? That's not a problem because you can always use both! That is, you can set up a Boot Camp partition to dual-boot Windows and OS X, *and* you can install virtualization software, thus giving yourself the best of both worlds. The good news is that Parallels Desktop, which I discuss in this chapter, can use the same version of Windows that you've installed using Boot Camp, so you only have to configure and maintain one version of Windows.

Guarding Against Malware

Whichever method you choose to run Windows on your Mac, remember that where's there's Windows, there's malware, such as viruses and spyware. Therefore, your first chore after you get Windows running on your Mac is to install a top-of-the-line antivirus program. Here are some good ones to check into:

Norton Internet Security (www.symantec.com)

McAfee Internet Security Suite (http://mcafee.com)

AVG Internet Security (http://free.avg.com)

avast! antivirus (http://avast.com)

Windows Vista comes with the antispyware program Windows Defender, but if you're running Windows XP, you need a third-party antispyware utility. The Norton, McAfee, and AVG suites that I mention here all come with antispyware components.

If you do happen to catch a virus or other form of malware on Windows, the good news is that the malware isn't contagious. That is, it's not possible for the virus (or whatever) to also infect your Mac.

Dual-Booting with Boot Camp

If you decide to go the dual-boot route, it's just a matter of installing and configuring Boot Camp, and then installing Windows in the partition created by Boot Camp. The next few sections take you through the details.

What you need to run Boot Camp

Before you strike out for Boot Camp territory, you should take a second and double-check that you've got everything you need for a successful and trouble-free trip. Fortunately, Boot Camp is a relatively simple affair (at least on the surface; it's quite complex behind the scenes), so you don't need much to make it happen. In fact, you need just six things:

Mac OS X 10.5

Boot Camp is available only as a Leopard (Mac OS X 10.5) utility, so you're out of luck if you're still using Mac OS X 10.4 or earlier. It is likely Boot Camp will be a standard part of future OS X releases. To install Boot Camp you need either the Leopard installation disc or the Mac OS X Disc 1 that shipped with your OS X 10.5–equipped Mac.

Note

The original version of Boot Camp was a beta (prerelease) version designed to work with Tiger (Mac OS X 10.4). On the off chance that you have one of those beta versions of Boot Camp kicking around, I'm sorry to report that you can't use it, because the beta expired as soon as Apple released Leopard in October 2007.

Windows XP or Windows Vista

If you want to install Windows XP, you need a 32-bit version of Windows XP Home or Windows XP Professional and it must have Service Pack 2 or later. If you want to run Windows Vista, instead, you need a 32-bit version of Windows Vista Home Basic, Windows Vista Home Premium, Windows Vista Business, or Windows Vista Ultimate.

Actually, you *might* be able to use a 64-bit version of Windows Vista. Apple included support for 64-bit Vista versions in the new Mac Pro and MacBook Pro models that it introduced in early 2008. So if you have one of those Macs, you can install 64-bit Vista in Boot Camp.

Whether you go the Windows XP or the Windows Vista route, note that whatever version you're installing, you must have the installation disc for the *full* install. If all you've got is an upgrade instal- lation disc, Boot Camp won't work.

Caution

If all you have is a full Windows XP Service Pack 1 disc, you might think you can get away with installing that and then upgrading to Service Pack 2 (or Service Pack 3, which is now available). Nope, sorry, that won't work. The disc has to be a full install of Windows XP with either Service Pack 2 or Service Pack 3.

DVD or CD drive

You need an optical drive so you can insert the Windows installation disc. The Windows XP installa- tion disc is a CD, whereas the Windows Vista disc is a DVD. Almost all Macs come with optical drives, so you should be safe here. The major recent exception is the MacBook Air, which doesn't come with a built-in optical drive. If you plan on dual-booting Windows on your MacBook Air, you need to connect a MacBook Air SuperDrive (or some other external drive).

Note

Unfortunately, you can't use MacBook Air's Remote Disc feature to install Windows using a DVD on a network computer. Bummer.

Intel-based Mac

Boot Camp isn't fussy about what Mac it gets installed on, except that it insists the Mac have an Intel processor. That makes sense because Windows is an Intel operating system, which means it works only with Intel processors. Because Boot Camp gives Windows direct access to the Mac's processor, that processor needs to be of the Intel variety.

Internal hard disk with enough free space

Boot Camp will install Windows only to an internal hard disk. If you've connected an external USB or FireWire hard disk to your Mac, you can't use it for the Windows partition. The Mac Pro supports multiple internal hard disks, so if you have a Mac Pro with two or more internal hard disks, you can use one of them for the Windows installation. (That is, you'd leave Mac OS X as is on the startup hard disk — usually called Macintosh HD — and you'd install Windows on one of the other internal hard disks.)

Your Mac needs to have enough room on its hard disk to create a partition big enough to hold Windows and whatever Windows applications you plan on using. At a bare minimum, your Mac's hard disk needs about 1.5GB free to install Windows XP, and about 15GB free to install Windows Vista. I show you how to check hard disk free space and decide on a partition size later in this chapter.

Caution

For some strange reason, Boot Camp refuses to install if your Mac hard disk already has two or more partitions. If you have multiple partitions, you'll need to delete the secondary partitions (that is, everything but the main Macintosh HD partition). Use a partitioning tool such as iPartition (see www.coriolis-systems.com/) to do this.

Wired mouse and keyboard

To work with the Windows installation program, you need a mouse to click stuff and a keyboard to type stuff. Unfortunately, the Windows installer (like the Mac OS X installer) has no way of recognizing wireless mice and keyboards, particularly Bluetooth devices. If you're installing Windows on a Mac notebook, the built-in trackpad and keyboard do just fine. Otherwise, you need to connect a USB mouse and keyboard when you install Windows.

Getting your Mac ready for Boot Camp

If your Mac meets all the requirements that I spelled out in the previous section, you're pretty much good to go. However, I suggest you first pay a visit to the Look Before You Leap department, because there are a few things you should do to make sure your Mac is ready, willing, and able to install Windows.

Check your free hard disk space

I mentioned earlier that you need a certain amount of free hard disk space to fit Windows comfortably on your Mac. Just how much constitutes "a certain amount" is discussed a bit later. For now, you need to know just how much free space you have to work with.

One easy way to do this is to open any Finder window and then either click Macintosh HD in the Devices list, or click any folder that resides on Macintosh HD (such as your user folder). As you can see in figure 11.1, Finder displays the amount of free space in the status bar at the bottom of the open window (55.16GB in this case — lots of room for Windows!).

11.1 In Finder, click any Macintosh HD folder and check out the status bar to see the hard disk's free space.

Make sure you're running the latest version of Mac OS X

The major releases of Mac OS X — 10.0, 10.1, 10.2, and so on — come out every 18 months to 2 years, give or take. In between these major versions Apple puts out minor versions of Mac OS X — 10.5.1, 10.5.2, and so on — every few months. These updates (as they're called) include, as Apple always says, "general operating system fixes that enhance the stability, compatibility, and security of your Mac."

It's always a good idea to install these updates as soon as possible, and it's a particularly good idea to ensure you have the latest update installed before you take on any major tasks, such as installing Boot Camp and Windows.

If your Mac is configured to check for software updates automatically, chances are you're running the latest version of Mac OS X. If you want to be certain, or if you've set up your Mac to not check for updates automatically, follow these steps to run Software Update and look for a new Max OS X update:

1. **Click the Apple icon in the menu bar.**

2. **Click Software Update.** Alternatively, click System Preferences in the Dock, click Software Update, and then click Check Now. Software Update checks the Apple servers for pending updates.

3. **If you see Mac OS X Update (or perhaps Mac OS X Update Combined), as shown in figure 11.2, select its Install check box.**

4. **If any other updates are available, deselect their Install check boxes.**

5. **Click Install 1 Item.** Software Update prompts you to enter your administrator account password.

6. **Use the Password text box to type your password and then click OK.**

7. **If you see the License Agreement dialog box, click Agree.** Software Update tells you that the new software requires a restart.

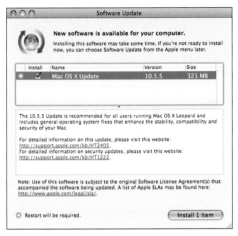

11.2 Look for either Mac OS X Update or Mac OS X Update Combined in the list of available updates.

8. **Click Restart.** Software Update restarts your Mac and installs the Mac OS X update.

Make sure you've installed the latest firmware for your Mac

Your Mac comes with *firmware*, a small program that's embedded with your Mac's hardware and helps control the hardware's internal functions. The well-being of your Mac's hardware is crucial with Boot Camp because it gives Windows full access to that hardware. So if your Mac's firmware has any bugs or glitches, that could cause problems when you try to run Windows.

Apple periodically releases new firmware versions for each Mac, and these new versions are almost always more stable and less buggy. So to help ensure that Windows can coexist peacefully with your Mac's hardware, always make sure that your Mac has the latest version of its firmware installed. In particular, look for updates to the EFI firmware. EFI is the Extensible Firmware Interface, and it's the code your Mac uses to (among other things) help the operating system boot. As such, it's used extensively by Boot Camp at startup, so having the latest EFI firmware can help Boot Camp do its job.

Follow these steps to locate, download, and install the latest EFI firmware for your Mac:

1. **Use Safari or another Web browser to go to www.apple.com/support/downloads.**

2. **In the Search box, type the name of your Mac model, type firmware, and then press Return.** Apple Support displays a list of matches, as shown in figure 11.3.

11.3 Go to Apple Support's Downloads page and search for firmware updates for your Mac model.

3. **If you see an EFI Firmware Update link for your Mac model, click the link.** You see details about the firmware update.

4. **Click the link to download the update.** Your Mac downloads the disk image and then mounts it on the desktop.

> **Note**
>
> Once the disk image mounts, it launches the EFI Firmware Update installer, which checks to see if your Mac needs the update. If not, you see an Alert message telling you your Mac doesn't need the update. In which case, click Close and skip the rest of these steps.

5. **Click Continue.** The License Agreement appears.

6. **Click Continue and then click Agree.** The Installation Type dialog box appears.

7. **Click Install.** The installer prompts you to enter your Mac's administrator password.

8. **Use the Password text box to type your password and then click OK.** The program loads the firmware installer.

9. **Click Close.**

10. **Click Shut Down.** The installer prompts you to enter your Mac's administrator password.

11. **Use the Password text box to type your password and then click OK.** The Installer shuts down your Mac.

12. **Press and release your Mac's power button.** Your Mac powers up and installs the firmware update. When the update is complete, your Mac restarts.

13. **When the firmware update program tells you your Mac's firmware is now up to date, click OK.**

Back up your Mac

The data you create on your Mac is as precious as gold not only because it's yours, but mostly because it's simply irreplaceable. Macs are reliable machines, but they do crash, and all hard disks eventually die, so at some point your data will be at risk. To avoid losing that data forever, you need to back up your Mac, early and often.

However, it's also important to back up your Mac before any major operation. Using Boot Camp to dual-boot with Windows definitely qualifies as major because, in most scenarios, you must use Boot Camp to carve out part of your Mac's hard disk to use as the Windows partition. Anytime you mess with your hard disk partitions you run a small risk of having everything trashed. It's a small risk, but it's not a nonexistent one. Therefore, it's really important that you back up your Mac before you do anything with Boot Camp. See Chapter 8 for the details on backing up your Mac.

Creating a partition for Windows

With your Mac all ready for action, it's time to let Boot Camp do its thing. This is a two-stage process:

- Use Boot Camp Assistant to create a partition for Windows. This is the subject of this section.
- Install Windows into the new partition. I get to that a bit later.

Understanding partitions

When you install an operating system such as Mac OS X or Windows on a hard disk, the operating system reserves the hard disk for its own use. The OS is quite adamant about this, too, and it won't let you install another operating system on the same hard disk. If you force another OS on that disk, you'll only trash the original system. This is all quite sensible when you think about it because different operating systems have different ways of organizing files on the hard disk, so letting two different systems access the same disk is just a recipe for chaos and disaster.

All is not lost for would-be dual-booters, however. You may not be able to install two different operating systems on a single hard disk, but you *can* divide a single hard disk into two different sections. These sections are called *partitions*, and the key thing for us is that each partition looks, acts, and responds just as if it were an entire hard disk on its own.

Note You'll also often see a partition referred to as a *volume*. For our purposes, the two words are synonymous.

For example, suppose you have a 200GB hard disk and you divide it into, say, a 150GB partition and a 50GB partition. For all intents and purposes, you can treat the 150GB partition as a 150GB hard disk, and the 50GB partition as a *separate* 50GB hard disk. "Separate" is the operative word here because it means you can install one operating system on the 150GB partition and another on the 50GB partition. Both operating systems will be clam-happy because they *think* they've got their "hard disk" all to themselves. You'll be happy too, because as long as you have the right software (such as Boot Camp) you're free to dual-boot between the two systems as you please.

Genius If you have a Mac Pro with two internal hard disks, you don't have to worry about all this partition business. Instead, you can leave Mac OS X on its current hard disk, and use the other internal hard disk for Windows.

Deciding on a partition size

You see in the next section that the Boot Camp Assistant lets you choose the size of your Windows partition. So now the big question looms: How big should you make that partition? The answer depends on four factors:

- **Which version of Windows are you installing?** Windows XP requires only a minimum of 1.5GB, whereas Windows Vista needs a hefty 15GB at a minimum.

- **Will you be installing lots of Windows applications?** The more applications you want to use in Windows, the more space you need, particularly if you'll be installing behemoth programs such as Microsoft Office.

- **Will you be working with a large amount of data in Windows?** If you've got lots of huge video files and thousands of audio files and photos, you need lots of storage space to handle everything.

Genius If your data files already reside on another Windows PC and you're going to transfer them to your Mac, you can get an idea of how much room the files take up. On the Windows PC, open the folder that contains the data, select all the files, right-click any selected file, and then click Properties. In the dialog box that appears, read the Size on Disk value.

⬤ **How much free space is left on your Mac hard disk?** Ideally you want to leave your Mac with plenty of room to grow, so that may constrain the size of the Windows partition. For example, if your Mac hard disk has 50GB free, you probably don't want your Windows partition to be any larger than about 25GB.

If you won't be installing very many Windows applications and your data files aren't massive, I suggest a 10GB partition for Windows XP, and a 25GB partition for Windows Vista. Otherwise, if you have enough room on your Mac hard disk, go with a 25GB partition for Windows XP, and a 50GB partition for Windows Vista.

Running Boot Camp Assistant to create the partition

Okay, you're finally ready to get the Boot Camp show on the road. Follow these steps to launch Boot Camp Assistant and create a new partition for the Windows installation:

1. **If you're using a Mac notebook, connect the Mac to a power supply.**

2. **Log in to your Mac with an administrator account.**

3. **In Finder, choose Applications ⇨ Utilities.** You can also press Shift+⌘+U. The Utilities folder appears.

4. **Double-click Boot Camp Assistant.** Boot Camp Assistant runs and displays the Introduction window.

5. **Click Continue.** The Create a Partition for Windows screen appears, as shown in figure 11.4.

11.4 Use the Create a Partition for Windows screen to set the size of the Windows partition.

6. **Click and drag the dot separating the two partitions until the Windows partition is the size you want.** You can also click Divide Equally to make the two partitions the same size, or click Use 32 GB to set the Windows partition size to 32GB.

7. **Click Partition.** Mac OS X partitions the hard disk (this may take a while, depending on the size of the disk).

When the partitioning is complete, you see a new desktop icon named BOOTCAMP (see figure 11.5), which represents the new partition.

Installing Windows

When Boot Camp Assistant finishes creating the Windows partition, it displays the Start Windows Installation screen. If you're not ready to install Windows now, click Quit & Install Later. When you're ready, follow these steps to get Boot Camp Assistant back on track:

11.5 When the Boot Camp Assistant has completed its partition labors, the new partition appears on the desktop as the BOOTCAMP icon.

1. **Log in to your Mac with an administrator account.**

2. **In Finder, choose Applications ⇨ Utilities.** You can also press Shift+⌘+U. The Utilities folder appears.

3. **Double-click Boot Camp Assistant.** Boot Camp Assistant runs and displays the Introduction window.

4. **Click Continue.** The Select Task window appears.

5. **Select the Start the Windows installer option.**

6. **Click Continue.**

With the new partition ready to go, it's time to install Windows to that partition. The exact procedure varies according to which version of Windows you're using. The following are just the generic steps:

1. **Insert your Windows disc into your Mac's DVD drive.** Wait until you see an icon for the disc appear on your Mac's desktop.

2. **In Boot Camp Assistant, click Start Installation.** Your Mac reboots and the Windows installation program begins.

3. **Follow the Windows installation screens as they appear.** Here are some things to bear in mind:

307

● When the Windows setup program asks you where you want to install Windows, be sure to choose the BOOTCAMP partition.

In Windows XP. Choose C: Partition 3 <BOOTCAMP>.

In Windows Vista. Choose Disk 0 Partition 3 BOOTCAMP.

● Boot Camp formats the BOOTCAMP partition using the FAT32 file system, which is fine for Windows XP partitions 32GB or less, but it won't work for Windows Vista, which requires a different file system called NTFS. During the Vista install, when you get to the Where Do You Want to Install Windows? dialog box, click the BOOTCAMP partition, click Drive Options, and then click Format.

Note

In case you're wondering, a *file system* is a technology used by the operating system to keep track of the files stored on a disk, such as a hard disk. FAT32 (The FAT part is short for File Allocation Table) is a relatively simple file system used by some versions of Windows, while NTFS (New Technology File System) is a more sophisticated file system used by Windows Vista and other higher-end versions of Windows (such as Windows Server). For the record, your Mac uses a file system called HFS+ (where HFS is short for Hierarchical File System).

● When the Windows XP setup program asks you to select a file system, be sure to choose the following option: Format the partition using the FAT file system.

Caution

In the Windows XP install, do *not* choose the option that says Leave the current file system intact (no changes). For the Boot Camp partition to work with XP, it must be formatted during the install.

● The Windows Setup program automatically reboots your Mac a few times during the installation, and each time you'll see a screen that says the following:

Press any key to boot from CD/DVD

When you see this message, do *not* press any key or you just start the installation process all over again.

● Specify your user name, password, time zone, and any other preferences that the setup program asks for.

4. **When the Windows installation is complete, insert your Leopard installation disc or Mac OS X Disc 1.** Windows prompts you to run setup.exe.

5. **Run the setup.exe program.** If you're running Windows Vista, you need to provide User Account Control credentials to continue. The Boot Camp installer appears, as shown in figure 11.6.

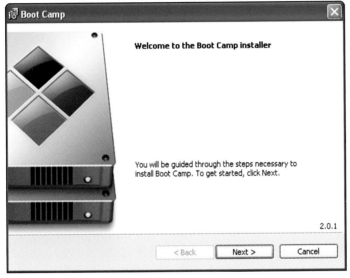

11.6 Insert your Mac OS X DVD to run Boot Camp in Windows.

6. **Click Next.** The License Agreement dialog box appears.

7. **Select the I accept the terms in the license agreement option, and then click Next.**

8. **Make sure the Apple Software Update for Windows check box is selected, as shown in figure 11.7, and then click Install.** Boot Camp installs Apple Software Update for Windows.

9. **Click Finish.** Boot Camp lets you know that you need to restart the computer to put the changes into effect.

10. **Click Yes to restart your Mac.**

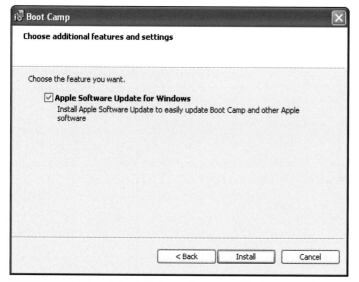

11.7 You need to install Apple Software Update for Windows to make sure your Mac hardware works properly with Windows.

Switching between Mac OS X and Windows

In an ideal world, you switch between Mac OS X and Windows by restarting the Mac and then booting into whichever operating system you want to use. Unfortunately, right after you install Windows via Boot Camp you find that you're living in a Windows world. That's because Windows somewhat rudely sets itself up as the default startup volume! This means that every time you restart your Mac, it always boots you directly into Windows.

Not to worry, there are a couple of ways that you can work around this problem.

Booting to Mac OS X from Windows

You can follow these steps to exit Windows and boot directly to Mac OS X:

1. **Click the Boot Camp icon that appears in the Windows notification area.**

2. **Click Restart in Mac OS X, as shown in figure 11.8.** Boot Camp asks you to confirm.

3. **Click OK.** Boot Camp shuts down Windows and then boots into Mac OS X.

11.8 To get back to the friendly confines of Mac OS X, click the Boot Camp icon and then click Restart in Mac OS X.

310

Dual-booting with the Startup Manager

If your Mac is off and you want to boot into Mac OS X, it seems awfully inefficient to have to boot into Windows first. Fortunately, you don't have to do this. Instead, you can invoke your Mac's Startup Manager, and you can then choose whether you want to boot to Mac OS X or Windows.

Here are the steps you need to follow to switch between Mac OS X and Windows using the Startup Manager:

1. **Start your Mac.**

2. **Hold down the Option key until you see the Startup Manager.** All you see are two hard disk icons: one for Macintosh HD and one for Windows.

3. **Double-click the Macintosh HD icon.** Alternatively, if you want to boot into Windows, double-click the Windows icon.

Booting to Windows from Mac OS X

You saw earlier that the version of Windows on your Boot Camp partition comes with a Boot Camp icon that enables you to boot your Mac to OS X from Windows. What about the opposite scenario: booting to Windows from OS X? That's less obvious because OS X doesn't come with a "Restart in Windows" command. Instead, you have two choices:

- If Windows is still the default OS, restart your Mac and it will boot to Windows automatically.

- If you reinstated Mac OS X as the default OS, as described in the next section, restart your Mac, invoke the Mac's Startup Manager, as described in the previous section, and then double-click the Windows icon.

Reinstating Mac OS X as the default OS

If you usually boot to Mac OS X and only boot to Windows occasionally, it's a hassle to have to invoke Startup Manager every time you want to use Mac OS X. To fix this, follow these steps:

1. **Boot to Mac OS X.**

2. **Click System Preferences in the Dock.** The System Preferences appear.

3. **Click the Startup Disk icon.** The Startup Disk preferences appear.

4. **Click Mac OS X *Ver* on Macintosh HD (where *Ver* is your OS X version number).**

Renaming the Boot Camp partition

When you install Windows, it formats the Boot Camp partition, so you lose the original BOOTCAMP name. In its place, you end up with either UNTITLED (if the partition was formatted using NTFS) or NO NAME (if the partition was formatted using FAT or FAT32). Here's how to rename the partition:

- **In Windows.** Click Start ⇨ Computer (or My Computer in XP), right-click the hard drive, click Rename, type the new name, and then press Enter. In Vista, you need to enter your User Account Control credentials to make the change.

- **In Mac OS X.** If the partition is formatted as FAT or FAT32, Control+click or right-click the partition's Desktop icon, click Get Info, and then edit the Name & Extension text. If the partition is formatted using NTFS, you can't edit the partition name in Mac OS X. In which case, you must use Windows to change the name.

Sharing files between Mac OS X and Windows

The major drawback with using Boot Camp is that you're limited in the amount of data you can share between Mac OS X and Windows, particularly if the Boot Camp partition is formatted using NTFS.

- **In Mac OS X.** You can see your Windows files by selecting the Boot Camp partition in Finder. For example, figure 11.9 shows Finder displaying the Windows Vista ⇨ Users ⇨ Paul folder (where Windows Vista is the name I'm using for my Boot Camp partition). If the partition is FAT or FAT32, you can work with the files just like they were local files: You can open files (assuming you have a compatible Mac application), edit files, add and delete files, and so on. If the partition is NTFS, you can only view the files; you can't make any changes to the existing files or add new files.

- **In Windows.** Unfortunately, Windows can't work with the Macintosh HD format, so it's not possible to see the Mac hard drive in Windows. Here are a couple of alternatives for sharing files:

  - **Use an external hard drive.** Format the drive as FAT32, move files from your Mac's hard drive to the external hard drive. Then you can see the drive and the files from Windows (and Mac OS X, too).

  - **Use a common network share.** Store the files in a shared network folder accessible from both Mac OS X and Windows.

11.9 In Mac OS X, you can view the Windows files on the Boot Camp partition, and you can edit those files if the partition is FAT or FAT32.

Boot Camp keyboard techniques

One of the conundrums you face when you boot into Windows using your Mac is how you press Windows-specific keys using your Mac keyboard. If you happen to have a USB PC keyboard lying around, connect it to a USB port on your Mac and your problems are solved because the PC keyboard works as advertised in Boot Camp. (This is also true if you connect a wireless PC keyboard to Windows.)

If you have only your Mac keyboard to deal with, all is not lost because Boot Camp installs a keyboard driver that translates certain Mac keyboard combinations into equivalent Windows keys. Table 11.1 lists the key combos you can use.

Table 11.1 Mac Keyboard Techniques to Use in Windows

Windows Key	Mac External Keyboard	Mac Notebook Keyboard
Windows Logo	⌘	⌘
Alt	Option	Option
Right Alt	Control+Option	Control+Option
Control	Control	Control

continued

313

Table 11.1 Continued

Windows Key	Mac External Keyboard	Mac Notebook Keyboard
Control+Alt+Delete	Control+Option+Fwd Delete	Control+Option+Delete
Enter	Return	Return
Backspace	Delete	Delete
Delete	Fwd Delete	Fn+Delete
Insert	Fn+Enter	Fn+Enter
Num Lock	Clear	Fn+F6
Print Screen	F14	Fn+Shift+F11
Print active window	Option+F14	Fn+Shift+Option+F11
Scroll Lock	F15	Fn+F12
Pause/Break	F16	Fn+Shift+F12

Removing the Boot Camp partition

If you decide you no longer want to dual-boot your Mac and Windows, you should delete the Boot Camp partition to reclaim the hard disk space. Note that you'll lose any data you have stored in Windows, so be sure to back up that data to a safe place before continuing.

Here are the steps to follow:

1. **Log in to your Mac with an administrator account.**
2. **In Finder, choose Applications ⇨ Utilities.** You can also press Shift+⌘+U. The Utilities folder appears.
3. **Double-click Boot Camp Assistant.** Boot Camp Assistant runs and displays the Introduction window.
4. **Click Continue.** The Select Task window appears.
5. **Select the Create or remove a Windows partition option.**
6. **Click Restore.** Boot Camp Assistant prompts you to enter your Mac's administrator password.
7. **Type your password in the Password text box and then click OK.** Boot Camp Assistant removes the Windows partition.
8. **Click Quit.**

Running Windows with Parallels Desktop

If you'd rather have your Mac running all the time and just load Windows into a window whenever you need it, virtualization software is the way to go. I mentioned earlier that several virtualization applications are available, but the best of them (at least as I write this) is Parallels Desktop, so that's the one I'll discuss first. (I also talk about VMware Fusion later in this chapter.)

Installing Parallels Desktop

Purchase the Parallels Desktop for Mac software from the Parallels site (www.parallels.com), or download the free trial if you just want to check it out. Don't bother with the Premium Edition, which is more expensive but doesn't offer anything you really need that the regular edition doesn't have.

Once the download is complete, follow these steps to install Parallels Desktop for Mac:

1. **Open Safari's Downloads window, if it's not already on-screen, by choosing Window⇨Downloads.** You can also display the Downloads window by pressing Option+⌘+L.

2. **Double-click the Parallels Desktop icon.** Your Mac mounts the Parallels Desktop partition.

3. **Double-click the Install Parallels Desktop icon.** The Parallels Desktop Installer appears.

4. **Click Continue.** The Parallels Desktop Installer displays its release notes.

5. **Click Continue.** The Parallels Desktop Software License Agreement appears.

6. **Click Continue and then click Agree.**

7. **Click Install.** The Parallels Desktop Installer prompts you for your Mac administrative password.

8. **Type the password and then click OK.** Parallels Desktop Installer installs the program. If you see a dialog box telling you that New network interfaces have been detected, click Cancel.

9. **Click Close.**

Running Parallels Desktop

With Parallels Desktop installed, start the program by opening a Finder window and then choosing Applications ⇨ Parallels ⇨ Parallels Desktop. The first time you do this, you're prompted for your activation key, which you should have received via e-mail if you purchased the software. Click Enter Activation Key. (If you're using the trial version, click Later, instead.) Copy and paste the key in the Activation Key text box, click Activate, and then click OK.

Setting up Parallels Desktop with a Boot Camp virtual machine

If you previously installed Windows in a Boot Camp partition, the Parallels Desktop Installer recognizes that partition and sets it up as a virtual machine called My Boot Camp. Here are the steps to follow to set up Parallels Desktop to use that virtual machine:

1. **When you launch Parallels Desktop for the first time, the New Virtual Machine window appears and prompts you to select a virtual machine.**

2. **Click the My Boot Camp virtual machine.**

3. **Click Select.** Parallels Desktop sets up the virtual machine, as shown in figure 11.10.

11.10 Parallels Desktop with Boot Camp's Windows partition set up as a virtual machine

Installing Windows in a new virtual machine

If you don't already have a Boot Camp partition, the first time you start Parallels Desktop you see the OS Installation Assistant, as shown in figure 11.11. You have three choices:

- **Windows Express.** This option installs Windows XP or Windows Vista in automatic mode, which means you're not prompted for any information during the installation. If you choose this option, you need to enter your Windows product key before starting the install. This is a good option to choose if you want to run the installation unattended, or if you want to create a new Windows installation.

- **Typical.** This option installs Windows XP or Windows Vista using a default virtual machine. I don't recommend this route because you don't get to customize the virtual machine.

- **Custom.** This option installs Windows XP or Windows Vista in a virtual machine that you can customize. No Windows information is specified in advance, so you must enter your Windows preferences during the installation. This is a good option to choose if you already have a Windows installation on your Mac (such as a Boot Camp Windows installation).

11.11 The OS Installation Assistant appears automatically when you first start Parallels Desktop.

Note If you see the New Virtual Machine window at startup, you can launch the OS Installation Assistant by clicking New. If Parallels Desktop displays an existing virtual machine at startup, launch the OS Installation Assistant by choosing File ⇨ New.

The following steps take you through the Custom option:

1. **In the initial OS Installation Assistant dialog box, select the Custom option and click Next.** The OS Installation Assistant asks you for the OS Type and OS Version.

2. **Choose Windows in the OS Type list, choose the version of Windows you want to install in the OS Version list, and then click Next.** The OS Installation Assistant asks you to specify how much RAM you want to give to the virtual machine, as shown in figure 11.12.

```
┌─────────────────────────────────────────────────┐
│            OS Installation Assistant              │
├─────────────────────────────────────────────────┤
│ Custom Installation                               │
│                                                   │
│           Specify the amount of memory (RAM) for your virtual │
│           machine:                                │
│                                                   │
│           ┌──────┐ ⬍                              │
│           │ 512  │    MB                          │
│           └──────┘                                │
│                                                   │
│           ────────────●──────────────────────    │
│           4 MB                          2048 MB   │
│                                                   │
│           Recommended size: from 512 MB up to 604 MB │
│                                                   │
│           Optimal size: 512 MB                    │
│                                                   │
│                                                   │
│            ( < Back )  ( Next > )  ( Cancel )     │
└─────────────────────────────────────────────────┘
```

11.12 Specify the amount of RAM you want to give to Windows.

3. **Type the number of MB you want Windows to use, or click and drag the slider, and then click Next.** The OS Installation Assistant asks you to choose a virtual hard disk option.

Genius The amount of RAM you specify depends on the version of Windows you're using and how much total RAM your Mac has to offer. If you have only 1GB total, give Windows XP and earlier 256MB and Windows Vista 512MB (which is the Vista minimum). If you have 2GB, give Windows XP and earlier 512MB and Windows Vista 1GB.

318

Caution

Don't specify a RAM amount that's larger than the highest recommended amount or the virtual machine won't be able to start.

4. **Select one of the following options and then click Next:**

   ● **Create a new hard disk image.** Select this option to set up a new virtual hard disk on which to install Windows. This is usually the preferred option for an initial install of Windows, unless you want to use an existing Boot Camp partition.

   ● **Use an existing hard disk image.** Select this option if you previously created a hard disk image and want to reuse it to save space on your Mac's hard drive.

   ● **Use Boot Camp.** Select this option if you want Parallels Desktop to use an existing Boot Camp partition as a virtual hard disk. This is the best option if you've already installed and configured Windows using Boot Camp because it allows Parallels Desktop to use the same Windows installation.

   ● **Do not add any hard disk.** This option is for an operating system (such as some versions of Linux) that can run off a CD instead of a hard drive. This doesn't apply to Windows, so you can ignore this option.

5. **If you opted to create a new hard disk in Step 4, the OS Installation Assistant asks you to specify the size and format of the hard disk, as shown in figure 11.13.**

   ● **Size.** Type the size in MB of the hard disk. How big should the hard disk be? That depends on the version of Windows you're installing and how much data you'll be adding to Windows. See "Deciding on a partition size," earlier in this chapter for some pointers.

   ● **Format.** I recommend selecting the Expanding option, which gives the hard disk only as much room as it needs. This is better than the Plain option, which sets aside the full amount of hard disk space right away, which takes longer to create and may waste unused disk space in the short term.

   Click Next when you've made your choices.

6. **In the networking options, select Shared Networking and click Next.**

```
                    OS Installation Assistant
 Custom Installation

                    Specify a size of the virtual hard disk:

                     [ 32000  [⇕] ]  MB       ☐ Split Disk

                    Select a format of the virtual hard disk:

                    ⦿ Expanding (recommended)
                       Such virtual hard disk is of zero size when created, can grow
                       up to the specified size as you use it. Saves space on real hard
                       disk.

                    ◯ Plain
                       Such virtual hard disk reserves the whole space at the
                       moment it is created. It always has room (up to its full size)
                       for new applications or data.


                    (  < Back  )   ( Next > )    (  Cancel  )
```

11.13 Specify the size and format of the new virtual hard disk.

7. **Type a name for the virtual machine and select the sharing options you want to use.**

   ● **Enable file sharing.** Select this check box to enable Windows to see your Mac home folder.

   ● **Enable user profile sharing.** Select this check box to use your Mac user profile folders (including the desktop) in Windows. Note that this option is disabled if you're using a Boot Camp partition as your Parallels Desktop virtual machine.

   Click Next when you're done.

8. **In the optimize options, select Virtual machine and click Next.**

9. **Insert your Windows installation disc.**

10. **Click Finish.** Parallels Desktop installs Windows.

11. **Follow the Windows installation screens as they appear.**

Note To use your mouse inside the virtual machine during the installation, click inside the Parallels Desktop window to activate the mouse. To use your mouse outside of the virtual machine, press Control+Alt.

12. **Install Parallel Tools by choosing Actions ⇨ Install Parallel Tools.** These tools ensure that all device drivers are installed correctly, and they make it easier to share data between Mac OS X and Windows.

Figure 11.14 shows Windows Vista running in a virtual machine window on the Mac OS X Desktop.

11.14 Windows Vista running in a virtual machine in Mac OS X

Configuring the virtual machine

If you need to make changes to the Windows virtual machine, first shut down the virtual machine by choosing Actions ⇨ Stop, and then click Yes when Parallels Desktop asks you to confirm.

When the virtual machine is stopped, choose Edit ⇨ Virtual Machine to open the Configuration Editor, shown in figure 11.15. Use the Resource list on the left to choose the item you want to configure, and then use the options on the right to make your changes. Click OK when you're done.

11.15 Use the Configuration Editor to make changes to the Windows virtual machine.

Exchanging files between Mac OS X and Windows

Sharing files and data between Mac OS X and Windows is much easier and more versatile when Windows is running in a virtual machine. Here's a summary of the main ways that you can share files and data:

- **Clipboard.** Parallels Tools has a feature called Clipboard Synchronization. When you cut or copy a file, folder, or other data in either Windows or Mac OS X, you can switch to the other operating system and then paste the data.

- **In Windows.** If you selected the Enable user profile sharing check box, choose Start ⇨ Computer and you see an icon called Home. Double-click this icon to see your Mac user profile folders and work with the files.

- **In Mac OS X.** Parallels Tools creates a device for the Windows hard drive named [C] *Virtual Machine*, where *Virtual Machine* is the name you supplied for the virtual machine. Click this device in Finder to access the Windows files, as shown in figure 11.16.

- **Drag and drop.** Select the object you want to share in either Windows or Mac OS X, click and drag the object from the source location, and then drop it inside a window in the other operating system (or on the desktop).

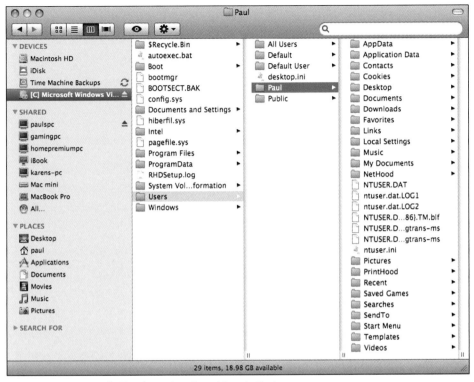

11.16 You can access the Windows virtual machine via Finder.

Running Windows with VMware Fusion

Besides Parallels Desktop, the other popular virtualization software for running Windows on a Mac is VMware Fusion, and that product is the subject of the rest of this chapter.

Installing VMware Fusion

Purchase the VMware Fusion software from the VMware site (www.VMware.com/mac), or download the free trial if you just want to check it out. Once the download is complete, follow these steps to install VMware Fusion:

1. **In the VMware Fusion window, double-click the Install VMware Fusion icon.** Your Mac asks you to confirm.

2. **Click Open.**

3. **Click Continue.** The Install VMware Fusion window appears.

4. **Click Continue.** The VMware Fusion Software License Agreement appears.

5. **Click Continue and then click Agree.** The installation program asks to install a program called MacFUSE, which VMware uses to create virtual disks and mount them in Finder.

6. **Make sure the Install MacFUSE check box is selected, click Continue.** The VMware Fusion installation program prompts you for your Mac's administrative password.

7. **Type your Mac's administrative password and then click OK.** The installation program installs MacFUSE.

8. **Click Install.** The VMware Fusion installation program prompts you for your Mac's administrative password.

9. **Type the password and then click OK.** The program installs VMware Fusion and then prompts you for your serial number if you purchased VMware Fusion. You should have received a serial number (which may be called an "activation code) in an e-mail message.

10. **If you have a serial number, type it in the Serial Number text box.** If you're using the trial version, instead, leave the Serial Number text box blank.

11. **Click Continue.**

12. **Click Close.**

13. **Restart your Mac.**

With VMware Fusion installed, start the program by opening a Finder window, opening the Applications folder, and then double-clicking the VMware Fusion icon.

Setting up VMware Fusion with a Boot Camp virtual machine

If you previously installed Windows in a Boot Camp partition, the VMware Fusion installer recognizes that partition and adds it to the Virtual Machine Library window, as shown in figure 11.17.

11.17 VMware Fusion's Virtual Machine Library with the Boot Camp partition added

Here are the steps to follow to set up VMware Fusion to use the Boot Camp partition as a virtual machine:

1. **If this is the first time you've started VMware Fusion, click Cancel in the Welcome window that appears.**

2. **In the Virtual Machine Library, double-click the Boot Camp virtual machine.**
   VMware Fusion prompts you for your Mac's administrative password.

3. **Type your password and then click OK.** VMware Fusion sets up the Boot Camp partition as a virtual machine, starts the virtual machine, and installs the VMware Tools software.

4. **Click Restart Now to put the changes into effect.**

> You may find that the mouse point is "stuck" inside the virtual machine window and so you can't click the Virtual Machine menu. In that case, press Control+⌘ to return mouse control back to your Mac, and then run the menu command.
>
> **Note**

Installing Windows in a new virtual machine

If you don't have a Boot Camp partition or if you prefer to run Windows on a separate partition, you need to install Windows in a new virtual machine. How you get started depends on whether you're starting VMware Fusion for the first time:

- **If this is the first time you've started VMware Fusion:** In the Welcome window that appears, click Create Virtual Machine.

- **If you have started VMware Fusion before:** In the VMware Fusion window, choose File ⇨ New (or click New in the Virtual Machine Library window).

Either way, VMware launches the New Virtual Machine Assistant. From there, follow these steps to install Windows in a new virtual machine:

1. **Insert your Windows installation disc.**

2. **Select the Install this operating system option.**

3. **Click Continue.** The Windows Easy Install window appears.

4. **Select the Use Easy Install check box.**

5. **Type the administrator Account Name and Password you want to use.**

6. **Type your Windows Product Key.**

7. **Click Continue.** The Sharing window appears.

8. **Select the sharing option you want to use.**

   - **Share home folder.** Select this option to enable Windows to see your Mac home folder.

   - **Mirror folders.** Select this option to use your Mac user profile folders (including the desktop) in Windows.

   - **None.** Select this option if you don't want to share files between Mac and Windows.

9. **Click Continue.** The Finish dialog box appears.

10. **Click Finish.** VMware prompts you to save the virtual machine.

11. **Use the Save As text box to edit the name of the virtual machine and then click Save.** VMware Fusion installs Windows.

12. **Follow the Windows installation screens as they appear.** Note that you won't need to specify your user name, password, or product key because you supplied that data to VMware earlier, and it automatically passes that data along to Windows.

Note
To use your mouse inside the virtual machine during the installation, click inside the VMware Fusion window to activate the mouse. To use your mouse outside of the virtual machine, press Control+⌘.

Figure 11.18 shows Windows Vista running in a VMware Fusion virtual machine window on the Mac OS X desktop.

11.18 Windows Vista running in a VMware Fusion virtual machine in Mac OS X

Configuring the virtual machine

If you need to make changes to the Windows virtual machine, first shut down the virtual machine by choosing Virtual Machine⇨Shut Down Guest, and then click OK when VMware Fusion asks you to confirm.

When the virtual machine is stopped, click Settings (or choose Virtual Machine⇨Settings, or press ⌘+E) to open the Settings dialog box, shown in figure 11.19. Click the item you want to configure, and then use the settings that appear to make your changes.

11.19 Use the Settings dialog box to make changes to the Windows virtual machine.

Exchanging files between Mac OS X and Windows

Sharing files and data between Mac OS X and Windows is much easier and more versatile when Windows is running in a virtual machine. Here's a summary of the main ways that you can share files and data:

- **Clipboard.** VMware Fusion sets up a common Clipboard between Mac and Windows. When you cut or copy a file, folder, or other data in either Windows or Mac OS X, you can switch to the other operating system and then paste the data.

- **In Windows.** If you elected to share folders on your Mac, double-click the desktop's VMware Shared Folders icon to see your Mac's shared folders and work with the files.

- **Drag and drop.** Select the object you want to share in either Windows or Mac OS X, click and drag the object from the source location, and then drop it inside a window in the other operating system (or on the desktop).

Appendix A
Mac Online Resources

The Internet is chock full of Mac-related sites, many of which are exceptionally good and reflect the passion that most Mac users feel toward their beloved machines. This appendix lists a few of the best sites for great information on all things Mac, from tips to troubleshooting and more. Most of these sites have been online for a while, so they should still be up and running when you read this. That said, things do change constantly on the Web, so don't be too surprised if one or two have gone sneakers up.

Official Apple Sites

If you like your information straight from the horse's mouth, here are a few useful Mac sites maintained by the good geeks at Apple.

www.apple.com/mac/

This is your starting point for Mac-related stuff on the Apple site. You'll find the latest Mac news, the top downloads, and the latest Mac ads (always a great time-waster).

www.apple.com/imac/

This is the official Apple site for the stylish iMac.

www.apple.com/macmini/

This is Apple's official page for the almost-too-cute Mac mini.

www.apple.com/macbook/

Head to this page to learn more about the MacBook.

www.apple.com/macbookair/

This is the home page of the MacBook Air, "the world's thinnest notebook."

www.apple.com/macbookpro/

This is the official page of the technolust-inducing MacBook Pro.

www.apple.com/macpro/

This is the home page for the mighty Mac Pro.

www.apple.com/support/hardware/

Head here for user guides, software updates, how-to articles, and troubleshooting tips for each different type of Mac.

discussions.apple.com

This site contains Apple's discussion forums, where you can talk to other Mac fans and ask questions.

More Mac Sites

If you feel like surfing off the beaten track, there are plenty of third-party Mac sites maintained by Mac enthusiasts.

db.tidbits.com

This is the best place to find news and commentary related to what's going on in the Mac universe.

www.download.com

This site has a huge selection of Mac software downloads.

www.macfixit.com

This site offers troubleshooting solutions for your Mac.

www.macintouch.com

You'll find the latest news from the world of Mac here.

www.macosxhints.com

This site provides a massive database of user-generated tips for the Mac.

www.macrumors.com

You'll find more news, and more than a few rumors, about the Mac on this site.

www.macworld.com

Go to this site to find articles, tips, and discussions from the publisher of *Macworld* magazine.

www.tucows.com/Macintosh

This site has thousands of Mac-related software downloads.

www.ultimatemac.com

Go to this site for Mac news, tips, troubleshooting, software reviews, and much more.

www.xlr8yourmac.com

You'll find hundreds of great tips and how-to articles for getting more out of your Mac here.

Appendix B

Mac Shortcut Keys

Although the Mac was built with the mouse in mind, it comes with lots of keyboard shortcuts that can save you time and make many operations easier and faster. The sections in this appendix summarize the most useful Mac keyboard shortcuts.

Startup Shortcuts

Table B.1 details shortcuts you can use for alternate booting techniques.

Table B.1 Startup Shortcuts

C	Press and hold to boot from the inserted CD or DVD
T	Press and hold to invoke FireWire Target Disk mode
Option	Press and hold to display the Startup Manager
Shift	Press and hold before the Apple screen comes up to boot into Safe Login mode
Shift	Press and hold after the Apple screen comes up but before login to bypass login items
Shift	Press and hold after login to boot into Safe Login mode

Restart and Shutdown Shortcuts

Table B.2 gives you some different options for the various dialog boxes you see when you restart or shut down your Mac.

Table B.2 Restart and Shutdown Shortcuts

Shortcut	Description
Shift+⌘+Q	Log out (with confirmation dialog box)
Option+Shift+⌘+Q	Log out (without confirmation dialog box)
Control+Eject	Display the Restart/Sleep/Shut Down confirmation dialog box
Power	Display the Restart/Sleep/Shut Down confirmation dialog box
Option+⌘+Eject	Put your Mac into Sleep mode (without confirmation dialog box)
Control+⌘+Eject	Restart your Mac (without confirmation dialog box, but you can save changes in open documents)
Control+Option+⌘+Eject	Shut down your Mac (without confirmation dialog box, but you can save changes in open documents)
Control+⌘+Power	Force your Mac to restart (without confirmation dialog box, and you can't save changes in open documents)
Power	Press and hold to force your Mac to shut down (without confirmation dialog box, and you can't save changes in open documents)

Application Shortcuts

Table B.3 shows you how to cycle through your current application's icons, how to open the application's preferences, and how to maneuver through windows without resorting to your mouse.

Table B.3 Application Shortcuts

Shortcut	Description
⌘+Tab	Cycle forward through active application icons with each press of the Tab key; release ⌘ to switch to the selected application
Shift+⌘+Tab	Cycle backward through active application icons with each press of the Tab key; release ⌘ to switch to the selected application
⌘+`	Cycle forward through the current application's open windows
Shift+⌘+`	Cycle backward through the current application's open windows
⌘+,	Open the current application's preferences
⌘+H	Hide the current application
Option+⌘+H	Hide all applications except the current one
⌘+M	Minimize the current window to the Dock
Option+⌘+M	Minimize all windows in active application to the Dock
⌘+Q	Quit the current application
Option+⌘+Esc	Display the Force Quit Applications window

Finder Shortcuts

Use the shortcuts in Table B.4 to switch Finder window views, open a new Finder window, eject a disc, duplicate files and folders, maneuver through Finder's Sidebar, and manage your Trash.

Table B.4 Finder Shortcuts

Shortcut	Description
⌘+1	Switch the active window to Icons view
⌘+2	Switch the active window to List Flow view
⌘+3	Switch the active window to Columns view
⌘+4	Switch the active window to Cover Flow view
⌘+A	Select all items in the current window
⌘+D	Duplicate the selected item
⌘+E	Eject the current disc
⌘+F	Display the Find dialog box
⌘+I	Display the Get Info window for the selected item
⌘+J	Display the View options
⌘+L	Create an alias for the selected item
⌘+N	Open a new Finder window
⌘+O	Open the selected item
⌘+R	Show the original item for the current alias
⌘+T	Add the current item to the Sidebar
⌘+W	Close the current Finder window
Shift+⌘+A	Go to the Applications folder
Shift+⌘+C	Go to the Computer folder
Shift+⌘+D	Go to the Desktop folder
Shift+⌘+G	Display the Go to Folder dialog box
Shift+⌘+H	Go to the Home folder
Shift+⌘+I	Go to the iDisk folder
Shift+⌘+K	Go to the Network folder
Shift+⌘+N	Create a new folder in the current Finder window
Option+⌘+N	Create a new Smart Folder in the current Finder window
Shift+⌘+U	Go to the Utilities folder
Option+⌘+W	Close all open Finder windows
⌘+Delete	Move the selected item to the Trash
Shift+⌘+Delete	Empty the Trash (with the confirmation dialog)
Option+Shift+⌘+Delete	Empty the Trash (without the confirmation dialog)

Safari Shortcuts

Table B.5 details the shortcuts you can use to maneuver through Safari windows, manage your bookmarks, send e-mails, and perform Google searches.

Table B.5 Safari Shortcuts

Shortcut	Description
⌘+I	E-mail the contents of the current page
⌘+L	Select the Address bar text
⌘+N	Open a new window
⌘+O	Open a file
⌘+R	Reload the current page
⌘+T	Open a new tab
⌘+W	Close the current tab
⌘+n	Open the nth item on the Bookmarks bar, where n is a number between 1 and 9
⌘+}	Select the next tab
⌘+{	Select the previous tab
⌘+.	Stop loading the current page
⌘++	Make the text bigger on the current page
⌘+0	Make the text normal size on the current page
⌘+-	Make the text smaller on the current page
⌘+D	Add the current page to the Bookmarks
Option+⌘+D	Add the current page to the Bookmarks (without the Bookmark dialog box)
Option+⌘+B	Display the Bookmarks window
Option+⌘+L	Display the Downloads window
⌘+[	Navigate back
⌘+]	Navigate forward
Shift+⌘+H	Navigate to the Home page
Shift+⌘+T	Toggle the Tab bar on and off (works only if you have one tab open)
Shift+⌘+W	Close the current window
Shift+⌘+I	E-mail a link to the current page
Shift+⌘+K	Toggle pop-up blocking on and off

Shortcut	Description
Shift+⌘+L	Run a Google search on the selected text
⌘+Return	Open the Address bar URL in a background tab
Shift+⌘+Return	Open the Address bar URL in a foreground tab
⌘	Click a link to open it in a background tab
Shift+⌘	Click a link to open it in a foreground tab
Option+⌘	Click a link to open it in a background window
Shift+Option+⌘	Click a link to open it in a foreground window
Option+⌘+Return	Open the Address bar URL in a background window
Shift+Option+⌘+Return	Open the Address bar URL in a foreground window

Miscellaneous Shortcuts

Use the shortcuts in Table B.6 to cut, copy, and paste materials, undo recent actions, manage the dock, and capture screenshots.

Table B.6 Miscellaneous Shortcuts

Shortcut	Description
⌘+X	Cut the selected objects or data
⌘+C	Copy the selected objects or data
⌘+V	Paste the most recently cut or copied objects or data
⌘+Z	Undo the most recent action
Option+Volume up/down/mute	Display the Sound preferences
Option+Brightness up/down	Display the Display preferences
F12	Press and hold to eject an inserted disc
Fn+Control+F2	Give keyboard control to the menu bar
Fn+Control+F3	Give keyboard control to the Dock
Option+⌘+D	Toggle Dock hiding on and off
Shift+⌘+3	Capture an image of the screen
Shift+⌘+4	Drag the mouse to capture an image of the selected area of the screen
Shift+⌘+4	Press Spacebar and then click an object to capture an image of that object

Glossary

access point A networking device that enables two or more Macs to connect over a wireless network.

Address Book Your Mac's default contact management application.

alias See *file alias*.

Apple menu. Click the Apple icon on the left side of the *menu bar* to see this menu, which is home to a few key commands, such as Software Update and System Preferences. Since this menu also includes Sleep, Restart, Show Down, and Log Out commands, it's the closest thing you'll find to the Windows Start menu in Mac OS X.

application menus This is the part of the *menu bar* that sits between the *Apple menu* icon and the *menu extras*. This area displays the menus associated with the current application.

application preferences The options, settings, and other data that you've configured for a particular application via the Preferences command. See also *system preferences*.

Bluetooth A wireless networking technology that enables you to exchange data between two devices using radio frequencies when the devices are within range of each other (usually within about 10 meters).

Bonjour A technology that scours the local network looking for other computers and devices that provide services, and then configures those services without requiring any input from you.

bookmark An Internet site saved in Safari so that you can access the site quickly in future browsing sessions.

bounce message An e-mail message that a mail server automatically fires off to the sender of a message when a problem occurs with the delivery of the message.

Command (⌘) The Mac's main *modifier key*.

Cover Flow A Finder view that shows a split screen, with a List view of the contents on the bottom, and a preview of the current item on the top.

cycling Letting a Mac notebook battery completely discharge and then fully recharging it again.

Dashboard A Mac application that you use to access mini applications called *widgets*.

data source The information required to connect to a database.

discoverable Describes a device that has its Bluetooth feature turned on so that other Bluetooth devices can connect to it.

disk image A file that acts as a kind of virtual disc or hard drive where launching the file is just like inserting a disc: You get an icon on your desktop, the disk image appears in Finder's Sidebar in the Devices section, and the installation program starts automatically.

Dock The strip of icons that runs across the bottom of the Mac screen that acts roughly as an amalgam of the Windows' Quick Launch toolbar and taskbar.

dual-boot To configure your Mac with two different operating systems (such as Mac OS X and Windows) running on two separate *partitions* on your Mac's hard drive.

dual-link A DVI cable that uses two transmitters. See also *single-link*.

Eject (⏏) Press this key (or, on some Macs, hold down the key for a second or two) to eject the currently inserted CD or DVD.

emulator A software application that simulates a hardware device or system.

event An appointment or meeting that you've scheduled in iCal.

Exposé A window-management program that temporarily shrinks all your running windows and then arranges them on your screen so that nothing overlaps.

extended desktop mode An external display mode where your Mac's desktop is extended onto the external display. See also *video mirroring*.

fast user switching A Mac feature that leaves your programs running when you log out, and reinstates them just as they were when you log back in.

female connector A cable connector with holes. See also *male connector*.

file alias A special type of file that does nothing but point to an original file, so that if you double-click an alias, your Mac locates the original and opens it.

file system A technology used by the operating system to keep track of the files stored on a disk, such as a hard disk.

Finder The Mac application that you use to view and work with (rename, move, copy, delete, and so on) your files, folders, and disk drives. Finder is more or less the Mac equivalent to Windows Explorer.

FireWire The Apple term for the IEEE 1394 hard drive interface. FireWire 400 (IEEE 1394a) offers 400Mbps data throughput; FireWire 800 (IEEE 1394b) offers 800Mbps data throughput.

FireWire target disk mode A startup mode that enables you to use a Mac to view the hard disk of another Mac via a FireWire connection.

firmware A small program that runs inside the device and controls its internal functions.

GarageBand A Mac application that you use to create songs, podcasts, and other audio files.

Gbps Gigabits per second (billions of bits per second).

group A collection of Address Book contacts. See also *smart group*.

guest operating system An operating system that runs inside a virtual machine using virtualization software.

home folder The folder associated with each Mac user account where you can store your documents, photos, music, and other personal data.

HTML See *Hypertext Markup Language*.

Hypertext Markup Language A collection of codes — called tags — that define the underlying structure of, and to some extent the formatting on, a Web page.

iCal Your Mac's default scheduling application.

iChat A Mac application that you use to converse with other people in real time by sending each other online text messages.

iDisk Online file storage that comes with a MobileMe account.

iDVD The DVD-burning software that comes with Apple's iLife suite.

iLife A suite of applications that you can install on your Mac and that includes programs such as iDVD, iPhoto, and iWeb.

Image Capture The Mac application that you use to connect to a device such as a digital camera or digital camcorder and download the device's photos or videos to your Mac.

iMovie The video-editing application that comes with Apple's iLife suite.

iPhoto The iLife application that you use to import photos from your digital camera and organize those photos into albums.

iTunes Your Mac's default media player application.

iWeb. An iLife application that you use to create Web pages.

iWork A productivity suite that comes with three programs: Pages, a word processor; Numbers, a spreadsheet program; and Keynote, a presentation program.

keychain A list of saved passwords.

login items The applications, files, folders, network shares, and other items that start automatically when you log in to your user account.

Macintosh HD This is the default name of your Mac's hard disk.

Mail Your Mac's default e-mail application.

male connector A cable connector with pins. See also *female connector*.

memory effect The process where certain types of batteries lose capacity over time if you repeatedly recharge them without first fully discharging them.

menu bar This is the strip that runs across the top of the Mac screen and it includes the *Apple menu* icon, the *menu extras*, and the *application menu*.

menu extras These icons appear on the right side of the *menu bar*, and the number of icons you see depends on the configuration of your Mac. You use these icons to see the status of certain Mac features (such as your wireless network connection) and to configure other features, such as the Mac's sound volume.

modifier key A key that you press in conjunction with one or more other keys to launch some action. On the Mac, almost all keyboard shortcuts involve the *Command* (⌘) key.

multithreading Running two or more threads in a single program at the same time.

package A Mac file system object that includes not only folders and files, but other data as well (the iPhoto library is an example of a package).

pair To connect one Bluetooth device with another by entering a passkey.

partition A subset of a hard disk onto which you install an operating system (such as Mac OS X in one partition and Windows in another).

permissions A collection of settings that determines what users or groups of users can do with a file.

power cycle To turn a device off, wait about 30 seconds for its inner components to stop spinning, and then turn it back on again.

preferences See *system preferences* and *application preferences*.

preferences file A document that stores options and other data that you've entered using an application's Preferences command.

process A running instance of an executable program.

QuickTime Player Your Mac's default digital video player.

Return This is the Mac equivalent of the Enter key, so you use it for the same kinds of things.

Safari Your Mac's default Web browser.

Safe Boot To start your Mac in Safe Mode.

Safe Mode A startup mode where your Mac doesn't load most of its behind-the-scenes components.

Safe Login A login that doesn't load any of your login items.

Server Message Block See *SMB*.

Sidebar The pane on the left side of any Finder window that offers a number of shortcuts to objects such as devices, network shares, and local folders.

single-link A DVI cable that uses one transmitter. See also *dual-link*.

sleep mode A low-power state where your Mac uses only marginally more electricity than if it were powered off altogether, while still preserving all your running applications, windows, and documents.

smart album A collection of photos that iPhoto maintains automatically based on data such as event names and keywords.

smart folder A kind of virtual folder where the contents depend on the criteria you specify, and your Mac adjusts the contents automatically as your files change.

smart group A collection of Address Book contacts where each member has one or more things in common, and where Address Book adds or deletes members automatically as you add, edit, and delete contacts.

smart mailbox A Mail folder that consolidates all of your messages that meet one or more conditions, and where Mail Book adds or deletes messages automatically as you receive and delete messages.

SMB A networking layer that enables a computer to share folders on the network and access folders that other computers have shared.

spaces Virtual desktops created using the Spaces application.

spinning wait cursor The icon that you see on your Mac when the system is busy with another task.

Spotlight The Mac feature that you use to search for files, folders, applications, Mail messages, images, and other data.

synchronization A process that ensures that data such as contacts, e-mail accounts, and events on your Mac is the same as the data on other devices such as cell phones and PDAs.

system preferences The options, settings, and other data that you've configured for your Mac via the System Preferences application (the Mac equivalent to Control Panel). See also *application preferences*.

TextEdit Your Mac's default word processor.

thread A program task that can run independently of and (usually) concurrently with other tasks in the same program. See also *multithreading*.

Time Machine A Mac application that you use to create and access backups of your files.

twisted-pair cable Network cable, so-called because it consists of four pairs of twisted copper wires that together form a circuit that can transmit data.

user agent A string that a Web browser uses to identify itself to a Web server.

video mirroring An external display mode where the same image that appears on the Mac's main or built-in display also appears on the external display. See also *extended desktop mode*.

virtualization Running a guest operating system (such as Windows on a Mac) in a virtual machine.

virtual machine A software environment that simulates a physical computer.

volume See *partition*.

widget A small program that runs in your Mac's Dashboard application.

Index

The Genius is in.

Macs PORTABLE GENIUS
978-0-470-29052-1

Mac OS X Leopard PORTABLE GENIUS
978-0-470-29050-7

iPhone 3G PORTABLE GENIUS
978-0-470-42348-6

Final Cut Pro PORTABLE GENIUS
978-0-470-38760-3

iMac PORTABLE GENIUS
978-0-470-29061-3

MacBook Air PORTABLE GENIUS
978-0-470-38108-3

MacBook PORTABLE GENIUS
978-0-470-29169-6

MacBook Pro PORTABLE GENIUS
978-0-470-29170-2

The essentials for every forward-thinking Apple user are now available on the go. Designed for easy access to tools and shortcuts, the *Portable Genius* series has all the information you need to maximize your digital lifestyle. With a full-color interior and easy-to-navigate content, the *Portable Genius* series offers innovative tips and tricks as well as savvy advice that will save you time and increase your productivity.

Available wherever books are sold.

WILEY
Now you know.